IO127702

THE ILLUSION OF THE FREE PRESS

This book explores the relationship between truth and freedom in the free press. It argues that the relationship is problematic because the free press implies a competition between plural ideas, whereas truth is univocal. Based on this tension the book claims that the idea of a free press is premised on an epistemological illusion. This illusion enables society to maintain that the world it perceives through the press corresponds to the world as it actually exists, explaining why defenders of the free press continue to rely on its capacity to discover the truth, despite economic conditions and technological innovations undermining much of its independence. The book invites the reader to reconsider the philosophical foundations, constitutional justifications, and structure and functions of the free press, and whether the institution can, in fact, realise both freedom and truth. It will be of great interest to anyone concerned in the role and value of the free press in the modern world.

The Illusion of the Free Press

John Charney

·HART·

OXFORD · LONDON · NEW YORK · NEW DELHI · SYDNEY

HART PUBLISHING

Bloomsbury Publishing Plc

Kemp House, Chawley Park, Cumnor Hill, Oxford, OX2 9PH, UK

HART PUBLISHING, the Hart/Stag logo, BLOOMSBURY and the Diana
logo are trademarks of Bloomsbury Publishing Plc

First published in Great Britain 2018
First published in hardback, 2018
Paperback edition, 2020

A catalogue record for this book is available from the British Library.

Library of Congress Cataloging-in-Publication data

Names: Charney, John, author. Title: The illusion of the free press / John Charney.
Description: Oxford [UK]; Portland, Oregon: Hart Publishing, 2018. | Includes bibliographical references and
index. | Description based on print version record and CIP data provided by publisher; resource not viewed.
Identifiers: LCCN 2017045282 (print) | LCCN 2017045671 (ebook) | ISBN 9781509908882 (Epub) |
ISBN 9781509908875 (hardback: alk.paper)
Subjects: LCSH: Freedom of the press. | Freedom of speech. | Truth.
Classification: LCC K3255 (ebook) | LCC K3255.C43 2017 (print) | DDC 342.08/53—dc23

LC record available at https://lccn.loc.gov/2017045282

ISBN: HB: 978-1-50990-887-5
PB: 978-1-50993-824-7
ePDF: 978-1-50990-889-9
ePub: 978-1-50990-888-2

Typeset by Compuscript Ltd, Shannon

To find out more about our authors and books visit www.hartpublishing.co.uk. Here you will
find extracts, author information, details of forthcoming events and the option to sign up for
our newsletters.

To Constanza and Rita

PREFACE

On 30 October 1938, Orson Welles aired over the Columbia Broadcasting System an adaptation of HG Wells's science-fiction novel, *The War of the Worlds*.[1] The adaptation consisted of a 60-minute radio programme, in which simulated press bulletins were inserted over a regular musical show being broadcast live from New York's Park Plaza Hotel. These bulletins interrupted the show on a regular basis, with increasingly alarming news about a series of strange events connected with a burning object that had allegedly fallen from the skies and landed somewhere in New Jersey. What was considered at the beginning of the show by (fake) scientists interviewed by (fake) reporters to be the most improbable explanation of such events, turned out to be the fatal outcome: Martians (and not the good sort) were invading the Earth.

Some speculation about the reaction of the public to the programme, and more specifically about the extent to which panic took over listeners in New York and other American and Canadian cities, followed the show. Sceptics claimed that fewer than 20 per cent of listeners believed that the Earth was actually under Martian attack.[2] The *New York Times*, on the other hand, opened its front page the next morning with the headline 'Radio Listeners in Panic, Taking War Drama as Fact', and claimed that a 'wave of mass hysteria seized thousands of listeners … and disrupted households, interrupted religious services, created traffic jams and clogged communications systems'.[3] Regardless of disputes over the scale of the effect that the programme had on its listeners, there was no doubt about the underlying message behind it. Welles's experiment not only clearly showed the power that technology could exert over its audiences, at a time when people were only beginning to get used to the effects of technological progress, but also warned about the potential for the media to deceive the public. By describing a non-reality, opening a chasm between media descriptions of reality and the reality they describe, Welles revealed the distance that separates these two realms and exposed the fragility of one of the central institutions of liberal democracies. He was severely criticised for attempting to undermine confidence in the system and had to make public apologies.

---

[1] O Welles, 'Orson Welles—War Of The Worlds—Radio Broadcast 1938—Complete Broadcast', available at www.youtube.com/watch?v=Xs0K4ApWl4g&feature=youtube_gdata_player.

[2] S Lovgen, '"War of the Worlds": Behind the 1938 Radio Show Panic', *National Geographic News* (17 June 2005), available at http://news.nationalgeographic.com/news/2005/06/0617_050617_warworlds.html.

[3] 'Radio Listeners in Panic, Taking War Drama as Fact', *New York Times* (31 October 1938).

What Welles unveiled with his experiment is a central theme of this book. It refers to what will be called the 'illusion of the free press'. The word 'illusion' means a 'deceptive appearance or impression', or 'a false idea or belief'. Although this meaning is not all there is to the word, and is not the one that will be generally used in this book (as will be explained shortly), it is the one used by the relevant critical literature to describe the state of the media in contemporary societies, among them one of its most influential critiques, the critique of the political economy of the press (CPEP). The CPEP has provided consistent valuable research about the structure and functioning of the press in advanced capitalist societies.[4] It has shown, among many other things, that the property of the means of communication is concentrated in a few hands, that the press responds to the interests of those who finance it (advertisers) and that these last are not necessarily aligned with the public interest but are sometimes in open contradiction. From this point of view, the CPEP has argued that the press is not free and independent but is subject to a series of financial, economic and political constraints, which necessarily affect its communications and hence the way in which it portrays social reality. The free press is thus a mere illusion, a deceptive idea of what it really is. The central purpose of the CPEP is thus to unveil the illusion, to show the *real* face of the press in order to raise awareness and consciousness about the distance separating appearances from reality.

Other thinkers, usually associated with the postmodern tradition, have argued, on the other hand, that the inability of the media to represent reality as it is, exceeds the material conditions in which it functions.[5] Their point is that regardless of the way in which it is structured, the media will never be able to reproduce reality because reality is not reproducible. From an ontological perspective, the argument is that the world (in the broad sense of the term) is pure chaos, pure antagonism, and that any effort to give meaning or sense to it will always be condemned to failure. The texture of reality is, in other words, so different from the texture of language that the latter is not only unable to reproduce it, it cannot even represent it. Any representational attempt is viewed as the consequence of power struggles, where disputing forces fight to construct a reality that best fits their interests, with the aim of making those constructions the dominant view of reality. Accordingly, representations of reality are mere illusions. At best, they would only show the power interests involved in those representations.

---

[4] Among some of the authors under this label that will be explored in ch 1 are R McChesney, *The Political Economy of Media: Enduring Issues, Emerging Dilemmas* (New York, Monthly Review Press, 2008); N Chomsky and E Herman, *Manufacturing Consent: The Political Economy of the Mass Media* (London, Vintage, 1994); B Bagdikian, *The New Media Monopoly*, 7th edn (Boston, MA, Beacon Press, 2004); H Marcuse, 'Repressive Tolerance' in A Feenber and W Leiss (eds), *The Essential Marcuse: Selected Writings of Philosopher and Social Critic Herbert Marcuse* (Boston, MA, Beacon Press, 2007).

[5] Among some of the theorists whose work will be analysed in ch 1 are M McLuhan, *Understanding Media*, 2nd edn (New York, Routledge, 2001); J Baudrillard, *Simulacra and Simulation*, tr S Glaser (Ann Arbor, MI, The University of Michigan Press, 1994); N Postman, *Amusing Ourselves to Death* (London, Methuen Publishing Ltd, 1987).

From another point of view, thinkers from this tradition have emphasised the relevance of technology in the process of mediation. They maintain that technologies offer different forms of communication, forms that diverge in the way in which they approach their objects, in their point of views and in the aspects they tend to emphasise or ignore about them. This is why they argue that the world of typography was completely different from the world of television, and the latter completely different from the digital world. Technologies themselves, with their particular codes, languages and modes of communication, have epistemological implications because they affect our perception and understanding of the world. But the way we perceive the world also changes the way in which we relate to it and the way in which we relate to each other. This is why postmodernists argue that technologies shape and mould reality.[6] Accordingly, not only have technologies altered our perception and understanding of the world, they have gone much further: they have modified the world itself. From this point of view, the illusion consists in believing that the media, through their technological platforms, mediate a reality that exists in itself, when the fact is that they construct the very reality they are supposed to mediate.

The critiques offered by the CPEP and by postmodernism will be explored in detail in Chapter 1. Not only have they enriched academic discussion, they have also permeated the broader public opinion. The events that led in Britain to the formation of the Leveson Inquiry opened debate over and discussion of the problems associated with media empires, corrupt editors, the collusion of politicians and media moguls, obscure manipulation of the political agenda and so on. More recently, the dissemination of fake news during the Brexit campaign and Donald Trump's election in the United States, both in 2016, brought media regulation to the fore in public discussion. The deep gulf that separates the idea of a free press from its real functioning was exposed, and the effects of that understanding are yet to be seen. What we still do not know (and perhaps never absolutely will) is to what extent these events will modify the way in which mass audiences relate to the news they receive from the media. How does our knowledge about its real conditions affect our epistemic attitude towards its contents and discourses? To what degree will these events alter the legitimacy of its claim to adequately and accurately portray reality?

Given the first meaning assigned to the concept of illusion, that is, as a false representation of reality, some would answer that nothing would really change. According to Peter Sloterdijk, for example, this would be so because the prevalent attitude of postmodernism is cynicism, which is reflected in what he calls the 'enlightened false consciousness'.[7] In relation to the 'illusion of the free press', the cynical subject would know very well the distance separating the idea of a free press and the actual conditions in which it functions in capitalist societies.

---

[6] See especially McLuhan, above n 5; Postman, above n 5.

[7] See P Sloterdijk, *Critique of Cynical Reason*, tr M Eldred (Minneapolis, MN, University of Minnesota Press, 1987) 5.

She knows about media concentration, she knows the huge political, commercial and financial pressures influencing its discourses, she knows that its depictions of reality fall far short of reality, and so on. Nevertheless, the cynical subject keeps on acting *as if* she did not know all these things. She keeps on informing herself through the news, using that information as part of her general knowledge about the world she lives in and using it, usually as a matter of fact, in her daily conversations. From this assumption, Sloterdijk concludes that we live in a post-ideological era in which our knowledge of the hidden mechanisms of the system does not affect the way in which we relate to it. The enlightened false consciousness is as servile to ideological commandments as the ignorant one. In this sense, ideology, after all, would be completely irrelevant.

However, do we truly live in a post-ideological era? Is ideology completely irrelevant, now that we have discovered that our knowledge about how things *really are* does not necessarily affect our attitudes towards them? These questions—which will be tackled in the first chapter—lead us to the central point of this book. The point is that in order to think about the 'illusion of the free press', it is not enough to focus merely on the first meaning of the word 'illusion'. Indeed, if the illusion is that the press is free and independent, or if the illusion is that there is a deep fissure that separates reality from the way in which the media portray it, one would be forced to conclude (with Sloterdijk) that ideology is irrelevant, because once those illusions are dispelled, once we know how things really are, nothing really changes. The system continues reproducing itself, regardless of our insight into the way in which it works. But the real problem is that the media still form an ideological apparatus and that we are still subservient to that apparatus in so many ways. So the question that needs to be asked is: why, despite our knowledge of the conditions of the press in capitalist societies and its consequent distance from the ideal of a free press, is it still such a central institution and the idea of a free press one of the central principles in liberal democracies?

A second meaning of the word 'illusion' provides a better answer to this question. For the fact is that the illusion is not merely a false idea of what the media really are. Neither is it solely the wrong belief that social reality corresponds to the way in which the media portray it. There is something more. Something that is ingrained in the history of the 'free press', in the fight for its recognition and in public expectations of it. It is not necessary to go very far to discover this additional element. It is inscribed in the meaning of the word 'illusion' itself. In fact, illusions are not only false ideas or beliefs, they are also the expression of a desire. We refer to a belief as an illusion, according to Freud, when 'wish-fulfilment plays a prominent part in its motivation'.[8] I could have the illusion, for example, that the world will be a fair place, that substantial inequality will be overcome or that there will be no more wars. From the point of view of the press, the illusion is connected to an epistemological desire. The desire to understand the world in which we live, to grasp our political contingency with all its nuances and subtleties, and so on.

---

[8] S Freud, *The Future of an Illusion*, tr JA Underwood et al (London, Penguin Books, 2008) 38.

Illusion, as desire, insists on affirming the ontological independence of social reality, but more importantly, the potential of gaining cognitive access to it. If, despite our knowledge of the actual conditions of the press, the illusion does not recede, it is because this 'other' illusion is necessary. We need the illusion in order to preserve the idea that there is a correspondence between reality *qua* reality and that same reality as the media portray it. The illusion is necessary if an important part of our experience is to retain consistency. Otherwise, if we renounce the illusion, we lose the grounding of a relevant portion of our social reality. In fact, most—if not all—of any common individual's knowledge about political contingency, international affairs, economic trends and crises, technological and scientific developments, culture, sports and so many other things comes directly or indirectly from the news he receives from the media. Whenever we engage in conversations about these topics, form an opinion or share our ideas about them, we need to assume that our knowledge is a reflection of a reality that exists independently of the media and not knowledge about how the latter construct that reality. If we do not retain this illusion, if we do not stick to this desire, then our social reality loses consistency. If we cannot represent to ourselves that a building, which stands before our eyes, has a backside that corresponds to its front, as Žižek argues, '[our] perceptual field disintegrates into an inconsistent, meaningless mess'.[9] The history of the free press itself reveals this necessity. It is contained mainly in its pseudoscientific aspiration of communicating reality as it is, of discovering the truth through its narratives. The *Observer*, the *Daily Mirror*, *The Times*, and even the Plato-conjuring *Sun* are all names of newspapers that reflect this aspiration. But behind these names there is much more than a self-contained ambition. There is a social expectation that the world that appears through the news is an adequate representation of the world as it is in itself, and this expectation, as will be argued, is contained in the illusion of the free press.

This approach to the illusion has a fundamental methodological consequence. In fact, in order to understand the origins, scope and implications of the illusion of the free press, it is necessary to explore the relationship between truth and freedom. More specifically, what needs to be investigated is how the free press is supposed to be an adequate means for the discovery of truth. Now, if the illusion is not merely a deceptive idea of what the press really is but something that is inherent to the institution of the free press itself, the best place to observe the relationship between truth and freedom is in the liberal theory. Indeed, this is the theory that has studied more closely than any other the notion of the free press.[10]

Two central themes will emerge from this analysis. The first is that truth has played a central function in literature on free speech from the seventeenth century on. Truth, however, has not always been understood in the same way. It will emerge that the classic theory has defended truth as a correspondence between reality and

---

[9] S Žižek, *Tarrying with the Negative: Kant, Hegel and the Critique of Ideology* (Durham, NC, Duke University Press, 1993) 85.

[10] See J Raz, 'Free Expression and Personal Identification' (1991) 11 *OJLS* 303.

its descriptions. Therefore, the purpose of expressive freedoms is to provide an adequate depiction of the world in which we live. In democratic theories, expressive freedoms are conceived of as a means of advancing political truths. Truth here is no longer correspondence with an outer reality but instead coherence between a central judgement (a political truth) and a set of judgements and institutions subordinated to this truth. In the case of autonomy theories, truth takes the form of authenticity, where expressive freedoms are conceived of as a mechanism contributing to the discovery of the true self. As will be argued throughout this book, the connection between freedom and truth in free-speech literature is the consequence of the desire to know and understand the world in which we live, the functioning of our political communities and to validate our own identity.

The second theme that will emerge from this book is the inherent tension that exists between truth and freedom. The point is that—as Hannah Arendt argues—while the discovery of truths or the advancement of knowledge supposes modes of thought and communication that are necessarily domineering,[11] no such modes are supposed to guide a free debate of ideas. If the modes of communication proper to the discovery of truths are used as standards of public discussion, free expression would be utterly and unacceptably precluded. This is why some argue that universities, journals, the scientific community, research communities and not the press would hence be the institutions best fitted for attaining this purpose. On the other hand, to consider the free press an adequate standard for the discovery of truth is to degrade truth to subjective or relative conceptions, where any view would be as valid as any other as long as it was coherently sustained. The inherent tension between truth and freedom manifests itself in the different theories that will be explored in the book.

This book consists of five chapters. Chapter 1 will analyse the concept of the illusion of the free press through the critique of the political economy of the press and cultural critiques. It will be argued that although they have contributed valuable insight to the debate, they are unable to explain why, regardless of our knowledge about how it works, the press remains a central institution in liberal democracies. The problem of these theories is that they conceive of the illusion of the free press as false consciousness. Under this logic, they assume that the illusion is removable or disposable. However, as will be shown, the illusion is not a problem of false consciousness but one of necessity. As a consequence, it is not possible to renounce the illusion, because as soon as we do that, we lose our sense of reality. Using Kant's notion of 'transcendental illusions' as an analogy, Chapter 1 will close by explaining the necessity for maintaining a connection between reality and appearances. This notion will be crucial to understanding the non-renounceable and non-disposable character of the illusion of the free press, and hence the necessity of exploring the relationship between truth and freedom from within free-speech literature.

---

[11] H Arendt, 'Truth and Politics' in *Between Past and Future: Eight Exercises in Political Thought* (New York, Penguin Books, 1977) 241.

Chapter 2 will explore the place of truth in free speech literature from the seventeenth to the nineteenth century in England. It will start with John Milton's *Areopagitica*—a pamphlet addressed to the English Parliament opposing the institution of licensing—in which Milton defends with great eloquence freedom of opinion and a free press as mechanisms for the discovery of truth. Despite the increasing political importance of the role of the free press in the eighteenth and nineteenth centuries, its truth-seeking purpose remained a fundamental argument for its justification. The latter achieved its chief expression with John Stuart Mill's 'theory of the truth', which, as it will be argued, was a revival of Milton's defence.[12] A central issue that will run through Chapter 2 will be the model of truth involved in these developments. Milton's theory emerged in a theocentric age, and his notion of truth follows a correspondence model that has been commonly referred to as a 'god's-eye view' of things. Although Mill is theoretically committed to this notion of truth, as will be shown, he also needs a subjective or perspectival truth in order to justify his argument that every opinion is as valuable as any other. This ambiguous approach to truth that shows itself in the text is the way in which Mill deals with the tension between freedom and truth, and this ambiguity is symptomatic of the illusion of the free press.

The reception of the classic theory in the United States and its application to the press will be explored in Chapter 3. The analysis will start with a jurisprudential product developed on the other side of the Atlantic Ocean in the form of a dissenting opinion given by Justice Oliver Holmes Jr in *Abrams v United States*. Under the name of the 'marketplace of ideas', it became a central justification of the First Amendment. But just like its predecessor, it embodied an irreconcilable tension between truth and freedom, a tension that led to a bitter repudiation of the truth-seeking purpose of expressive freedoms within the liberal theory itself. In the course of this dispute with truth-seeking justifications, two central theories emerged that proposed a different approach. On the one hand, democratic theories justified the protection of expressive freedoms because they considered them to be essential to the development and strengthening of a democratic polity.[13] Some of these theories stressed the point that expressive freedoms should guarantee that everything worth saying in a democratic society, that is, everything that contributes to the discussion about how to live our lives in common, should be said. Other democratic theories emphasise the value of political autonomy, recognising expressive freedoms as the right of every individual to contribute to the formation of public opinion.[14] Despite their differences, both approaches coincide in

---

[12] See A Haworth, *Free Speech* (London, Routledge, 1998) 3.

[13] Among those who defend this approach are A Meiklejohn, 'Free Speech and its Relation to Self-Government' in *Political Freedom: The Constitutional Powers of the People* (New York, Oxford University Press, 1965); O Fiss, *The Irony of Free Speech* (Cambridge, MA, Harvard University Press, 1996); CR Sunstein, *Democracy and the Problem of Free Speech* (New York, The Free Press, 1995); R Post, 'Participatory Democracy and Free Speech' (2011) 97 *Virginia Law Review* 477.

[14] See especially Post, above n 13.

the importance they assign to political speech over any other form of speech, and in the fact that their theories are supported by particular conceptions of democracy, conceptions that define the scope and understanding of the free press. On the other hand, autonomy theories (which will be analysed in Chapter 4) criticise the consequentialist nature of both democratic and truth-seeking justifications. According to autonomy theorists, expressive freedoms are not instruments for the achievement of particular goals but a proper manifestation of the autonomous character of human beings.[15] Accordingly, it is not the form of speech or its goals that define and justify constitutional protection; only the dignity of the autonomous individual counts as a valid justification for the protection of these freedoms.

The purpose of Chapters 3 and 4 is not simply to describe how democratic and autonomy theories, respectively, rejected truth-seeking justifications but to show that whenever truth has been denied access through the front door, it has entered through the back. In Chapter 3, it will be argued that although the theocentric model of truth advanced by Milton and its secularised version defended by Mill were rejected by democratic theories, an understanding of truth in the form of 'coherence' emerged. Within these theories the scope, meaning and purpose of the free press was subjected to particular conceptions of democracy, or to what some authors have called 'the plan contained in the Constitution'.[16] These conceptions present themselves as truths that define admissible discursive practices and with them the form and functions of a free press in a democratic society. They serve as a mirror to reproduce the democratic system itself and to guarantee its legitimacy. What is true and what is false is not necessarily the relation to some objective reality but is reduced to the internal coherence of the democratic system itself. Rather than reflecting a reality that exists in itself, truth as coherence has a constitutive dimension that defines the discursive conditions of societies and the practices associated with them according to particular conceptions of democracy.

Chapter 4 will analyse the space of truth in autonomy theories of free speech and its application to the free press. It will be argued that regardless of a general scepticism by autonomy theorists about the truth-seeking purpose of expressive freedoms, truth emerges in these theories in the form of authenticity or the discovery of the true self. Truth, in this context, is no longer something that must be searched for in the outer world. It is not correspondence with an external reality, as it is in the classic tradition of free speech; neither is it coherence with a central judgement, as it is with democratic arguments. By contrast, in autonomy theories,

---

[15] Influential autonomy theories have been developed by T Scanlon, 'A Theory of Freedom of Expression' (1972) 1 *Philosophy & Public Affairs* 204; T Scanlon, 'Freedom of Expression and Categories of Expression' (1979) 40 *University of Pittsburgh Law Review* 519; Raz, above n 10; CE Baker, *Human Liberty and Freedom of Speech* (New York, Oxford University Press, 1989); R Dworkin, 'The Coming Battles over Free Speech' *The New York Review of Books* (11 June 1992), available at http://www.nybooks.com/articles/1992/06/11/the-coming-battles-over-free-speech/.
[16] See Meiklejohn, above n 13, 70.

truth is located within the subject himself and takes the form of authenticity. Chapter 4 will show the relationship between the discovery of the 'true self' and expressive activities, and how this relationship manifests itself in some influential autonomy theories of free speech.[17] The tension between truth and freedom is manifest here in an ambiguous conception of the subject and the role of a free press in the public validation of subjectivity.

Chapter 5 is an attempt to harmonise truth and freedom. This is an important challenge, because despite their tension, the relationship between truth and freedom, as expressed in free-speech literature, responds to an epistemological necessity that is driven by our desire to understand the world in which we live, our political contingency and our own identity. In Chapter 5, it will be argued that at the basis of the tension between truth and freedom is the concept of freedom as non-interference. Invented by Thomas Hobbes to justify absolute forms of government, this concept has been crucial in shaping and legitimising a media environment governed by radical market logics hostile to the truth-seeking purpose of the press. A republican version of freedom (freedom as non-domination) will be presented as a conceptual alternative that is tolerant of forms of interference with the market aimed at shaping the structure and functioning of the press in order to stimulate truth-seeking practices.

Before moving forward, a methodological warning must be made. This book uses indistinctively and interchangeably the concepts of 'free speech' and 'free press'. It does so not because there are no distinctions between them, but because the level of generality at which the argument works throughout most of the book (Chapters 2 through 4) does not require such fine distinctions. The book explores the rationales that justify press freedoms and their inherent connection to truth. The rationales under scrutiny apply without distinction to both individual freedoms (free speech) and institutional freedoms (free press). The democratic argument (Chapter 3) that claims that free speech is a necessary tool for enhancing public deliberation applies to both individual speakers and the media. The same can be said about the classic argument (Chapter 2), which maintains that expressive freedoms are a means for the discovery of truth and the advancement of knowledge. From this argument's point of view, expressive freedoms, regardless of their source, would enhance the truth-seeking purpose. Things get a bit more complicated with arguments that justify expressive freedoms on autonomy grounds (Chapter 4). The type of argument that claims, for example, that free speech is valuable because protecting self-expression is a way of enhancing the speaker's personal autonomy, is clearly not applicable to the media. As Onora O'Neill has argued, the press is not in the business of self-expression and should not be in it.[18] What we expect from the press is for it to communicate information

---

[17] Mainly Scanlon, 'Freedom of Expression and Categories of Expression', above n 15; and Raz, above n 10.

[18] O O'Neill, 'News of This World' *Financial Times* (18 November 2011).

that is in the public interest, and to do so in a way that provides resources that allow everyone to make adequate judgements about the world in which we live. Although it makes perfect sense that free-speech rationales of this sort are not applicable to the media, there are free-speech theories that, while grounded on autonomy grounds, are also applicable to the media. These will be dealt with in Chapter 4. These theories argue that free speech is a public good. As such, its protection is justified by audiences' interest rather than by speakers' interests. According to Raz, for example, free speech contributes to enhancing individual identity because public portrayals and expressions of specific sorts of life are a form of validation while their censoring is a form of condemnation.[19] Just as in democratic and classic rationales, speech is protected not as a consequence of *who* expresses it but as a consequence of *what* is expressed. Therefore, these rationales apply to both institutional and individual speech.

If no distinctions between the concepts of free press and free speech are necessary at the level of the rationales justifying them (at least the ones analysed in this book), it is necessary to make some distinctions in order to construct the idea of the *illusion of the free press* (Chapter 1) and to defend media regulation aimed at enhancing its truth-seeking practices (Chapter 5). The illusion of the free press as an epistemological necessity applies only to communications that are delivered by the media. If we are prone to believing that the world shown by the press corresponds to the world itself, it is because we need to assume that press freedoms are designed or have the ability to direct institutional communications towards that goal. The same is not always true about self-expression, which can be orientated towards goals that have nothing to do with truth discovery. This marks an important distinction between free speech and the free press. In fact, although some of the rationales that justify free speech may coincide with the rationales that justify the free press, the latter is expected to perform certain functions that are vital to democratic societies which are not necessarily expected from individual speakers. If the latter is true, as Phillipson seems to claim, the media should be endowed with certain privileges and carry the weight of certain responsibilities that should not be endorsed to individual speakers.[20] The distinction between free speech and free press has important legal consequences.[21] In fact, media regulation is justified

---

[19] Raz, above n 10.

[20] G Phillipson, 'Leveson, the Public Interest and Press Freedom' (2013) 5 *Journal of Media Law* 220.

[21] Eric Barendt identifies three different models that deal with the relationship between free speech and free press. The first argues that the two freedoms are equivalent: freedom of the press refers to the free speech rights of owners, editors and journalists. Therefore, no special privileges are justified to the media. The second position, by contrast, maintains that the free press is a distinct freedom from that of free speech, hence special privileges should be recognised. The third perspective, like the first, claims that the two freedoms are equivalent. However, by contrast with the first position, it adds that the free press should be endowed with special privileges when it promotes (and only when it does) the values of freedom of speech. Philipson adds a fourth model that recognises not only special privileges to the media in order to promote the public interest, but also specific forms of regulation in order to promote the same interest. See E Barendt, *Freedom of Speech*, 2nd edn (Oxford, Oxford University Press, 2007) 417–50; ibid 227.

on the basis of this distinction. If certain forms of regulation apply to the institutional speech of the media and not necessarily to individual speech, it is precisely because the former is distinct from the latter. Chapter 5 defends media regulation on the basis of the fundamental distinction between free speech and media freedoms.

There is one further difficulty that must be acknowledged at this stage. As the distinction between free speech and the free press affects the content and scope of these rights with important legal consequences, it is necessary to define 'media freedom' as a legal concept in order to identify who is going to be affected by this distinction. This issue is of special relevance considering the emergence and development of digital technologies. The Internet, in particular the blogosphere and social media, has blurred the traditional distinction between professional journalism (endowed with institutional rights and particular responsibilities) and non-professional free speech. The ability to reach mass audiences is not an exclusive asset of the media industry any longer. In line with these developments, Oster has proposed a functionalist approach to define what constitutes the media. According to him, '*if* a person or institution contributes to matters of public interest in accordance with certain standards of conduct, then they are to be conceived of as media'.[22] This book will follow Oster's approach, especially in Chapter 5, where media regulation will be justified as a way of enhancing the truth-seeking purpose.

Finally, it is important to clarify what this book is not about. First, it is not about proposing an adequate theory for the protection of speech, nor identifying which forms of speech deserve constitutional protection and which do not according to a general framework. Secondly, it is not about arguing that truth-seeking justifications are the only relevant justifications in liberal theory, or to ignore the relevance of democratic or autonomy defences. On the contrary, the purpose is to assess and to explore why the press remains such a central institution in the mediation of social reality in liberal democracies, despite all the limitations it faces in the exercise of this function. To do this, it is necessary to explore the illusion of the free press in its fullest dimension. It is necessary to overcome (without disregarding) the limitations of external critical standards, and to explore the inherent complexity in the relationship between truth and freedom from within the liberal theory itself. The final aim is not simply to contribute to a critical appraisal of the notion of the free press, but also to provide a theoretical instrument aimed at improving our understanding of what is still a fundamental notion in any democratic polity.

---

[22] J Oster, 'Theory and Doctrine of Media Freedom as a Legal Concept' (2013) 5 *Journal of Media Law* 57.

ACKNOWLEDGEMENTS

This book is the product of a long process that started almost a decade ago when I began my doctoral studies at King's College London, which were funded by the Chilean Government through the Becas-Chile programme administered by CONICYT (Comisión Nacional de Ciencia y Tecnología). Since that time, I have met persons who have inspired my work and to whom I am deeply indebted. I would like to thank my PhD supervisor, Christoph Kletzer for his support and advice. I am also grateful to Alan Norrie and Andrew Scott, my thesis examiners, who encouraged me to publish the thesis as a book. My gratitude also goes to my friends at KCL, with whom I shared joys and miseries during a remarkable season of our lives. Special thanks go to Diego Acosta, Henrique Carvalho, Anastasia Chamberlen, Hayley Gibson, Tom Goldup, Sabrina Gilani, Hin-Yan Liu, Stefan Mandelbaum, Katerina Maniadaki, Billy Melo Araujo, Nova Miao, Harry Nikolaidis, Korina Raptopulou, Rachel Seoighe and Jingyi Wang.

A significant part of this book was written in the British Library. The building and the people who work there are somehow part of the words and ideas contained in the volume. I am indebted to Noémie Oxley, Victoria Pereyra, Cecilia Sosa and Tomás Undurraga for all the conversations we had there. I am also indebted to Luna Montenegro, Adrian Fisher, Cristóbal Bianchi, and Juan Pablo Rioseco for all their kind support and friendship.

Part of the book was written and presented in the School of Law of Warwick University, where I most gratefully spent a research sabbatical as a visiting fellow in the summer of 2016. I would like to thank Henrique Carvalho for hosting me on that occasion, and for all the generous support and wise advice that he has given me throughout the years. I am also grateful to academics of the School of Law whom I met on that occasion, especially Jayan Nayar, John Snape, Tom Flynn and Tomaso Ferrando.

Parts of this book were also presented at the City University School of Law's external research seminar, at the research seminar hosted by Instituto de Ciencia Política of Pontificia Universidad Católica de Chile and at the VII Congreso de Derecho y Cambio Social (Valdivia-Chile). The suggestions, comments and constructive critiques raised on those occasions have enriched this book, and I would like to thank all those who participated and generously contributed in those instances.

I would also like to thank Alfonso Donoso, Sasha Mudd, Enzo Solari and Nelson Rosas, who generously commented on parts of this book. A special thanks to Nikolai Stieglitz for his great work and patience. My gratitude also goes to Manuel

Nuñez and to the School of Law of Pontificia Universidad Católica de Valparaíso. I appreciate the comments of two anonymous reviewers for suggestions that have contributed to strengthen the argument of this book. My special gratitude to the Hart Publishing team, specially to Bill Asquith, Catherine Minahan, Francesca Sancarlo and Anne Flegel, for their professionalism and their attention to detail.

For having always supported and encouraged every project I have undertaken during my life, I would like to thank my parents, Daniel and Vivian.

Lastly, the most special thanks of all go to Constanza, my companion and my guide. Not only this book, but an important part of my life would be unimaginable without her.

John Charney
Valparaíso
July 2017

CONTENTS

1

Free Press: Necessary Illusions[*]

I. Introduction

One of the most influential justifications of the free press is the one that maintains that it is an instrument for the discovery of truth and the advancement of knowledge. The argument is as old as the press itself and claims, basically, that government restrictions on the freedom of discussion and of the press prevent or dilate the emergence of truth. Consequently, if these restrictions are diminished or abolished, truth will emerge. This justification originated in John Milton's *Areopagitica* and appeared in its most sophisticated version in JS Mill's *On Liberty*. It has also been used as a central justification of the First Amendment in the United States since Justice Oliver Wendell Holmes so eloquently introduced it in *Abrams v US*.[1]

Regardless of its influence, the truth argument is problematic and has been subjected to severe criticism. Some of its critiques maintain that it is based on an illusion. The Critique of the Political Economy of the Press (henceforth CPEP) suggests that the economic structure of the press in capitalist societies makes the press servant to a series of economic, political and financial interests that necessarily affect its independence and freedom, and hence the way in which it depicts social reality. The free press is just an illusion, according to these theories, because there is an unbridgeable gap separating ideal conceptions of the free press from its actual conditions, a gap that necessarily affects the way in which the press portrays reality. The purpose of these theories is to expose this gap in order to show what the press *really is*. As will be analysed in section II the strategy of exposure assumes that the illusion is a problem of false consciousness—a false idea of what the press really is—and its removal a necessary (if not sufficient) condition for its transformation.

[*] This chapter appeared originally in J Charney, 'Free Press: Necessary Illusions' in *Law, Culture and the Humanities*, at http://journals.sagepub.com/doi/abs/10.1177/1743872116659845, and is used by kind permission of SAGE Publications.
    [1] *Abrams v US* 250 US 616, 630 (1919). In an eloquent passage, Justice Holmes claims that '[w]hen men have realized that time has upset many fighting faiths, they may come to believe even more than they believe the very foundations of their own conduct that the ultimate good desired is better reached by free trade in ideas—that the best test of truth is the power of thought to get itself accepted in the competition of the market, and that truth is the only ground upon which their wishes can be safely carried out'.

Some cultural theorists, on the other hand, do not view the illusion as the structural impossibility of the press providing adequate depictions of reality due to the conditions of news production in capitalist societies. For these authors, as will be examined in section III, the illusion is the consequence of the chaotic character of social reality itself, which admits of no representations. From this point of view, any attempt to depict reality is either a failure or a mere social construct necessarily detached from the reality it is supposed to represent. In other words, the illusion is redundant. As Baudrilliard put it, the illusion is no longer a question of ideology (false representations of reality) *but of concealing the fact that the real is no longer real.*[2]

To some extent, both the CPEP and cultural theorists have provided tools relevant to the understanding of the limitations of the truth argument. However, these theories are insufficient to explain why the latter still holds a prominent place in free speech literature,[3] particularly in the United States where some scholars claim that it has been the canonical interpretation of the First Amendment.[4] This chapter will examine the problematic relationship between truth and freedom through the CPEP and the cultural critique of the press. Its purpose is not only to unveil the central flaw of the truth argument in liberal justifications of the free press, but to explain why, despite its flaws, the truth argument continues to be so relevant. Building upon but superseding these approaches, this chapter affirms that the relevance of the truth argument is based on an illusion. However, the illusion of the free press, as will be argued in the last section, is not merely a false idea of what the press really is. The illusion is—in contrast—an epistemological necessity: we need the illusion of the free press in order to retain the belief of a possible correspondence between the world that appears through the press and that same world as it is in itself. If we abandon the illusion, we lose a fundamental instrument for understanding social reality.

II. The Critique of the Political Economy of the Press

The press, that is, the system of mass communication that continually produces and delivers regional, local and global news, has undergone enormous transformations since the CPEP began to expose its problems in capitalist systems.

---

[2] J Baudrillard, *Simulacra and Simulation*, tr S Glaser (Ann Arbor, MI, The University of Michigan Press, 1994) 13.

[3] See, eg, E Volokh, 'In Defense of the Marketplace of Ideas/Search for Truth as a Theory of Free Speech Protection' (2011) 97 *Virginia Law Review* 595; S Shiffrin, 'A Thinker-Based Approach to Freedom of Speech' (2011) 27 *Constitutional Commentary* 283.

[4] V Blasi, 'Holmes and the Marketplace of Ideas' 2004 *The Supreme Court Review* 1.

The emergence of the Internet, blogging and social media has radically transformed not only the platforms of communication, but also—and perhaps more
importantly—the way in which news is mediated and the participation of the
public in the process of mediation.[5] Despite all these changes, the central critique of the CPEP—as it will be seen—has remained basically unchanged. One
of its fundamental assertions is that there is an unbridgeable gap between the
free press as an ideal and the actual functioning of the press in capitalist systems.
The CPEP has argued that under capitalism, the idea that the press is free and
independent, committed to the discovery and reporting of truth, to the advancement of knowledge and the strengthening of democracy, is just an illusion.[6] The
urgent task is, accordingly, to show this illusion in order to 'debunk some of
the mythology that impedes scholars from undertaking clear analysis, and prevents citizens from being effective participants in media and communication
policymaking'.[7]

The CPEP is mainly a critique of ideology. For Chomsky and Herman, for
example, mass media are 'effective and powerful ideological institutions that carry
out a system-supportive propaganda function by reliance on market forces, inter-
nalized assumptions, and self-censorship'.[8] This propaganda model 'suggests that
the "societal purpose" of the media is to inculcate and defend the economic, social,
and political agenda of privileged groups that dominate the domestic society and
the state'.[9] In a similar way, Marcuse stresses the point that, by effectively block-
ing dissident views, the media contribute to the creation of a mentality 'for which
right and wrong, true and false are predefined wherever they affect the vital interests of the society'.[10] For Bagdikian, in turn, the institutional bias of the media
'does more than merely protect the corporate system. It robs the public of a chance
to understand the real world'.[11] More recently Nick Davies stated that 'we are deep
into a third age of falsehood and distortion, in which the primary obstacles to
truth-telling lie inside the newsrooms, with the internal mechanics of an industry which has been deeply damaged'.[12] The list can go on and on, with similar
descriptions of the media and their effects on audiences. All of them, however,
share a common element, especially when it comes to the press. This is its ability
to select, produce, censor and spread information that contributes to reproducing

[5] See M Castells, *Communication Power* (Oxford, Oxford University Press, 2009).

[6] See D Berry, 'Radical Mass Media Criticism, History and Theory' in J Klaehn (ed), *The Political
Economy of Media and Power* (New York, Peter Lang, 2010) 324.

[7] R McChesney, *The Political Economy of Media: Enduring Issues, Emerging Dilemmas* (New York,
Monthly Review Press, 2008) 306.

[8] N Chomsky and ES Herman, *Manufacturing Consent: The Political Economy of the Mass Media*
(London, Vintage, 1994) 306.

[9] ibid 298.

[10] H Marcuse, 'Repressive Tolerance' in A Feenberg and W Leiss (eds), *The Essential Marcuse:
Selected Writings of Philosopher and Social Critic Herbert Marcuse* (Boston, MA, Beacon Press, 2007) 42.

[11] B Bagdikian, *The New Media Monopoly*, 7th edn (Boston, MA, Beacon Press, 2004) xviii.

[12] N Davies, *Flat Earth News* (London, Vintage, 2009) 23.

existing social practices and aligning public opinion with the tenets of prevailing ideologies.

The type of critique favoured by the CPEP assumes that the illusion of the free press is a problem of false consciousness: the illusion consists in the belief that the press is free and independent, when in fact it is subject to a series of economic, political and financial constraints that severely limit its freedom and hence its capacity to provide adequate depictions of reality. Chomsky and Herman originally developed this influential critique back in the 1980s in *Manufacturing Consent*. There they identified a *propaganda model* that 'describes the forces that cause the mass media to play a propaganda role, the process whereby they mobilize bias, and the patterns of news choices that ensue'.[13] One of the central problems they identified of media markets in general and of the press in particular was that of their tendency towards concentration of ownership. This tendency, it has been argued, affects the ability of the press to develop its functions freely and independently.[14] Concentration affects 'the routes by which money and power are able to filter out the news fit to print, marginalize dissent, and allow the government and dominant private interests to get their messages across the public'.[15] Concentration has also been generally associated with the reduction of diversity, not only of media content, but also of viewpoints. In general, concentration has been identified as a serious threat to democracy and a serious impediment to the communicative functions of the press.[16]

Another focus of this critique has been the strongly profit-orientated character of media markets, manifested in their heavy reliance on advertising as the main source of revenue. Adorno and Horkheimer claim that advertising is the cause of media *production of sameness*.[17] This is so because, as content needs to appeal to the tastes of mass audiences in order to attract advertisement financing, the media in general and the press in particular need to lower their standards so as to find a common denominator, something which might be shared by largely heterogeneous groups of people with different interests. Moreover, as media providers are competing to attract the same mass audiences, not only do they lower their standards, but each also tends to replicate the content offered by the others. Media content thus tends to look very similar irrespective of the existence of a multiplicity of media providers. Economists have referred to this phenomenon as 'competitive duplication'.[18] They have argued that minority tastes will only be served if media companies in a specific market are able to exhaust the profits

---

[13] Chomsky and Herman, above n 8, xi–xii.

[14] For a thorough analysis of and debate about the extent and effects of media concentration, see EM Noam, *Media Ownership and Concentration in America* (New York, Oxford University Press, 2009); CE Baker, *Media Concentration and Democracy* (Cambridge, Cambridge University Press, 2007).

[15] Chomsky and Herman, above n 8, 2.

[16] See in general Baker, above n 14.

[17] TW Adorno and M Horkheimer, *Dialectic of Enlightenment* (London, Verso Books, 1997) 124.

[18] G Doyle, *Understanding Media Economics* (London, Sage Publications Ltd, 2002) 74.

generated by majority programming and pursuing minority audiences becomes more profitable than making marginal gains with the majority.[19] Although this effect applies to the media in general, the press is particularly affected because advertisers usually prefer to show their products on platforms that are able to reach massive audiences. In these circumstances, not only does news content tend to be relatively homogeneous across the spectrum, but serious journalism is also usually eclipsed by programmes and content designed to amuse and entertain rather than to inform the public.

Further problems have been identified in the strong dependence of the media on advertisement. According to Chomsky and Herman, advertisers have become the patrons of the media. Accordingly, they do not simply stimulate the production and diffusion of content that appeal to massive audiences, they are also 'normative reference organizations, whose requirements and demands the media must accommodate if they are to succeed'.[20] This is how advertisers, for example, tend to control dissident views. Indeed, as it is unusual for them to *subsidise* those who tend to prejudice their interests, they would naturally not tend to advertise their products in unfriendly business media. The radical press, which canalises dissidence and is generally antagonistic to the interests of big corporations, is one of the victims of a media system heavily reliant on advertisement. Similarly, advertisement can also work as immunity from bad publicity, as the press will usually have second thoughts before denouncing any scandal that might be linked to its advertisers.

The media environment has radically changed since Chomsky and Herman first articulated the propaganda model. With the emergence and spread of digital technologies, platforms of communication have multiplied; the amount of and access to information has exploded; participation in the public sphere has increased in ways that were unthinkable just a few years ago, and so on. Sources of information have also varied. Most breaking news, like the Ferguson, MO demonstrations, now appears on Twitter before newspapers pick it up. Although these changes have affected the financial viability of the press and its relevance in the formation of public opinion vis-à-vis other news providers, the CPEP has remained as vital as ever. This is because despite radical transformations of the public sphere, '[t]he tremendous promise of the digital revolution has been compromised by capitalist appropriation and development of the Internet'.[21] While the production and distribution of news remains under the logics of capitalism, the central assumptions of the CPEP will remain unaltered and the critique relevant.

There are different manifestations of capitalist appropriation of the digital sphere. Analysing them in detail would distract us from the central aim of this

---

[19] ibid.

[20] Chomsky and Herman, above n 8, 16.

[21] RW McChesney, *Digital Disconnect: How Capitalism is Turning the Internet against Democracy* (New York, The New Press, 2013) 97.

chapter. However, a simple sketch of this issue might better illustrate this point. First of all, the Internet has consistently increased as a source of news consumption. In the UK at least, the Internet was the second platform for news consumption (41 per cent) after television (67 per cent) and before newspapers (31 per cent) and radio (32 per cent) in 2015.[22] Most news consumed on the Internet comes from traditional news media (64 per cent). The most popular among them (apart from the BBC) are the *Daily Mail*, the *Guardian*, the *Telegraph*, the *Independent* and the *Mirror*, all newspapers that existed before the emergence of the Internet and, most of them, even before television.[23] It is true that their business models have been radically affected in the last years. However, most of the problems originally detected by the CPEP have remained unaltered—some of them have even got worse.[24] The press has become more dependent on advertisement as it has seen its revenues substantially affected by free access to online content. Moreover, competition over classified advertisements (Craigslist and Gumtree)— one of the press's most important sources of revenue—has also radically affected its income, making it even more dependent on (fewer) advertisers.[25] The financial pressure of newspapers has affected one of their most celebrated products: investigative journalism. Therefore, while the old problems of the political economy of the press have sharpened, their watchdog role has weakened.

Although the CPEP has been adjusted to the current conditions of the press, its central line of argument has remained unchanged. The basic idea is that the press in capitalist systems is subject to a series of constraints that substantially define the type of news distributed in the marketplace. Thus, the news tends to reproduce prevalent ideologies and hence provide a misleading picture of social reality. The solution given by the CPEP to this problem is to expose the actual conditions of the press in capitalist systems. The purpose is to show that under capitalist conditions of production, the idea that truth will find its way through a free market of ideas is a myth; it is an illusion that needs to be unveiled.

A. Strategic Limitations of the Epistemological Approach

The CPEP has made substantial contributions to the field. Chomsky's 'propaganda model' alone has been essential to understanding the main problems of the press in capitalist systems. However, there is a central flaw in the CPEP. This flaw can be

---

[22] See 'News Consumption in the UK: Research Report', Ofcom, 2015, available at https://www.ofcom.org.uk/__data/assets/pdf_file/0020/77222/News-2015-report.pdf.

[23] ibid.

[24] For an ethnographical exploration of this issue, see D Boyer, *The Life Informatic: Newsmaking in the Digital Era* (London, Cornell University Press, 2013).

[25] See R Kaiser, 'The Bad News about News' (2014) *The Brookings Essay*, available at http://csweb.brookings.edu/content/research/essays/2014/bad-news.html.

traced back to its critique of ideology and explains why its strategy of unmasking is ineffective. According to the CPEP, the illusion of the free press is a problem of false consciousness. The press remains an ideological apparatus because citizens are ill informed about what the press really is. Thus, knowledge about the real conditions of the press in capitalist systems, according to the CPEP, is a necessary—if not a sufficient—condition for transforming the structure and functioning of the press. Once the structure of the press is radically transformed—that is once ownership concentration, its profit-orientated character, its dependence on advertisement and so on, are overcome—the press will be able to fulfil its truth-seeking purpose.

The logic of false consciousness implied in the CPEP's critique of ideology is problematic. There is, nowadays, abundant information about the vices and problems of the press in capitalist systems. In fact, we know that the press is controlled by a few extremely powerful persons; we know that the flow of information is both subject to and responds to huge commercial, political and economic pressures; we are aware that rather than providing proper representations of the reality it describes, the press has a crucial role in their construction, and so on. However, despite our knowledge of its material conditions and regardless of ever-increasing distrust in the institution of the press itself, in our social relations we still act as if we were unaware of all this.[26] The press is still a fundamental instrument in the mediation of social reality and remains a central institution in democratic societies. Most of our knowledge about politics, economics, technology, scientific developments, culture, sport, among so many others topics, is directly or indirectly sourced from the press. We use these sources in our daily conversations, they affect our interpretation of the world we live in, they affect people's political commitments and they are the main point of entrance into social reality.

What is the problem then? Why, despite our knowledge about the conditions of the press in capitalist systems, does nothing really change? According to Peter Sloterdijk, we live in a post-ideological era where the prevalent attitude is cynicism.[27] The cynical subject is able to see through the illusion. He or she is conscious of the way in which the system works, knows the lack of consistency between ideological discourses and political practices, understands that the discourse of freedom is often used to legitimate an exploitative system, and so on. However, and despite this knowledge, the cynical subject *acts* as if unaware of it. From this assumption, Sloterdijk draws his conclusion. In this context, the traditional critique of ideology as false consciousness seems to be completely ineffective. In fact,

---

[26] See 'US Distrust in Media Hits New High' (2012) *Gallup*, available at http://www.gallup.com/poll/157589/distrust-media-hits-new-high.aspx?utm_source=alert&utm_medium=email&utm_campaign=syndication&utm_content=morelink&utm_term=All%20Gallup%20Headlines.

[27] P Sloterdijk, *Critique of Cynical Reason*, tr M Eldred (Minneapolis, MN, University of Minnesota Press, 1987) 5.

the main assumption behind the ideological strategy of false consciousness is that once the subject knows how the system works and recognises its effective conditions, illusions will dissolve. Only then will the subject be ready to rebel against the system and push for its transformation.

Slavoj Žižek argues that Sloterdijk's conclusion of the end of ideology is too quickly derived from his thesis of the enlightened false consciousness.[28] According to Žižek, despite the fact that the cynical subject is too astute, too clever to be trapped by the ideological mystification of the official rhetoric, the system keeps on functioning and ruling ideologies continue to serve the interests of dominant powers. He suggests that this is possible because 'in contemporary societies, democratic or totalitarian ... cynical distance, laughter, irony, are, so to speak, part of the game. The ruling ideology is not meant to be taken seriously or literally'.[29] Thus, although the illusion has receded in the discursive sphere, it has not receded at the level of practice. Consequently, dominant ideologies can be naked and exposed in their sheer brutality without running the risk of losing their strength. If we are to locate ideology on the side of knowledge, we are in fact in a post-ideological era. But this would be so only from the point of view of the traditional critique of ideology, which assumes that social practices are real while the beliefs that justify them are illusory. A reverse reading of this formula would be to suggest that while social practices are structured by an illusion, the beliefs that justify them might or might not be true. Ideology is, in other words, on the side of practice and not on the side of knowledge. This interpretation is plausible from the standpoint of the Marxian conception of ideology developed in the chapter on the fetishism of commodities in *Capital*. There Marx argues that the fetishism is not removable by the exposure of the illusion because it is the commodity form itself which before any (mis)representation already embodies the social relations of production. According to Marx, 'its discovery destroys the semblance of the merely accidental determination of the magnitude of the value of the products of labour, but by no means abolishes the determination's material form'.[30] In capitalist systems the illusion (ideology) is not just a false representation of reality; it is, rather, the product of reality itself. That is why if the fetish were to be removed, the whole system of production and the social relations on which it is structured would have to be radically transformed.

B. Marcuse's Radical Way

Up to now, perhaps the most radical attempt to break with the illusion of the free press is that contained in Marcuse's essay 'Repressive Tolerance', written almost

---

[28] S Žižek, *The Sublime Object of Ideology* (London, Verso Books, 2008) 27.
[29] ibid 24.
[30] K Marx, *Capital: Critique of Political Economy* (London, Penguin Classics, 1990) 168.

50 years ago. In this essay Marcuse portrays the *illusion of the free press* as the reflection of real contradictions existent in capitalist systems rather than as false consciousness.[31] Marcuse's identification with a materialist theory of ideology is inferable not only from the fact that his ideological strategy supposes a radical break with the prevailing conditions of production of the media (and not just knowledge of how the system works), but also because he argues that the communications produced by media systems in advanced capitalist societies reflect the real contradictions of the system itself and of the principles upon which it rests. This will be analysed shortly. First, however, it must be acknowledged that Marcuse's project does not completely abandon the idea of false consciousness. On the contrary, he maintains a clear distinction between truth and appearances, and claims that the removal of the latter will lead to the discovery of the former. But for that to happen the systems needs to be radically transformed. So the question is how Marcuse can propose a break with illusions if he considers them part of the system itself? Or to put it in other terms, how can a materialist critique of ideology cohabit with a critique based on false consciousness?

First of all, it is important to state the obvious. For a materialist critique of ideology, real contradictions in social reality will be reproduced through ideology as long as the system responsible for those contradictions prevails. The fetishism of commodities will continue to exist as long as products are produced for the market as commodities, and it will cease to exist only when this process is radically reversed. In fact, there cannot possibly be a *fetishism of commodities* without commodities. In other words, the radical transformation of capitalism supposes the transformation of the contradictions inherent in the system itself. Marcuse's aim in 'Repressive Tolerance' is precisely to radically change the conditions of communications proper to liberal democracies so as to remove the contradictions of the system. I shall now describe these contradictions and how, according to Marcuse, they work, and finish by analysing the benefits and problems of his ideological strategy before moving to the next section.

The first important difference between Marcuse and other critiques of the CPEP is the *level* at which the analysis takes place. While the critiques already explored focus mainly on the material conditions of the press (on its structure, functioning and so on), and on that basis show how they contradict the idea of a free press, Marcuse's analysis works the other way around. He starts analysing the principles upon which the idea of a free press is grounded so as to conclude that the application of those principles to the actual conditions of the press in capitalist systems invariably fails.

Marcuse's analysis starts with the 'abstract framework of tolerance' that regulates and justifies the protection of the free press in liberal democracies. Within this framework, every point of view deserves a hearing, every opinion might be

---

[31] See generally Marcuse, above n 10.

submitted for public deliberation and no discriminations are allowed on the basis of content or viewpoint. The ultimate purpose of this regime of tolerance is, according to Marcuse, the discovery of truth. He expressly claims that '[t]he telos of tolerance is truth';[32] thus agreeing on this specific point with Mill and the tradition that follows him, Marcuse justifies tolerance of free speech as a means to discover truth:

> Tolerance of free speech is the way of improvement, of progress in liberation, *not* because there is no objective truth, and improvement must necessarily be a compromise between a variety of opinions, but because there *is* an objective truth which can be discovered, ascertained only in learning and comprehending that which is and that which can be and ought to be done for the sake of improving the lot of mankind.[33]

Marcuse's notion of truth has a very specific content in 'Repressive Tolerance'. It is limited to the sphere of the political, and more specifically to the progressive movement towards human emancipation, to the need to create a society in 'which man is no longer enslaved by institutions which vitiate self determination from the beginning'.[34] He claims that there are true and false solutions that become distinguishable in the process of constructing an emancipated society, and *progressive tolerance* of freedom of speech is a necessary tool for the discovery of the true solutions. However (and it is here that his main critique of the liberal tradition of freedom of speech starts), the sort of tolerance that is required in order to build this society cannot be indiscriminate. At least it cannot be indiscriminate under the conditions within which liberals defend this freedom, the conditions of capitalism. In fact, according to Marcuse, as has already been shown, under the 'rule of monopolistic media—themselves the mere instruments of economic and political power—a mentality is created for which right and wrong, true and false are predefined wherever they affect the vital interests of the society'.[35] This does not mean that there is an invisible hand controlling the discourses and expressions that should or should not enter media markets. On the contrary, according to Marcuse, it is the system itself that reproduces real contradictions existent in social reality.

Marcuse's point is that in a society where power remains unequal, countervailing forces trying to fight against dominant ideas are integrated into the whole by increasing standards of living and concentration of power. In this way, he argues that the interests of workers tend to become conflated with those of management, the interests of consumers with those of producers, the interests of the intellectual with those of their employer, and so on.[36] The same contradictions existing in social reality and their apparent pacification emerge in the sphere of

---

[32] ibid 39.
[33] ibid 38.
[34] ibid 37.
[35] ibid 42.
[36] ibid 40.

communications. Consequently, although different voices are accepted in the public sphere, the meaning of those that defy prevalent conditions of inequality loses its vitality in favour of a general meaning which pacifies social conflict. In fact, when a newspaper presents the slaughter of thousands of people by some dictatorship and on the next page there is a full page advertisement for cosmetics, or when a reporter communicates the closure of a factory with hundreds of families affected in the same tone of voice as that used when the weather forecast is communicated, the meaning of injustices loses its strength. Meaning is, accordingly, predefined according to the terms of the whole. In these circumstances the truth is precluded because there is no space left for the 'rational development of meaning'.[37]

Liberal tolerance is thus something that, in Marcuse's scheme, reproduces real contradictions existing in capitalist systems: 'contradiction is not simply stipulated, it is not simply the product of confused thinking or fantasy, but is the logical development of the given, the existing world'.[38] This is why Marcuse concludes that liberal tolerance is regressive. Instead of advancing the true conditions of emancipation, instead of serving as a tool for a progressive movement towards liberation, it reproduces social inequality, injustice and misery, because the meaning of progressive voices is pacified under the weight of the whole. The trend will continue, according to Marcuse, until conditions are radically modified. The truth will be concealed while the system remains unchanged:

> To find for themselves what is true and what is false for man in the existing society, they would have to be free from the prevailing indoctrination. But this means that the trend would have to be reversed: they would have to get information slanted in the opposite direction ... the truth, 'the whole truth' surpasses the facts and requires the rupture with their appearance.[39]

Ideology for Marcuse is not simply false consciousness. It is not simply a mask hiding real contradictions. Indeed, for Marcuse, even if the mask is removed, even if we get to know how the system *really is*, nothing will change because contradictions are part of the system itself.

However, as was argued at the beginning of this sub-section, false consciousness is still important in Marcuse's theory, although it acquires a completely different meaning and requires different strategies in order to be surmounted. The strategy of unmasking favoured by the CPEP is not enough for Marcuse because the *falsity* is not simply a wrong idea about what the press is: the falsity is already contained in its functioning and in the principles to which the press responds. It is part of the framework of abstract tolerance itself. Thus, the system will keep on reproducing prevailing discourses regardless of our knowledge of how it works. This is why, according to Marcuse, it becomes necessary to subvert the framework

---

[37] ibid 42.
[38] ibid 52.
[39] ibid 44.

altogether. Accordingly, Marcuse's project amounts to the suspension of the liberal creed of freedom of speech and its replacement by a system in which only progressive voices are allowed. This strategy, according to Marcuse, will stop the process of indoctrination and will lead to the discovery of truth.

Marcuse believes that the truth will find its way by suppressing regressive speeches and stimulating progressive ones. For him truth is related to the process of human emancipation. He claims that it is possible to distinguish policies that might rationally lead societies to the achievement of that end from those that would not be fitted for purpose. He refers to the former as progressive, identifying them with the truth, and refers to the latter as regressive, identifying them with what is false.[40] These distinctions can be made, he argues, on rational grounds, based on empirical evidence.[41] Accordingly, if reason can distinguish progressive and regressive policies, it can also identify the movements and speeches committed to truth from those which are not, and so decide, accordingly, which will be admitted and which will be rejected from public discussion. His proposal is that only progressive discourses should be admitted in the public sphere, while regressive discourses should be rejected.

Marcuse's theory surmounts the theoretical and practical difficulties of the strategy of *unmasking*, and is also able to provide a proper response to Sloterdijk's thesis of the enlightened false consciousness. In fact, Marcuse would answer that knowledge of the real conditions of the system does not remove the illusion because the illusion is not false consciousness but is part of the system itself. This is why the illusion will only be removed if the conditions of the system are radically transformed. Marcuse's theory is also an adequate response to the ineffectuality of liberal attempts to favour adequate depictions of reality by reinforcing objectivity, neutrality, impartiality and accuracy. Media policies designed to apply these principles, catalogued by Baker under the name of 'market failure theories', are condemned to failure under capitalist conditions.[42] Indeed, when true and false are predefined, any attempt to discover the former only tends to intensify appearances.

However, despite the strengths of Marcuse's ideological strategy in relation to the one generally defended by the CPEP, his proposal is a recipe for a different form of indoctrination. Indeed, if, as Marcuse himself recognises, ideology is not just about false consciousness but is rooted in social practices, it is difficult to see why the practices he favours would not themselves be contaminated by ideology. Marcuse's response would be his distinction between progressive and regressive tolerance, which is equivalent to the distinction between true and false.[43] Progressive

---

[40] ibid 47.

[41] ibid 48.

[42] See CE Baker, *Human Liberty and Freedom of Speech* (New York, Oxford University Press, 1989) 37–46.

[43] Marcuse, above n 10, 47.

tolerance would be free from ideology because it favours discourses and practices that are true to the spirit of human emancipation, and which can be rationally determined on empirical grounds.[44] Regressive tolerance, by contrast, favours discourses and practices that are against that same spirit. As a consequence, societies that only accept discourses designed to stimulate progressive tolerance will be free from indoctrination, or—what is the same—they will be faithful to truth. With this answer we are back, however, in the logics of false consciousness.

According to the logic of false consciousness, and in order to justify the magnitude of the restrictions he proposes, Marcuse needs to show how progressive tolerance is in fact related to truth. The problem, however, is that although the arguments he gives are strong, they are not strong enough to support the tough restrictions that he proposes. His arguments are mainly historical. He defends the thesis that while historical violence emanating from the rebellion of oppressed classes has brought progress in civilization, no such progress is identifiable with respect to historical violence emanating from the dominant classes. To illustrate this he opposes the English civil wars and the French Revolution to fascism and Nazism.[45] Although there is no doubt about the progressive force of the former and the regressive power of the latter, from this it does not necessarily follow that the suppression of regressive voices necessarily leads to a progressive society. Moreover, Marcuse does not specify what exactly is to be considered regressive for the purpose of exclusion. In principle it seems that this would embrace much more than Nazism and fascism. His definition seems to include any movement that favours the status quo. The question is whether the repression of all these movements would really favour the type of progressive society that Marcuse is promoting. Is he not, on the contrary, creating conditions of intolerance that would favour the emergence or multiplication of forces that might be much more regressive than the ones against which he is fighting? The problem with Marcuse's theory is that for progressive tolerance to lead into a progressive society, a process of indoctrination similar to the one he is criticising would be required. Such a process of indoctrination might suppress individual differences and disagreement to the point where everyone coincides more or less with a particular form of understanding of human emancipation and the policies needed for its realization.

It seems that Marcuse's argument runs the risk of circularity. He is trapped in the logics of ideology and is not able to break the circle. Indeed, if he argues that ideology is embedded in social practices, he needs to prove why the practices he favours are not ideological. If, on the contrary, he defends the thesis that ideology is false consciousness while its opposite, the truth, is the movement towards human emancipation, he needs to show how the complete censorship of regressive voices will lead to a progressive society without the help of mechanisms of indoctrination. The answers provided by Marcuse to these problems are not

---

[44] ibid 48.
[45] ibid 49–50.

proportionate to the level of restrictions he suggests. Moreover, they do not provide an escape from the process of indoctrination. In other words, the illusion
remains intact, just as it remained intact in the strategy of unmasking generally
favoured by the CPEP.

III. Technological Progress and the Construction of Social Reality

A completely different way of thinking about the relationship between the
free press and truth has arisen that I refer to as the *cultural critique of the press.*
Although the cultural critique shares with the CPEP scepticism about the capacity of the press to provide adequate depictions of social reality, their reasons for
being sceptical are entirely different. As we have seen, the CPEP's scepticism is
based on the conditions of production of the press in capitalist systems. It believes,
however, that the press can be an instrument for the advancement of truth and
knowledge. It certainly requires radical transformations, but if these are correctly
implemented, truth might be achieved. The cultural critique, instead, is sceptical
about the very possibility of a truth-seeking press. This critique has taken several
forms. Here I want to explore in some detail the one that claims that reality is a
social construct fundamentally shaped by media technologies.

According to Marshall McLuhan, media technologies not only have altered the
way in which communications are processed, but, much more importantly, they
have changed the very world we live in.[46] Media technologies offer different forms
of communication, forms that diverge in the way in which they approach their
objects, in their point of views and in which aspects they tend to emphasise or
ignore. It is indeed very different to watch a football game on television than to listen to it on the radio. Both, in turn, are completely different from reading a report
of the game online. But technologies not only affect the way audiences perceive
the game, they have changed the game itself. Football would be played differently
if there were only radio. Media technologies have epistemological implications
because they affect our perception and understanding of the world. But the way
we perceive the world changes the world itself. Therefore, media technologies
not only have altered our perception and understanding of the world, they have
changed the world itself.

Since the media—from this point of view—play a central role in the construction of social reality, any serious understanding of the latter requires a serious
examination of the former. Accordingly, the cultural critique has divided modern history into a series of periods or epochs, all of which are shaped by the
prevalent media of their time. Neil Postman, for example, compares the *Age of*

---

[46] M McLuhan, *Understanding Media*, 2nd edn (New York, Routledge, 2001) 7–9.

Exposition, dominated by typography and controlled by the written press, with the *Age of Show Business*, dominated by the image and controlled by television.[47] According to Postman, the written media force a particular construction of public discourses—of truth telling—which responds to the requirements of its form. On the one hand, it forces writers, politicians, journalists and anyone who is involved in the production and communication of news to provide a coherent and structured exposition of ideas that need to be presented systematically to the public. Moreover, it requires its readers to develop certain basic skills in order to understand and engage with the complexity of the written form. When public discourse is dominated by the written word, there is no escape from meaning. Indeed, words devoid of meaning are nonsense, at least for the requirements of print. Hence, if written ideas are to be understood, they need to be coherently organised, properly arranged and adequately structured. These were central requirements of public expression in the typographic age, and this form, according to Postman, defined the epistemological conditions of societies in which the prevalent medium was the written language.

Broadcast television broke the rationality, uniformity, linearity and the sense of meaning that characterised communications in the Age of Exposition. The world of television, according to Bourdieu, is afraid of boring and anxious about amusing audiences.[48] News programmes are particularly affected by this trend. In fact, serious information, detailed argumentation and investigative journalism are all shadowed by the prominence television gives to scandal, violence and crime. The world shown by television is a world full of ethnic struggles, religious wars and racist hatred, 'a world full of incomprehensible dangers from which we must withdraw for our own protection'.[49] Moreover, it is a world that we cannot even begin to understand because it is shown in fragments, as parcels of information where there is no connection between one event and another, except for the fact that they all occurred within a similar period of time. Reality thus becomes a 'series of unrelated photos' or, according to Postman, 'a word [*sic*] of fragments, where events stand alone, stripped of any connection to the past, or to the future, or to other events—[a world in which] all assumptions of coherence have vanished'.[50] Television thus promotes political disengagement and favours the status quo by forming audiences alienated from their political and social reality.

The dystopian Age of Show Business gave way to the 'Network Society', a term coined by sociologist Manuel Castells to refer to a 'social structure that characterizes society in the early twenty-first century, a social structure constructed around (but not determined by) digital networks of communication'.[51] Two central aspects of this technology need to be emphasised for the purposes of this book.

---

[47] N Postman, *Amusing Ourselves to Death* (London, Methuen Publishing Ltd, 1987) 65.
[48] P Bourdieu, *On Television* (Cambridge, Polity Press, 2011) 2.
[49] ibid 8.
[50] Postman, above n 47, 112.
[51] M Castells, *The Rise of the Network Society* (Oxford, Blackwell Publishing, 2010) 4.

The first one is media convergence. From a technological point of view, 'telecommunication networks, computer networks, and broadcasting networks converged on the basis of digital networking and new data transmission and storage technologies, particularly optic fiber, satellite communication, and advanced software'.[52] By reducing information to binary codes, digital technology dismantled the old lines that used to separate mass media. Now, a single physical technology is able to carry multiple services that in the past were provided separately. On the other hand, a service that was provided through a single medium is now provided in a multiplicity of physical forms.[53] The mobile phone is the paradigmatic form of media convergence. Through a single device we can watch television, read the press, pay our bills and listen to our favourite songs, amongst many other things—including using the phone for the purpose for which it was originally conceived.

Media convergence is not simply integration of different forms of communication into one single technology. It is integration into an *interactive network*.[54] This second aspect of digital networks of communication is crucial. Indeed, those who used to be passive recipients of information flowing vertically from press agencies, newsrooms and broadcasting studios can now actively participate in the construction and circulation of news. Interaction has allowed people to communicate with one another and to express themselves in the public sphere in ways that were unthinkable only a few years ago. It has strengthened political activism, participation, and control over the acts of government and power, to mention just some of its consequences. Not everyone thinks, however, that the changes brought by digitization are necessarily for the good. What Nicholas Negroponte prophesied under the name of the 'Daily Me' back in the 1990s[55] and Castells explored more recently under the term 'mass self-communication' supposes that digitization is seriously eroding the public sphere.[56] The explosion of virtual communities and social media in which their members share common interests or desires; the emergence of a blogosphere, which is essentially a personal form of communication (to which some authors have referred as *electronic autism*); or collaborative filtering, which is used by a number of sites, such as Amazon, Spotify, Netflix and Facebook, to suggest their customers' content according to their own tastes—all are forms of mass self-communication that are affecting the vitality of the public sphere. In fact, they have fragmented audiences in such a way that the public sphere is rapidly being replaced by the subjective experience that each singular individual gets through media consumption. If television was once the cause of the loss of meaning, the transit to digital technologies is producing the loss of a shared world. And as we lose the space we have in common, the bonds that hold together a political community also get weaker.

---

[52] ibid 58.
[53] See R Jenkins, *Convergence Culture* (New York, NYU Press, 2006) 10.
[54] Castells, above n 51, 356.
[55] N Negroponte, *Being Digital* (New York, Knopf, 1995) 153.
[56] Castells, above n 51, 67.

The cultural critique does not merely analyse the effects that media has in culture. It contains an underlying assumption about the ontological character of reality itself. If the rational order of modernity (its linearity and sense of meaning) and the fragmentation of postmodernity are the consequence of the prevalent media technologies of their times, then these are not simply instruments that help us to get hold of reality. On the contrary, they configure the very reality they are supposed to communicate. This assumption is relevant to understanding how the cultural critique understands the relationship between truth and the free press. In fact, if reality is not independent of mediation but is precisely the product of mediation, then the press ceases to be an instrument of knowledge to become the fabric of knowledge itself. This assumption, in its most radical version, made Baudrilliard described Watergate and the Gulf War as products of the media. But there are subtler manifestations of this idea. When reality loses its objective and independent character so as to become a social construct, it also disappears as a referent by which media communications can be assessed as true or false, or as expressing an underlying meaning beyond the realm of appearances. From this point of view, knowledge of social reality can only be reduced to the interests and forces militating in its formation. Thus, the press—at best—would only be able to 'deconstruct' this reality by unveiling the different interests participating in its formation and thus privileging (as long as it is possible) the plurality of contingency over the singularity or identity of the 'meaning' assigned to this contingency. Although this strategy is designed to avoid ideological mystification, it can be as ideological as those that are supposedly committed to the discovery of an objective truth. The comparison between western media depictions of the 1991 Gulf War and the Bosnian war might be useful to exemplify this. According to Renata Salecl:

> Instead of providing information on social, political or religious trends and antagonisms in Iraq, the media ultimately reduced the conflict to a quarrel with Saddam Hussein, Evil Personified, the outlaw who excluded himself from the civilized international community. Even more than the destruction of Iraq's military forces, the true aim was presented as psychological, as the humiliation of Saddam who was to 'lose face'. In the case of the Bosnian war, however, notwithstanding isolated cases of the demonization of Serbian president Milosevic, the predominant attitude reflects that of a quasi-anthropological observer. The media outdo one another in giving us lessons on the ethnical and religious background of the conflict; traumas hundreds of years old are being replayed and acted out, so that, in order to understand the roots of the conflict, one not only has to know the history of Yugoslavia, but the entire history of the Balkans from medieval times ... In the Bosnian conflict, it is therefore not possible simply to take sides, one can only patiently try to grasp the background of this savage spectacle, alien to our civilized system of values ... Yet this opposite procedure involves an ideological mystification even more cunning than the demonization of Saddam Hussein.[57]

---

[57] R Salecl, *The Spoils of Freedom: Psychoanalysis and Feminism After the Fall of Socialism* (London, Routledge, 1994) 13, quoted in S Žižek 'The Spectre of Ideology' in S Žižek (ed), *Mapping Ideology* (London, Verso Books, 2012) 3–4.

The predominant form of communication involved in the Bosnian war follows, according to Žižek, the strategy of the 'externalization of causes'.[58] It is the radical opposite of the 'internalization of the external contingency' identifiable in the Gulf War, where the context and real causes of the conflict are ignored and everything is condensed into the figure of 'Evil Personified', Saddam Hussein. In the former case, on the other hand, it is the ethnic cleansing that is neglected in favour of the over-analysis of contingency and the particularities that serve to explain the Bosnian war. There are at least two major problems associated with this strategy. The first is that the more the emphasis is placed on the context, the more the major ethical issues involved in the conflict are relativized. Indeed, what should be the primary focus of attention, genocide, takes a secondary position in a debate that concentrates on the historical, ethnical and religious struggles in The Balkans. The more these conflicts are dug into, the more space is given to understanding, explaining and even justifying crimes which should be totally and absolutely condemned once and for all. Accordingly, a debate that at first sight appears to maintain a distance from particular positions turns out to be extremely ideological, because in the best case it provides a context for horrible crimes and in the worst scenario it gives grounds to justify them.

The second problem is that when the analysis of the circumstances of a conflict is taken to such radical extremes so as to relativise, for example, the gravity of crimes against humanity, subjects are relieved from the responsibility of acting. According to Žižek, the theoretical expression of this problem finds a homologous reversal in the notion of personal responsibility. Indeed, one way of concealing the web of social, economical, cultural and political circumstances involved in criminality is the idea of a fully responsible individual: 'the system can function only if the cause of its malfunction can be located in the responsible subject's guilt'.[59] When responsibility is fully condensed into the individual, the figure of the criminal tends to be demonised and the social context of criminality tends to be ignored. However, when the opposite is true, that is, when the *externalisation of causes* is radicalised and every action is seen as the product of those circumstances, it implies a notion of the subject that is completely detached from itself, completely determined by its environment and whose ability to act is thus radically stifled.[60]

The cultural critique of the press has important implications for the idea of the illusion of the free press. In fact, it turns on its head the modern idea that reality has an objective existence that is independent of us and which can be apprehended through sense perception or through the instruments created for that purpose. For the cultural critique, reality is a social construct, shaped and defined

---

[58] Žižek, above n 57, 4.
[59] ibid 5.
[60] For a similar argument see H Arendt, *Eichmann in Jerusalem: A Report on the Banality of Evil* (London, Penguin, 2006).

by the prevalent techniques of the time. As there is no longer a reality to be mediated because reality is the product of mediation, the illusion cannot possibly be
a blanket that prevents us from seeing reality, as the CPEP conceives it. For the
cultural critique, the illusion is that there is a reality beyond the sphere of appearances that can be captured by the press. This theory is thus incompatible with the
truth-seeking purpose of the press. Its fundamental mistake is that even though
it understands itself as standing in radical opposition to ideological discourse, it
actually holds fast to, while simply despairing of, the standards set up by ideology.
The cultural critique's goal of abandoning the possibility of a truth-seeking press
altogether is fundamentally an ideological move. As Eagleton argues, when reality
as a whole is thought of as merely the product of power struggles, rhetoric and
the protection of specific interests, when all viewpoints are just relative and talk
of truth, facts or objectivity is only a way of legitimising them, it is not possible
to make distinctions between discourse aimed at reproducing forms of domination and discourse aimed at subverting them.[61] And when these distinctions are
impaired, there is no space left for the struggle of human emancipation.

IV. Re-thinking the Illusion of the Free Press

Regardless of the problems of the CPEP and the cultural theories identified in this
chapter, they both challenged a fundamental social expectation with respect to the
idea of a free press. This is the possibility of the press achieving a correspondence
between its depictions of reality and that same reality, as it is, in itself, independent
of those depictions. We can no longer naively assume such correspondence. For
the CPEP, this is the consequence of the actual conditions of the press in capitalist systems; for cultural theorists, it is due to an ontological misunderstanding of
social reality: reality is the product and not the object of mediation. The illusion
of the free press consists, from these perspectives, in the possibility of securing a
continuity between both fields.

But although these critiques have exposed the illusion, although they have dem-
onstrated that there is a gap between reality *qua* reality and that same reality as
represented by the press, they have insisted on the possibility of bridging this gap
(in the best case) or on the futility of such an enterprise (in the worst). While
for the CPEP this illusion could be overcome by understanding the conditions
under which the press functions, for the cultural critique the illusion is redundant
because there is no underlying truth to be discovered beyond the sphere of appearances. Consequently, both critiques assume that the illusion is disposable.

The CPEP's strategy of exposing the actual conditions of the press in capitalist
societies in order to trigger transformations has proved to be ineffectual. Not even

---

[61] T Eagleton, *Ideology: An Introduction* 2nd edn (London, Verso, 2007) 165.

a growing awareness of these problems, an increasing public distrust of the press and the massive scandals affecting it, has changed its privileged role. On the other hand, the cultural critique seems to have dropped the illusion altogether. In fact, if, according to that critique, there is no reality to be mediated, neither can there be an illusion masking it. The illusion has been replaced with a thick blanket of scepticism, leaving a series of unanswered questions, such as what the role of the press would be if it had nothing more to offer than mere constructs detached from the reality it is supposed to mediate.

Although it is undeniable that the press, to a certain extent, constructs social reality rather than mediating it, and that many of the problems exposed by the CPEP affect the ability of the press to adequately depict social reality, if we do not cling to the illusion of a correspondence between both fields, an important part of our own sense of reality becomes a mess. This is why the truth-seeking justification of the press cannot be simply disposed of just by proving it wrong. In this final section I argue that the illusion of the free press is neither a false idea of what the press really is, nor an ontological misunderstanding of social reality. The illusion is, in contrast, an epistemological necessity. We need the illusion that a free press is able to mediate a world that exists in itself, because otherwise the very reality principle is under threat.

In *The Future of an Illusion*, Freud refers to the word 'illusion' when discussing religion. In this context, the illusion is not merely a deceptive appearance, or a false idea or belief about someone or something. Religions are illusions, according to Freud, in the sense that they provide us with comforting explanations for the most difficult cosmic questions. We might even renounce to our critical judgement if we can get, in return, the comforting feeling that religion provides.[62]

In a similar vein, Kant talks about the 'transcendental idea'. Kant's theory of transcendental idealism is based on the fundamental distinction between things as they appear to us (appearances or phenomena) and those same things as they are in themselves (noumena). Human beings can only know things in the former sense. There is no cognitive access to the thing in itself.[63] Whenever we use the transcendental categories to cognise things in themselves, rather than things as objects of sensible intuition, antinomies emerge and with them the sphere of illusions, which Kant calls transcendental illusions.[64] Hence, according to Kantian philosophy, we can never imagine in a consistent way the world as a whole: 'as soon as we do it, we obtain two antinomical, mutually exclusive versions'.[65]

---

[62] S Freud, *The Future of an Illusion*, trs JA Underwood et al (London, Penguin Books, 2008) 38.

[63] HE Allison, *Kant's Transcendental Idealism: An Interpretation and Defence*, rev'd edn (New Haven, CT, Yale University Press, 2004) 19.

[64] I Kant, *Critique of Pure Reason*, trs P Guyer and AW Wood (Cambridge, Cambridge University Press, 1998) A295.

[65] S Žižek, *Tarrying with the Negative: Kant, Hegel and the Critique of Ideology* (Durham, NC, Duke University Press, 1993) 83.

There is always a fissure, a break between things as they appear to us and those same things as they are in themselves.

The problem is that if experience is to retain its consistency, we cannot realistically renounce what lies beyond the sensuous realm of appearances. We need to believe that outer reality counts as a thing in itself, independent of us. In other words, we need illusions in order for experience to make sense; we need them in order to understand our world as a consistent whole, that is, as a world which is not just limited to our perception of objects of experience. Otherwise, if we renounce *illusions*, reality becomes inconsistent, fragmented and partial; reality becomes an artefact, it becomes virtual reality.[66] Although Kant exposes a necessary fissure between things in themselves and appearances, and denies cognitive access to the former, he recognises that we cannot avoid the illusion of thinking of those things as things in themselves *even if* we are perfectly aware that the product of this thought is an illusion. This illusion is as unavoidable as it is for the astronomer 'to prevent the rising moon from appearing larger to him, even when he is not deceived by this illusion'.[67]

This unavoidability of illusions, as Žižek argues, is based on the fact that 'the moment we subtract fictions from reality, reality itself loses its discursive logical consistency'.[68] And this is so because, as Kant himself states, in our reason

> lie fundamental rules and maxims for its use, which look entirely like objective principles, and through them it comes about that the subjective necessity of a certain connection of our concepts on behalf of the understanding is taken for an objective necessity, the determination of things in themselves.[69]

This is why the illusion that ideas refer to things that exist in themselves, beyond the realm of appearances, is inseparable from human reason, and this illusion does 'not cease even though it is uncovered and its nullity is clearly seen', as Kant himself remarked.[70]

Transcendental idealism's distinction between things in themselves and those same things as they appear to us is productive when used, as an analogy, to understand the notion of the *illusion of the free press* developed in this book. In fact, the press is, so to speak, a *space of appearances*, one that by breaking the barriers of time and space, opened up a new sphere of the sensible to human beings.[71] In this sphere the old Kantian distinction between appearances and things in themselves, and all the problems this distinction brought about, re-emerges in a different dimension. This time the press is a third actor in the epistemological table,

---

[66] ibid, 85.
[67] Kant, above n 64, B354.
[68] Žižek, above n 65, 88.
[69] Kant, above n 64, A297.
[70] ibid B354.
[71] R Silverstone, *Media and Morality: On the Rise of the Mediapolis* (Cambridge, Polity Press, 2006) 27.

and the main problem consists in identifying the relationship between the space of appearances or mediated reality and that same reality as it is in itself, independent of those mediations. In this context, the following questions arise: What is the nature of the world that appears through the press? Are these appearances constitutive of reality, or are they just mere representations of some reality that exists in itself, independent of the media and independent from us?

These questions have, in some way, already been answered in this chapter, at least from the point of view of the CPEP and the cultural critique. For the former tradition there is a reality that exists in itself, there is a true version of the world which the press aims at representing. The distortions between these two realms are, according to this critique, the consequence of the material conditions of the press in capitalist systems. This is a press whose ownership is concentrated in the hands of a few powerful media moguls, a press that does not represent the diversity of opinions and interests militating in contemporary societies, a press which, moreover, depends for its survival on the interests of advertisers, and so on. In these circumstantes, the idea that the free press is a transparent mediator of social reality is just an illusion.

What characterises cultural critiques, on the other hand, is their epistemological scepticism. The space of appearances cannot possibly reflect a reality that exists in itself because there is no such thing. Instead of representing an independent reality, the press constructs the very reality it is supposed to represent. This is thus a world of appearances, of the image or the spectacle, where connections to a deeper realm of meaning or truth have forever been lost.

The CPEP and cultural critiques have re-enacted the Kantian dilemma of the relationship between appearances and things in themselves. Just as Kant definitely separated the thing as it is in itself from that same thing as it appears to us, the theories examined in this chapter radically separated the realm of appearances or mediated reality from that same reality as it is in itself. As a consequence, the narratives used by the press to describe and communicate a particular event seem to be forever displaced from the events they attempt to describe. But if our knowledge is limited to the sensuous products delivered by the media, and there is nothing beyond those images, words or sounds that our cognition can apprehend, then our knowledge of 'social reality' becomes impossible. Although we know, to some extent, that the press cannot provide access to the events it describes as they are in themselves, we need to stick to the illusion; we need, at the very least to *think* that those events exist in themselves, independently of how the press describes them. Otherwise one of our fundamental connections to social reality would be lost forever.

In the Kantian system, the transcendental idea maintains alive the illusion of thinking of things as things in themselves in order to retain the sense of reality; in the context of the press, the *illusion of the free press* is what keeps alive the connection between an independent reality and that same reality as it is described by the press. If the illusion of the free press is thought of in these terms, we can understand why, regardless of its obstacles and limitations, the truth argument in free speech doctrine and critique remains strong. Through this analogy we can also answer the questions that have been left unanswered by the CPEP and by the cultural critique. As a matter of fact, if the critique of the strategy of exposure of the conditions of the press favoured by the CPEP is not effective, this is not because, as Sloterdijk would claim, we live in a post-ideological world whose subjects are cynical and whose knowledge of the conditions of the world they live in does not affect their practices. On the contrary, if we keep on granting such importance to the press, it is because we need the illusion just as we need the transcendental idea in order to *think* of the world as a consistent whole. We need the illusion of the free press in order to preserve the idea that there is an independent world beyond the space of appearances, and that a correspondence between reality as reality and mediated reality is achievable. Similarly, the *idea of the free press* has escaped the postmodern scepticism because it is not possible to effectively renounce the illusion. Otherwise, 'as soon as we renounce fiction and illusion, we lose reality itself'.[72] As soon as we renounce the *illusion of the free press*, we immediately lose connection to a fundamental aspect of our social reality that is mainly sourced by the press, and this explains the unavoidability of the illusion of the free press.

As will be shown in the chapters to come, this illusion is not just an empty idea. It is the product of social expectations that the people have placed on the functions and aims of the press in a free society. These expectations, as will be examined, have led to emancipatory struggles that, in turn, have triggered the recognition of the free press in modern constitutions and bills of rights. These expectations also explain the contemporary scepticism about the capacity of the press to fulfill its truth-seeking role and the complaints about the distance separating the free press as an ideal from the existing press in capitalist systems. The illusion of the free press, as we shall analyse, assumes in modern discourse a necessary connection between truth and freedom. This is most clearly expressed in the theories that have justified the importance of a free press, which we now begin to explore. From its very origins in the seventeenth century until our days, we shall see that freedom and truth have been combined in different ways. Looking at these theories closer will allow us to understand how deeply the illusion is grounded on free speech literature and discourse, the problems of the truth-freedom relation and the possible ways of overcoming them.

---

[72] Žižek, above n 65, 88.

2

The Classic Theory
and the Quest for Truth

I. Introduction

In the previous chapter it was argued that the illusion of the free press is not merely a problem of false consciousness: a false idea of what the press really is and of the products it delivers. Despite an expanding awareness of the actual conditions of the press in capitalist societies and of its inability to provide adequate depictions of reality, the illusion has not receded. Regardless of the fact that we are all well aware that not only is the press not free and independent but that even in the most advanced liberal democracies it is heavily affected by its modes of production and that its survival depends, in most cases, on fierce commercial pressures, the press still stands as a central institution in those systems and still plays a fundamental role in the mediation of social reality.

The illusion—it was argued—works at a different level. It is embedded in our social practices to such an extent that without it, social reality itself would fall apart. This is why we need what was called the *illusion of the free press*. We need it because it allows us to think that the press does not construct the realities it is supposed to mediate but that it portrays a reality that exists in itself, independent of its mediation. It allows us to think, in other words, that a correspondence is possible between reality *qua* reality and that same reality as the press portrays it. Without this illusion, without the illusion of the free press, the correspondence between the world and the way the press shows us the world would fall apart. Without this illusion our knowledge of social reality would become an incoherent, inconsistent and meaningless mess.

As the illusion is a structural problem rather than merely a problem of false consciousness, and is radically embedded in the institution of the press and in the idea of the free press itself, the best way to explore it is precisely by examining the theories of those who have studied this institution most intimately, that is to say, those who have analysed it from within. The purpose of this chapter is to commence the analysis of these theories, and to explore the historical context and the political circumstances in which the idea emerged that a free press is an adequate mechanism for the discovery of truth. This chapter also aims to analyse the internal contradictions embedded in the relationship between a free press and the discovery of the truth, and the connection between those contradictions and the illusion of the free press.

The analysis is set out in three further sections. Section II explores John Milton's *Areopagitica*. Written in the theocentric England of the seventeenth century, this pamphlet promotes the idea that truth—based on a theocentric mode of knowledge—would emerge if government restrictions on the liberty of discussion and of the press were lifted. Although this line of defence lost strength during the struggle for the free press in the eighteenth and nineteenth centuries in England, in favour of a defence based on political liberties, it remained relevant, as will be seen in section III. The truth-seeking purpose of the free press and of the liberty of discussion was, however, revived with much vigour in John Stuart Mill's *On Liberty*, and became known as the *theory of truth*. Section IV will explore the central features of this theory and its most persistent criticisms. From this analysis it will emerge that there is an inherent tension between truth and freedom. This tension appears in Mill's theory in an ambiguous conception of truth. On the one hand, Mill seems to defend a theocentric mode of knowledge for which truth is correspondence with the thing in itself. This conception of truth is the consequence of Mill's theoretical commitment.[1] On the other, Mill recognises a perspectival or subjective truth, according to which the opinion of every individual is as valid as the opinion of any other. This other truth is essential to Mill's defence of the liberty of discussion and opinion. As will be argued, Mill's ambiguity is not only the price he pays for mingling freedom and truth (two conflicting values); it is also a manifestation of the internal tension of the illusion of the free press.

II. John Milton: The Origins of the Theory

Milton's defence of the liberty of the press and discussion developed in *Areopagitica*[2] contains the original arguments of a number of defences that followed (including John Stuart Mill's) and which were later labelled as the 'classic defences of freedom of expression'.[3] Its analysis is of great importance to the general purpose of this book. This is so because it is, first of all, the earliest modern theoretical source in which government restrictions on freedom of expression and of the press are identified as clear threats to the discovery of truth and the advancement of knowledge. It is important, secondly, because Milton's notion

---

[1] This theoretical commitment is a form of empiricism that Mill follows not only in the field of physics, but also in the field of *human affairs*. See I Berlin, 'John Stuart Mill and the Ends of Life' in *Liberty*, ed H Hardy (Oxford University Press, 2002) 232.

[2] The title evokes Protagoras' burning of books, ordered by the judges of Areopagus in Athens. John Milton, *Areopagitica* (first published 1644; Champaign, IL, Standard Publications, Inc, 2008) 11.

[3] See A Haworth, *Free Speech* (London, Routledge, 1998) 3.

of truth is intrinsically connected to the theocentric mode of knowledge of the rationalist tradition, which assumes that, as we are God's creatures, our reason, if left to itself, will necessarily lead us to truth. This is an understanding of the truth that is modelled on and conceived from a point of view that has commonly been referred to as a 'god's eye view of things'. As will be shown in this section, it is in Milton's defence that it is possible to identify the first traces of the illusion of the free press in the form of a theory.

John Milton's *Areopagitica* has been described as the 'most perfect literary expression of the ideal of freedom' produced during the struggle of the press in 1644.[4] *Areopagitica* was Milton's response, in the form of a pamphlet, to the repressive political conditions of his time. It was, more specifically, an attack on the censoring powers of the state that were used to suppress the free expression of ideas and opinions through the institution of licensing.[5] But *Areopagitica* proved to be much more than an immediate response to the censoring powers of Milton's time. It contained the seeds of a profound and lasting defence of the freedom of the mind and of intellectual liberty. This is a defence that still resonates after more than 350 years. It is, moreover, one that saw, in the institution of licensing in particular and in government restrictions on freedom of speech and printing in general, a

> discouragement of all learning, and the stop of truth, not only by disexercising and blunting our abilities in what we know already, but by hindering and cropping the discovery that might be yet further made both in religious and civil wisdom.[6]

The central argument of *Areopagitica* is that restrictions on these liberties prevent the emergence of truth. This was Milton's response to a conflict that, by the time of his writing, already had a long history.[7] This conflict was one between political and religious powers trying to impose their views and conceptions of god, state and religion, on the one hand; and, on the other, individuals who attempted to oppose and criticise those views in newspapers, pamphlets, sermons or whatever tool was

---

[4] W Haller (ed), *Tracts on Liberty in the Puritan Revolution*, vol I (New York, Columbia University Press, 1934) 75.

[5] John Milton became a renowned victim of the Ordinance of 1643, when his unlicensed and unregistered pamphlet, *The Doctrine and Discipline of Divorce*, was found to contain blasphemous and pernicious opinions and, as a consequence, he was cited to the Committee on Printing and to the Westminster Assembly in November 1644. See F Siebert, *Freedom of the Press in England 1476–1776* (Urbana, IL, University of Illinois Press, 1965) 198.

[6] Milton, above n 2, 10.

[7] The introduction of the printing press in England by William Caxton in 1476 was followed by an almost immediate reaction on the part of the Crown. In 1487, only 11 years later, Henry VII instituted the Star Chamber Court, which amongst other functions had the power to 'make unlawful the writings that would harm the good rule of this realm'. What might be defined as the first regulation of the press was designed to prevent public questions about the king's ascension to the throne, but it also announced the tone in which the fight for recognition of freedom of expression and the free press was going to be framed in the centuries to come. See DA Copeland, *The Idea of a Free Press: The Enlightenment and Its Unruly Legacy* (Evanston, IL, Northwestern University Press, 2006) 22.

available for that purpose.[8] Milton's *Areopagitica* defined the terms of subsequent defences of these freedoms against the regulatory mechanisms devised by the state and the Church to control and restrict the diffusion of ideas that could threaten them. The argument, as has already been advanced, is that those restrictions prevent the emergence of truth and wisdom.

Milton believed that reason allowed men to distinguish good from evil and truth from falsehood. It was precisely his firm belief in the power of reason that explained his confidence in the benefits of open discussion. As a result of this belief, he claimed, 'Give me the liberty to know, to utter and to argue freely according to conscience, above all liberties.'[9] Truth, according to Milton, will reveal itself through the use of reason exercised in an open debate of opinions and ideas: 'See the ingenuity of Truth, who, when she gets a free and willing hand, opens herself faster than the pace of method and discourse can overtake her.'[10] As reason necessarily leads us to truth, there was no need, according to Milton, to fear the diffusion of ideas and opinions. On the contrary, there were good reasons to fight for it, as it was an essential tool for the progress of truth, religion and good government.

According to John Milton, licensing and licensors were the obstacles that had to be removed in order to discover the truth.[11] They were the central enemies of a nation committed to learning and improving knowledge in the widest range of disciplines and studies.[12] Milton's explicit purpose is, hence, to convince Parliament of the inadequacy of previous controls. Amongst his rhetorical efforts two arguments should be picked out. These are important not simply because they conveyed the theoretical basis previously sketched, but also because they were revived, two centuries later, in a completely different context in John Stuart Mill's *On Liberty*, another fundamental text in the construction of the illusion of the free press, and one which will be examined in section IV of this chapter.

The first argument is that of *infallibility*. According to this argument, entrusting to licensors the role of deciding what should and what should not be published is equivalent to assuming their infallibility. But human beings are all fallible creatures, prone to making mistakes. So, Milton asks, 'how shall the licensors themselves be

---

[8] During the 16th and 17th centuries in England, state control of speech took the form of previous censorship. Printing was restricted to members of the Stationer's Company, who had a monopoly on printing, and no work could be printed unless it received the imprimatur of certain judges or bishops. See WH Wickwar, *The Struggle for the Freedom of the Press, 1819–1832* (London, Allen & Unwin Ltd, 1928) 14.

[9] Milton, above n 2, 41.

[10] ibid 22.

[11] After an exceptional period of press freedom that followed Parliament's abolishment of the Star Chamber—the royal enforcement agency—in 1641, the institution of licensing was revived by the Ordinance of 1643. This was enacted for the purpose of 'suppressing the great late abuses ... in Printing many false, forged, scandalous, seditious, libellous, and unlicensed Papers, Pamphlets, and Books to the great defamation of Religion and Government'. See CH Firth and RS Rait (eds), *Acts and Ordinances of the Interregnum, 1642–1660*, vol 1 (London, Stationery Office, 1911) 184.

[12] Milton, above n 2, 37.

confided in, unless we can confer upon them, or they assume to themselves above all others in the land, the grace of infallibility and uncorruptedness?'[13] Like any other human beings, licensors are likely to commit errors and, in their erring, prevent the emergence of truth.

The second argument is that of *established truth*. According to Milton, truth needs to be constantly exercised: 'if her waters flow not in a perpetual progression, they sicken into a muddy pool of conformity and tradition'.[14] Anyone who holds a truth because it has been passed on to him by his master or an assembly, and who has not submitted it to the test of reason, is, according to Milton, a *heretic in the truth*: 'the very truth he holds becomes a heresy'.[15] Accordingly, the process of getting to know the truth, the process of reasoning, is as important as the truth itself. Without the former, the latter has no value. This is why, according to Milton, opinion and discussion are so essential to the discovery of truth. This same argument, under the label of 'dead dogma', was used by John Stuart Mill to defend the freedom of thought and opinion in *On Liberty*.[16]

The arguments and ideas developed in *Areopagitica* were ahead of their time. The tract was scarcely discussed or referred to by contemporary writers and public men, and was only republished in 1738, almost a century after it was written,[17] becoming for the first time in the eighteenth century a ubiquitous font of quotation for any defence of expression and of the press.[18] Something that might explain this 'late reception' is that the arguments given by Milton to support his thesis were based on rationalist premises that fitted well with the ideas of the Enlightenment, already well established in England in the eighteenth century but still incipient in 1644. And although Milton's ideas were inspiring for those fighting for political freedoms in the eighteenth century, there was a fundamental difference between the context in which Milton's *Areopagitica* was written and the one in which his ideas were later applied.

Milton's rationalism was framed in religious terms and conceived in a predominantly religious context, a context in which neither he nor his contemporaries could draw clear distinctions between the ethical, the political or the scientific. All these disciplines were influenced and shaped by a religious viewpoint, which took precedence in all human affairs.[19] This religious context not only defined Milton's ideas about the scope and limits of free discussion, but also shaped his rationalist epistemology, upon which the former ideas were grounded.

According to Milton, God gave man the ability to think and to discover the truth through the use of reason: 'God ... trusts him with the gift of reason to be

---

[13] ibid 21.
[14] ibid 33.
[15] ibid.
[16] JS Mill, *On Liberty* (New York, Cosimo Classics, 2005) 48.
[17] See Haller, above n 4, 135.
[18] For the influence of the tract on English and American writers, see Copeland, above n 7, 85.
[19] See Haworth, above n 3, 119.

his own chooser'.[20] This is why there is nothing to fear in the dissemination of ideas: 'Read any books whatever come to thy hands, for thou art sufficient both to judge aright and to examine each matter'.[21] Milton added that 'who destroys a book, kills reason itself, kills the image of God, as it were in the eye'.[22] This does not mean, however, that he was committed to discussion without limits: he believed in certain restrictions on speech, and these restrictions were framed, according to Copeland, in the light of his faith. Heresy, which included, for example, the doctrine of Roman Catholicism, should be excluded—according to Milton—from public debate.[23] However, what was central in his view was the idea that truth will always prevail over falsehood, and this was so because, as Copeland summarised, 'if public debate were open to all ideas, man, through his God-given reason, would naturally be led to God-revealed truths, and that was the only way of suppressing erroneous ideas'.[24]

In the previous chapter it was argued that the 'illusion of the free press', seen through the Kantian metaphor, is necessary because it contributes to preserving the 'order of things'. Just as 'the transcendental idea maintains alive the illusion of thinking of things as existing in themselves', the *illusion of the free press* is what keeps alive the connection between the realm of appearances and reality itself. Milton's conception of truth in turn is an early manifestation of this illusion in which the connection between liberty of discussion and the discovery of truth is framed within a divine mode of knowledge—that is, knowledge of things as they are in themselves. Lifting restrictions on expressive freedoms is for Milton a necessary measure for the advancement of god's given truths:

> Truth indeed came once into the world with her divine Master, and was a perfect shape most glorious to look on: but when he ascended, and his Apostles after him were laid asleep, then straight arose a wicked race of deceivers, who, as that story goes of the Egyptian Typhon with his conspirators, how they dealt with the good Osiris, took the virgin Truth, hewed her lovely form into a thousand pieces, and scattered them to the four winds. From that time ever since, the sad friends of Truth, such as durst appear, imitating the careful search that Isis made for the mangled body of Osiris, went up and down gathering up limb by limb, still as they could find them. We have not yet found them all, Lords and Commons, nor ever shall do, till her Master's second coming; he shall bring together every joint and member, and shall mould them into an immortal feature of loveliness and perfection. Suffer not these licensing prohibitions to stand at every place of opportunity, forbidding and disturbing them that continue seeking, that continue to do our obsequies to the torn body of our martyred saint.[25]

[20] Milton, above n 2, 18.
[21] ibid 17.
[22] ibid 10.
[23] See Copeland, above n 7, 85.
[24] ibid 87.
[25] Milton, above n 2, 36.

Milton's notion of truth anticipates a form of theocentric rationalism later developed by Spinoza through his distinction between the second and the third kinds of cognition. This is the distinction between discursive cognition or *ratio* and intuitive cognition or *scientia intuitiva*.[26] While the latter provides access to the essence of things in its outmost concreteness, and it is a divine form of knowledge, the former provides access to things as they are given to us, limited to their sensible properties, and it is a human form of knowledge. In Milton these forms of cognition do not differ from each other in their nature or origin. They are not two different and independent forms of knowledge. As Allison explains, in this mode of knowledge intellectual intuition 'functions as an implicit norm in the light of which human cognition is analysed and measured'.[27] Milton recognises that humans might never achieve intellectual intuition, never achieve a god's eye view of things. However, reason, which was given to us by God himself, allows us to see things with greater clarity, it allows us to get closer to a god's eye view of things. This is why, although the efforts to reconstruct the image of Osiris in its absolute form will be vain, nothing should prevent human beings from rendering tribute to this divine form of knowledge, the knowledge of things as they are in themselves.[28]

Milton's mode of knowledge supposes, in Kantian terminology, a form of transcendental realism that 'regards space and time as something given in themselves ... which would exist independently of us and of our sensibility and thus would also be outside us according to pure concepts of the understanding'.[29] In Milton there is a truth that is independent of us and has a divine origin, a truth that once came to earth in the form of Osiris and which will return with 'the Master's second coming'. In the meantime, all the doors should be left open, and nothing that might disturb the opportunities to advance and pay tribute to truth should be neglected. This is why reason—which is a god-given thing—should be left free. Ideas and opinions and the liberty of the press should not be stifled in the effort to advance truth and knowledge.

Milton's theory contains the central elements of the illusion of the free press. First of all, the conflict between government restrictions on speech and individuals trying to express their ideas is approached from an epistemological standpoint. Restrictions on speech are seen as preventing the emergence of truth. The central assumption is that those restrictions need to be lifted if there are to be no obstacles to the emergence of truth. Secondly, his transcendental realism evokes a truth that exists in itself, independently from us and from our sensibility. That truth,

---

[26] B de Spinoza, *Ethics*, tr E Curley (London, Penguin, 1996) ch 2, prop 40, scholium I.

[27] HE Allison, *Kant's Transcendental Idealism: An Interpretation and Defence*, rev'd edn (New Haven, CT, Yale University Press, 2004) 28.

[28] For the connection between things as they are for God and things as they are in themselves, see ibid 28–30.

[29] I Kant, *Critique of Pure Reason*, trs P Guyer and AW Wood (Cambridge, Cambridge University Press, 1998) A369.

which has a divine origin, although not accessible to human beings, is the very rod by which our knowledge is measured. The fact of its unavailability is thus not a sufficient reason to prevent its discovery. On the contrary, its discovery should be stimulated, and a central mechanism for doing so is to lift restrictions on expressive freedoms. Although we shall never reach it, we shall at least be under the *illusion* that there are no obstacles to impede its discovery.

III. The Struggle for the Freedom of the Press

A. The Political Dimension

From the predominantly religious context in which Milton's *Areopagitica* was written, England had moved into a largely secular one by the time John Stuart Mill's *On Liberty* was published. If at the roots of the yearning for a free press was 'the desire to know God and to worship according to the dictates of conscience', as Copeland remarks,[30] the struggle for the freedom of the press in the eighteenth century and at the beginning of the nineteenth century was framed within a wider fight for political emancipation, where the liberty of the press was seen as 'essential to the nature of a free state'.[31] However, it would be a mistake to think that as a consequence of this shift, the epistemological dimension of the free press— previously defended by Milton—was abandoned in favour of the political dimension that was gathering momentum. In fact, both elements are closely connected. This is not only visible in Milton, who, as will be seen in further detail in Chapter 5, challenges the political conditions of his time in order to defend the freedom of discussion. The same holds true in the centuries to come. For the advancement of knowledge and the discovery of truth were still seen as fundamental functions of a press that was, at the same time, committed to the wider struggle for political emancipation. Both were part of the same formula used by activists and philosophers in the eighteenth and nineteenth centuries to press for more freedoms.

By the beginning of the eighteenth century the liberty of the press in England was conceived of, according to Wickwar, as 'a right or liberty to publish without a license what formerly could be published only with one'.[32] In fact, prior restraints on publications ended in England in 1695, when the last Licensing Act expired without being renewed by the Commons. Restrictions on freedom of expression and on the freedom of the press did not end, however, with the expiration of Licensing Acts. Indeed, state control of speech in England took the form of ex post—rather than prior—censorship; it took the form of retribution rather than

---

[30] Copeland, above n 7, 22.
[31] See W Blackstone, *Commentaries of the Laws of England, 1765–1769*, vol 4, ed WC Jones (San Francisco, Bancroft-Whitenet, 1916) 151.
[32] Wickwar, above n 8, 15.

prevention.[33] Governments used two main mechanisms in order to control the diffusion of ideas and opinions.

One of these was stamp duties. Introduced for the first time in 1712, they became popularly known as *taxes on knowledge*, and their target was the country's newspapers and pamphlets.[34] The effects of these taxes are disputed among commentators, but what is certain is that a number of newspapers had to close as an immediate consequence of their implementation.[35] Taxes were extended to the American colonies, and were used throughout the eighteenth century and part of the nineteenth century as an overt mechanism of control over views that were critical of the Government, usually put forward in inexpensive newspapers. They were seen as a mechanism to drive these papers out of the market.[36] Suffice to say that the Preamble to the Publication Act of 1819 declared:

> Pamphlets and printed papers containing observations upon public events and occurrences, tending to excite hatred and contempt of the Government and Constitution of these realms as by law established, and also vilifying our holy religion, have lately been published in great numbers and at *very small prices*: and it is expedient that the same should be restrained.[37]

Another important mechanism used by the state during this period to exert control over the press and individual speakers was the laws of libel, particularly in the form of criminal libel. These laws were designed to sanction those who dared to defy the established order and to discipline future attempts to do so. Through these laws the state was giving a clear indication, a clear warning, about the limits of speech in the fields of politics, religion and morals. Anyone who stepped outside of those limits would face the full force of the law, in this case the force of the libel laws, which considered defamatory, obscene, blasphemous or seditious libel as identified by the persons or the institutions that were threatened by any given publication.[38]

The limits established by the libel laws as to what was to be considered acceptable or unacceptable speech during the eighteenth century and beginning of the nineteenth century were extremely narrow, especially in the field of politics. Any publication with a malicious intention that might cause a breach of peace

[33] ibid.
[34] See Copeland, above n 7, 97.
[35] See Siebert, above n 5, 316.
[36] John Toland—who proclaimed himself as a zealous defender of the free press—decried the 'licentiousness under which seditious insinuations were spread and public ministers abused with impunity. He urged an amendment to the Stamp Act to stop up the loophole whereby the six page newspapers were evading the tax, and in addition, he recommended that the evening newspapers, which were being published on post days and which were culling their news from the morning journals, be prohibited altogether.' Quoted ibid 318.
[37] Publications Act, or Act to subject certain Publications to the Duties upon Newspapers, and to make other Regulations for restraining the Abuses arising from the Publication of Blasphemous and Seditious Libels (60 Geo III c.9), quoted from Wickwar, above n 8, 138 (emphasis added).
[38] ibid 19.

was considered a crime under the common law.[39] As James Mill argued in an article published in the *Edinburgh Review* in 1811, 'if a publication be calculated to alienate the affections of the people, by bringing the government into disesteem ... the person so conducting himself is exposed to the inflictions of the law: it is a crime'.[40] The truth of the facts contained in a publication did not prevent criminal libel. On the contrary, 'the greater the truth, the greater the libel' was a strong dogma designed not to prevent arbitrary, unfounded or malicious criticisms but to stop altogether criticisms based on real facts and concrete evidence, and which, precisely for that reason, could have had much greater destabilizing effects politically.[41]

Severe limits were thus placed on the ability of the press to oppose the acts of government, to expose corruption or simply to criticise the Government if that criticism could cause a breach of peace. The problem is that the interpretation of what counted as a 'breach of peace' was extremely broad and imprecise. Anything could be considered to fall under this term, where even 'to disturb the King's peace of mind was probably a breach of the King's peace'.[42] As a consequence of all this, discontent increased among philosophers, intellectuals, activists and some politicians who considered that a free press was vital for achieving wider political freedoms. They vigorously defended the freedom of the press against repressive forms of state control. However, this was not merely a struggle for a free press but a wider struggle for political emancipation.[43]

Among those committed to the struggle for the free press and political and parliamentary reform were the Philosophical Radicals, an influential group from the first half of the nineteenth century led by the utilitarian philosophers Jeremy Bentham and James Mill.[44] They maintained that a good political system requires a strong representative body in order to check the functions of government and keep a proper balance between different powers (legislative, executive and judiciary).[45] But this representative body, they claimed, needs to have an identity

---

[39] ibid.

[40] Mill was citing Lord Ellenborough in *R v Cobbet* (1804) 29 How St Tr 49, quoted from KC O'Rourke, *John Stuart Mill and Freedom of Expression: The Genesis of a Theory* (London, Routledge, 2001) 11.

[41] See Wickwar, above n 8, 24.

[42] ibid 20.

[43] See, eg, Richard Carlile, a young radical activist in the early 19th century, who gave crucial support to the defence of a free press. In August 1819, Carlile published an article referring to the murder of 11 activists at a public gathering at Manchester, which contained a direct call to arms as a response to the murders. The Government reacted with the passing of the Six Acts, two of which were against the press, including the Publication Act 1819. The aggressive government response to Carlile's publications produced a huge impact on the intellectual circles that were arguing for more political freedoms. See ibid 67–75.

[44] In 1881 Henry Maine claimed that the Philosophic Radicals 'suggested and moulded the entire legislation of the fifty years just expired'. See H Maine, 'Radical Patriarchalism', *St James's Gazette* (18 June 1880) 259–60, quoted from W Thomas, *The Philosophic Radicals: Nine Studies in Theory and Practice, 1817–1841* (Oxford, Clarendon Press, 1979) 6.

[45] See J Mill, 'Government' in T Ball (ed), *Political Writings* (Cambridge, Cambridge University Press, 1992) 23.

of interests with the community. If it does not, it will only serve the interests of the ruling classes, thus defeating its own purpose. In order to materialise the identity of interests, the Philosophical Radicals advocated expanding the composition of the electorate to include a wider portion of the community.[46] Members of the community would be, according to the radicals, in a position to choose those who represented the community's interests as a whole in the best way possible.

The freedom of the press was fundamental in the political reforms advocated by the Philosophical Radicals. Indeed, if an identity of interests between the representative body and the community was to be achieved, if individuals were to make good political decisions at all, they needed to be properly informed about their choices. They needed to know the candidates and their ideas in order to elect those who were best fitted to represent their interests. An open debate of ideas guaranteed by a free press was essential to achieving those aims. But the free press was not only conceived of by the Philosophical Radicals as a space through which citizens could get to know the candidates and form an opinion of them. The press, like the representative body itself, was envisaged as a fundamental form of security and check against corrupt governments. It was conceived of as a sphere in which the actions of the governments could and should be held to account, a place in which even the most radical criticism should be tolerated if the defects of vicious governments were to be removed.[47] Bentham claimed that the 'press was ... the chief guarantee of the progressive happiness of the sovereign people, and their chief security against the sinister interests of their rulers'.[48] In 'Liberty of the Press', moreover, James Mill claimed that

> [s]o true it is, however, that the discontent of the people is the only means of removing the defects of vicious governments, that the freedom of the press, the main instrument of creating discontent, is, in all civilized countries, among all but the advocates of misgovernment, regarded as an indispensable security, and the greatest safeguard of the interests of mankind.[49]

The Philosophical Radicals viewed the free press as an instrument for improving the political conditions of their time. But it was no ordinary instrument; it was not another simple condition that should be met in order to satisfy the requirements of their political theories. On the contrary, the free press was an essential and a fundamental piece of the political system they proposed. Without the former, the latter would not be possible. Indeed, in 'Liberty of the Press', James Mill acknowledged that 'it is doubtful whether a power in the people of choosing their own rulers, without the liberty of the press, would be an advantage'.[50] More radically,

---

[46] ibid 26–35.

[47] J Mill, 'Liberty of the Press' in T Ball (ed), *Political Writings* (Cambridge, Cambridge University Press, 1992) 116.

[48] J Bowring (ed), *The Works of Jeremy Bentham*, vol IX (Edinburgh, William Tait, 1843) 275–95, quoted in Wickwar, above n 8, 251.

[49] Mill, above n 47, 116.

[50] ibid 117.

Bentham argued that revolution was preferable to the evils that might be caused by interferences with the freedom of the press.[51] Along these lines, as well as calling for structural parliamentary reform, which would assure a representative body aligned with the interests of the community, the Philosophical Radicals were committed to legal reforms that would remove the existing obstacles (libel laws and taxes on knowledge) to the materialization of the free press.

The political changes advocated by the Philosophical Radicals finally arrived. Whether these changes were a consequence of their influence in British politics, as asserted by Sir Henry Maine,[52] a product of the *spirit* of their *time*, or the natural outcome of an extended period of political struggle is not the object of this study. The fact is that in 1832 the Great Reform Act marked a radical turning point in the political conditions of Britain, initiating the 'beginnings of the democratic era in British constitutional history'.[53] By subordinating the House of Lords to the House of Commons and by extending voting rights (although on a limited basis), the Act permanently and radically modified the relationship between citizenry and government.[54] Citizens could now take part in a democratic process and were made responsible for their political decisions.

The necessary corollary to the Great Reform Act only came 10 years later. In 1843, what came to be known as Lord Campbell's Act removed some of the most burdensome obstacles that the law of criminal libel imposed on the press. New defences against libel actions were introduced by the Act in sections 2 and 6.[55] Crucial among these was the defence of justification, which recognised, for the first time, that the truth of a statement was a complete defence against libel actions if the libellous statement contained in a publication was for the public benefit.[56] The defence of justification removed from the common law the old dogma of 'the greater the truth, the greater the libel'. With it, new possibilities were opened to the press. Indeed, Lord Campbell's Act gave the press a powerful instrument, an instrument that allowed it to scrutinise with increasing liberty the actions of those in power if that scrutiny was based on the truth and was done for the benefit of the community. The defence of justification was thus the first big step taken to transform the press into a powerful check on the actions of the Government; it was a fundamental move towards materialising the objectives that the Philosophical Radicals expected the press to fulfil: security against corruption and guarantee of good governments.[57]

---

[51] Wickwar, above n 8, 251, fn 1.

[52] See Thomas, above n 44, 16.

[53] I Loveland, *Political Libels: A Comparative Study* (Oxford, Hart Publishing, 2000) 19.

[54] I Loveland, *Constitutional Law: A Critical Introduction* (London, Butterworths, 1996) ch 7.

[55] See C Duncan, *Duncan and Neill on Defamation* (London, Butterworths, 1983) 118 and 159.

[56] ibid 159.

[57] Although seditious libel and blasphemous libel were not reformed, by the 1830s some influential government authorities were of the mind that libel abusing the institutions of the country and incitement to general resistance to government did very little harm. However, they thought that the best way of dealing with them was through the discretionary activity of the Attorney-General, rather than removing these libels completely from the law. See Wickwar, above n 8, 308–9.

B. The Epistemological Dimension

The defence of a free press in the eighteenth century and at the beginning of the nineteenth century was not, however, exclusively circumscribed by political objectives. Its epistemological dimension, although overshadowed by the political context of the time, was still recognised as something fundamental, even by those who—like the Philosophical Radicals—defended the advantages of a free press on predominantly political grounds. The fact is that the epistemological dimension is not something that can easily be ignored in any defence of the freedom of the press, especially in the context of a struggle for political emancipation. This is because a political struggle necessarily involves the question about the relationship between power and knowledge.

This question had been raised as early as 1597, and answered by the English philosopher Francis Bacon with the formula 'knowledge itself is power'.[58] Although Bacon's formula was provided in his *Religious Meditations on Heresy*, where he was talking about the knowledge of God, it expresses a relationship between knowledge and power that has been often held during the modern period. This idea is that power is a function of knowledge. In its theological form this idea assumes that knowledge of God provides the person who holds it with a form of power. According to Bacon, one errs by not knowing the scriptures, and by erring one affects his capacity to act in the world.[59] Hence, the precept is to increase our knowledge of God and to learn the scriptures. This knowledge will necessarily increase our power.

Although the Philosophical Radicals were looking at the relationship between knowledge and power in a secular context, their understanding of this relationship was not so distant from Bacon's. For them, as for Bacon, power was a function of knowledge. And in a secular context this relationship supposed that the greater the knowledge about the world and social reality, the greater the political power. As John Stuart Mill clearly acknowledged in his essay 'De Tocqueville on Democracy':

> The knowledge which is power, is not the highest description of knowledge only: any knowledge which gives the habit of forming an opinion, and the capacity of expressing that opinion, constitutes a political power; and if combined with the capacity and habit of acting in concert, a formidable one.[60]

The formula provided by Mill supposes a causal relationship between knowledge and power. But in order to make this statement productive, it is necessary to define

[58] F Bacon, 'Religious Meditations, On Heresy' in *The Essaies of Sr Francis Bacon* (Edinburgh, AndroHary, 1614).
[59] See Bacon, *The Essaies of Sr Francis Bacon*, above n 58.
[60] JS Mill, 'De Tocqueville on Democracy in America [II]' in JM Robson (ed), *Essays on Politics and Society: Collected Works of John Stuart Mill*, vol XVIII (Toronto, University of Toronto Press; London, Routledge & Kegan Paul, 1977) 165.

the type of knowledge that constitutes political power. At the beginning of the nineteenth century it was clearly no longer knowledge about God that was important. For James Mill, the necessary knowledge was reduced to a specific ambit of the political, more specifically to the functions of government. A good government, according to him, is achieved when the interests of the rulers are aligned with the interests of the citizens.[61] In the case of rulers, their interest is reduced to their desire to remain in power regardless of their actions and plans. In order to succeed in this desire, bad governments will keep societies in a servile state of mind, segregated from truth.[62] The type of knowledge that is fundamental to preventing this from happening, and hence to increasing the power of the people by aligning the interests of their rulers with their own, is, according to James Mill, political knowledge: 'The people ought to know, if possible, the real qualities of the actions of those who are entrusted with any share in the management of their affairs.'[63] This is their security for the good conduct of government. The liberty of the press is an essential instrument for guaranteeing this.

For John Stuart Mill, however, the type of knowledge that constitutes political power was broader than the one envisioned by his father. It was not limited to the actions and opinions of politicians but encompassed issues as broad as 'morals, religion, politics, social relations and the business of life'.[64] John Stuart Mill observed that in the English society of the nineteenth century, which was in a process of secularisation, the old sources that gave authority or legitimacy to received knowledge, such as the dogmas of priests or philosophers, were receding.[65] He noted, not without discomfort, that a new form of authority was emerging. This new authority, which was already identified by De Tocqueville in America, derived its legitimacy from public opinion, and more specifically from the number of people that supported it. And in a society where everybody was considered to be equal to the rest, it appeared almost impossible that the opinion of everyone could possibly be wrong. As a consequence, this new authority lay, according to Mill (agreeing at this point with De Tocqueville), in a sort of 'faith in public opinion', which becomes 'a species of religion, and the majority is the prophet'.[66]

A *religion of public opinion* emerged in England—as in the United States—as a consequence of the struggle for the freedom of the press and for broader political freedoms. An ever-stronger public opinion was guided by a press that saw itself as heavily committed to contributing to the advancement of knowledge and to the discovery of truth. Richard Carlile was at the frontline of this struggle in England. He became renowned in the Reform Movement for being imprisoned for parodying the Church of England and for deliberately provoking the

---

[61] See Mill, above n 45, 4.
[62] See Mill, above n 47, 118.
[63] ibid 122.
[64] See Mill, above n 16, 44.
[65] Mill, above n 60, 179.
[66] A de Tocqueville, *Democracy in America*, as quoted ibid.

Government by publishing a serialised version of the works of Thomas Paine, challenging the authority of Christianity and the nature of revealed religion. He popularised the idea that knowledge is power[67] when he wrote in *The Republican:* 'Let us, then, endeavour to progress in knowledge, since knowledge is demonstrably proved to be power.'[68]

Knowledge, according to Carlile, was no longer to be received from the dogmas of the Church. In a free society, knowledge should be derived from the open discussion of opinions and ideas, and the press was the means by which this discussion should be administered: 'I tell Jehovah to his face that I will worship no other God but the Printing-Press! To that great power I will offer my matins and my vespers, and live alone for its glory and, to exhibit its powers omnipotent!'[69] As a result of his belief, the premises in Fleet Street where his paper *The Republican* was produced became known as the 'Temple of Reason', evoking the idea that the press was the instrument that had replaced the Church in the pursuit of truth. But the press, as Carlile acknowledged, also replaced the authority of the state, which used to frame the admissible scope of knowledge through restrictions on speech. These restrictions, symbolized in the figure of the monarch, were receding in favour of a new authority: the printing press, which was supposed to be the source of all social benefits and progress:[70] 'The Printing press has become the Universal Monarch; and the Republic of Letters will go on to abolish all minor monarchies, and give freedom to the whole human race, by making it as one nation and one family.'[71]

The idea of a press as a single nation, as a single family, united in the advancement of knowledge and progress through the instrument of open and free discussion, was indeed an idealised and mythical image of the free press. As we have seen, in this period, England achieved important political transformations, which, according to Loveland, radically altered the relationship between citizenry and government.[72] And these changes also radically affected the nature of the struggle of a free press in the years that followed. Indeed, the fading power of the state with respect to the control of speech was giving way to the increasing power of a public opinion, which, according to some, threatened to monopolise the scope of discussion. John Stuart Mill wrote his *On Liberty*, which contains what is perhaps the most important defence of the freedom of discussion, in this belief. And although the context and the nature of the conflict had changed, his defence revives with full strength the epistemological dimension of the free press, something that will now be analysed.

---

[67] See O'Rourke, above n 40, 167, fn 19.
[68] R Carlile, *The Republican* (26 April 1822) vol v, 514.
[69] R Carlile, *The Republican* (19 July 1822) vol vi, 227.
[70] R Carlile, *The Republican* (1 March 1822) vol v, 279.
[71] R Carlile, *The Republican* (6 September 1822) vol vi, 449.
[72] Loveland, above n 54, ch 7.

IV. John Stuart Mill and the Theory of Truth

Mill's central defence of the liberty of thought and discussion is contained in the second chapter of his famous work, *On Liberty*. Published in 1859, the political and social conditions of the time substantially differed from those prevailing only a few years before. While the Great Reform Act of 1832 initiated the democratic constitutional era in England, Lord's Campbell Act of 1843 gave a new breath to the freedom of the press.[73] As a witness to and as an active advocate of these transformations, John Stuart Mill was aware that the political and civil liberties gained during the first half of the nineteenth century had modified the way in which the questions of the freedom of discussion and of the press should be assessed. Indeed, when he referred in his *Autobiography* to the prosecutions of Carlile in 1819, he claimed that '[f]reedom of discussion even in politics, much more in religion, was at that time far from being, even in theory, the conceded point which it at least *seems* to be now'. With this conviction in mind, Mill opens Chapter 2 of *On Liberty* with a claim that:

> The time, it is to be hoped, is gone by, when any defence would be necessary of the 'liberty of the press' as one of the securities against corrupt or tyrannical government ... This aspect of the question, besides, has been so often and so triumphantly enforced by preceding writers that it needs not be specially insisted on in this place.[74]

The arguments once advanced by the Philosophical Radicals did not need to be pushed forward any longer. This was not simply because they were argumentatively exhausted but, more importantly, because the conditions of the time did not call for such a defence. The idea that a free press was a fundamental security against corrupted and tyrannical governments had permeated all political levels in such a way that, according to Mill, it would be highly unlikely that a government would use its powers to suppress political discussion.

This is the radical difference that distinguishes the political context in which Mill's defence was developed in *On Liberty* from the contexts of previous defences. The crucial point is that he was no longer reacting to government restrictions on the freedom of the press. In contrast with Milton's *Areopagitica*, which attacked the institution of licensing contained in the Ordinance of 1643,[75] Mill was not opposing a specific act. His purpose was not to argue against regressive political and legal conditions, which at the time of the Philosophical Radicals were manifest in stamp duties and ruthless libel laws.[76] Mill's defence of the freedom of discussion did not need to engage with government decisions anymore. And by freeing itself from strict political contingency, Mill's argument seemed to disengage itself from

---

[73] Loveland, above n 53, 19; Duncan, above n 55, 118.
[74] Mill, above n 16, 19.
[75] Siebert, above n 5, 198.
[76] See Wickwar, above n 8, 138.

pragmatic political objectives, creating instead a 'principled defence'. Many saw in this effort a new way of approaching the subject.

In fact, Mill's defence in *On Liberty* has been interpreted as a sound alternative to consequentialist defences previously put forward by the Philosophical Radicals and indeed by Mill himself.[77] It is seen as an alternative in which human enhancement, instead of security against corruption in government, was at the very core of the exercise of free and open discussion. Some authors have claimed that Mill's conception of freedom of thought and discussion, as presented in *On Liberty*, was designed to improve intellectual liberty, which is seen as the basis of *all* other liberties, including political liberties.[78] Others have claimed that freedom of thought and discussion was for Mill a way of strengthening individual autonomy,[79] while yet others have stressed that it is a form of self-expression.[80] Lastly, some have suggested, more radically, that Mill's doctrine of freedom of thought and discussion completely breaks with anything previously existing. Totally departing from previous views in both philosophy and religion, they argue that Mill's doctrine proposed a new type of society, one that was built and structured upon the value attributed to the liberty of thought and discussion.[81]

Mill's approach to the subject was not, however, completely new and original. Despite the fact that the political and social context of the publication of *On Liberty* was completely different from that prevailing in the times of Milton and even of the Philosophical Radicals, the *nature* of the conflict with respect to the free press was not so different. This conflict has always involved an external threat to the exercise of this freedom, which affects our capacity to know about and to reflect on the world in which we live. In his *Areopagitica*, Milton had identified government restrictions on free and open discussion as threats to the advancement of knowledge and the discovery of truth. His formula was simple, and can be reduced to the following statements:

(a) government restrictions on the freedom of discussion and of the press affect the discovery of the truth and the advancement of knowledge;
(b) if these restrictions are diminished then;
(c) the truth will emerge.

---

[77] See J Bowring (ed), *The Works of Jeremy Bentham*, vol II (Edinburgh, William Tait, 1843) 275–95.

[78] For an extended version of this argument, see O'Rourke, above n 40, 76–93 and 162.

[79] According to John Gray, the fact that Mill admitted restrictions on speech when the latter might induce violence, as in the case of incendiary speech addressed to an angry mob, shows that Mill's defence is justified on the basis of individual autonomy. Gray argues that the restriction is admissible in this case because the actions of the individual members of the mob will be the consequence of the circumstances of the moment and not of their autonomous decision. These restrictions were accepted on the basis of what Gray called the 'improbability of autonomous thought in excited mobs'. See J Gray, *Mill on Liberty: a Defence*, 2nd edn (London, Routledge, 1996) 194.

[80] O O'Neill, 'News of This World', *Financial Times* (18 November 2011).

[81] W Kendall, 'The "Open Society" and its Fallacies' (1960) 54 *The American Political Science Review* 972.

Although in the eighteenth century and at the beginning of the nineteenth century the epistemological dimension of the defences of free speech and the free press was overshadowed by the political context, it remained relevant. In fact, government restrictions on speech were considered to affect the knowledge that the community could have with respect to the actions and qualities of its leaders.[82] Accordingly, although heavily framed and designed to advance political freedoms, the Philosophical Radicals' defence still incorporated Milton's ideas to some extent. Government restrictions on expressive freedoms were considered to adversely affect the advancement of knowledge, something the Philosophical Radicals equated with political knowledge.

Shortly, it will be argued that John Stuart Mill revived and gave new strength to Milton's argument of truth. However, before that, it is important to underline that in the middle of the nineteenth century—when *On Liberty* was published— the Government was not, according to Mill, the exclusive threat to the freedom of the press. Mill identified a menace to freedom that had emerged in the context of the struggle for political emancipation, and which had grown stronger with the political and civil liberties gained as a consequence of that struggle. Mill referred to this threat as the *tyranny of the majorities*.[83]

Mill claimed that the tyranny of the majorities was as relentless a threat as the Government itself. According to Gertrude Himmelfarb, in *On Liberty* as in previous writings, Mill starts from the premise that while democracy is the salient fact of contemporary life, the overwhelming influence of public opinion is its greatest evil.[84] Indeed, as Mill argues on the first pages of *On Liberty*, the tyranny of the majority 'is now generally included among the evils against which society requires to be on its guard'.[85] In another statement he develops in more detail the risks of this new form of tyranny:

> Protection, therefore, against the tyranny of the magistrate is not enough; there needs protection also against the tyranny of the prevailing opinion and feeling, against the tendency of society to impose, by other means than civil penalties, its own ideas and practices as rules of conduct on those who dissent from them; to fetter the development and, if possible, prevent the formation of any individuality not in harmony with its ways, and compel all characters to fashion themselves upon the model of its own.[86]

Mill had identified his enemy: it had a name, was the product of democratic societies and was a menace to liberty. This enemy emerged together with or parallel to the reduction of government restrictions on the freedom of discussion and, as such, replaced or complemented the threat that was once condensed in governments alone. With such an identifiable enemy pullulating at the centre

---

[82] Mill, above n 47, 122.
[83] Mill, above n 16, 7.
[84] See G Himmelfarb, *On Liberty and Liberalism: The Case of John Stuart Mill* (New York, Knopf, 1974) 38.
[85] Mill, above n 16, 7.
[86] ibid.

of democratic societies, it is difficult to claim that Mill's defence was completely abstracted from political contingency. Although this enemy was more diffuse than the state, which has a structure or a body that speaks through its laws, for Mill the threat of the tyranny of majorities was, nonetheless, a danger of the same magnitude.[87] Consequently, Mill's defence of the freedom of thought and discussion shares with all previous defences of these freedoms a common starting point: a threat to their exercise posed by an identifiable enemy. Although the form of the enemy had changed, the nature of the threat itself—as will now be explained—was little different.

A. The Central Argument

Although the political, social and intellectual conditions prevalent in England when *On Liberty* was published were radically different from the ones prevailing two centuries before, Mill's argument did not abandon the substance (and even the form) of Milton's defence to the freedom of thought and discussion:

> [T]he peculiar evil of silencing the expression of an opinion is that it is robbing the human race, posterity as well as the existing generation—those who dissent from the opinion, still more than those who hold it. If the opinion is right, they are deprived of the opportunity of exchanging error for truth; if wrong, they lose, what is almost as great a benefit, the clearer perception and livelier impression of truth produced by its collision with error.[88]

The central argument employed by Mill in *On Liberty* is that freedom of discussion leads to the discovery of truth, while its suppression leads to its obfuscation. As different scholars have recognised, the epistemological dimension is crucial to Mill's defence.[89] The old argument of truth was revived and systematised with such strength and conviction by Mill that his theory is popularly known today as the *theory of the truth*,[90] and has been labelled *the classic version of the classic defence* in a clear reference to *Areopagitica*.[91] Mill himself recognised that the type of arguments employed in the second chapter of *On Liberty* belonged to a longstanding tradition of defence of this liberty: 'Those to whom nothing which I am about to

---

[87] In a letter sent to Theodor Gomperz before the publication of *On Liberty*, Mill said that the subject of the book is 'moral, social, & intellectual liberty, asserted against the despotism of society whether exercised by governments or by public opinion'. See JS Mill in FE Mineka and DN Lindley (eds), *The Later Letters of John Stuart Mill: Collected Works of John Stuart Mill*, vol XV (Toronto, University of Toronto Press; London, Routledge & Kegan Paul, 1972) 581.

[88] Mill, above n 16, 21.

[89] Himmelfarb argues that instead of defending the importance of preserving individuality against the despotism of the Government or of public opinion, as Mill proceeds to do in other chapters of *On Liberty*, in ch 2 he rejects these forms of despotism for the sake of truth. See Himmelfarb, above n 84, 24–25; see also Haworth, above n 3, ch IV.

[90] See Himmelfarb, above n 84, 25.

[91] See Haworth, above n 3, 3.

say will be new may therefore, I hope, excuse me if on a subject which for now three centuries has been so often discussed I venture on one discussion more.'[92] Mill's argument is structured in four parts that will be summarised briefly: (i) the argument of infallibility; (ii) the argument of rationality; (iii) the argument of dead dogma; (iv) the argument of half-truths.

Argument (i), known as the argument of infallibility, was already used by Milton in *Areopagitica* against the institution of licensing.[93] According to Mill, 'all silencing of discussion is an assumption of infallibility':[94] those who prevent the publication of an opinion do so in order to defend certain ideas that they consider to be true. Their certainty about the truth of an idea is justifiable, and even desirable. But when that certainty is used to decide for everyone what is to be heard and what is to be silenced, it amounts to absolute certainty. As fallible creatures, argues Mill, human beings have again and again censored and persecuted ideas that have hitherto proven their value and power to mankind. And they have done so because they have assumed their own infallibility. The greatest risk of this assumption is, according to Mill, that if certain doctrines generally accepted by a society are false, silencing opposing opinions may prevent the emergence of the truth, and consequently it may preclude the possibility of *exchanging error for truth*.[95]

Arguments (ii) and (iii) do not deal with the problem of silencing ideas or opinions that might be true. On the contrary, they are designed to respond to the problem of what is to be done with opinions that are false or contain error.[96] Should they be silenced for the sake of truth, or should they be openly admitted to public debate? Mill definitely inclines to the latter position. The argument of rationality (ii) asserts that even if some opinions contain the whole of the truth, if those who hold them do not understand the grounds on which they rest, they will hold them as prejudice, as mere superstition.[97] According to Mill, as important as the truth itself is the conviction with which it is held. And conviction can only be obtained if its arguments have been tested in the most rigorous way. Only in the confrontation of ideas, only in a permanent and fearless competition between truth and falsity, will those who are exposed to truth be able to understand it on rational grounds and to defend it with the required conviction against opposing views:

[N]o one's opinions deserve the name of knowledge, except so far as he has either had forced upon him by others or gone through of himself the same mental process which would have been required of him in carrying on an active controversy with opponents.[98]

[92] Mill, above n 16, 19.
[93] Milton, above n 2, 21.
[94] Mill, above n 16, 21–22.
[95] The silencing of Socrates' teachings, Jesus' conviction and the persecution of Christianity are some of the examples used by Mill to illustrate this point: ibid 29–33.
[96] ibid 43–55.
[97] ibid 64.
[98] ibid 55.

In Mill's view, even false ideas should be protected, because they are like a sparring partner in the exercise of reason and truth.

Some authors have suggested that the appeal to the value of rationality shows that Mill's defence of the freedom of discussion is grounded on the ideal of autonomy. According to Gray, Mill's repudiation of restrictions on freedom of speech 'is a consistent application of his ascription to human beings of an overriding interest in becoming and remaining autonomous agents'.[99] But the fact is that Mill is not protecting the expression of false ideas merely based on the autonomy of the individual who professes those ideas, or of the individual who is benefited by them because he is pushed to prove the truth through reasoned arguments. On the contrary, the value of rationality is here used as a tool, as a *necessary* mechanism for the discovery of truth. So clear is Mill on this point that he even claims that if no one opposes received truths, opponents should be invented: 'So essential is this discipline of moral and human subjects that, if opponents of all-important truths do not exist, it is indispensable to imagine them and supply them with the strongest arguments which the most skilful devil's advocate can conjure up'.[100] Mill is thus interested in the *use* of that opinion and not necessarily in the individual who holds it. This is why if the opinion holder does not exist, it must be imagined, it must be created.

Argument (iii), generally known as 'dead dogma', confirms the relevance of truth in Mill's defence. The first use of this argument appears in Milton's *Areopagitica*. According to this argument, if the truth of a doctrine is not constantly scrutinised it will become mere prejudice. 'In the absence of discussion', says Mill, 'not only the grounds of the opinion are forgotten, but too often the meaning of the opinion itself'.[101] Without discussion, truth loses its vitality, it relinquishes its meaning and, consequently, risks its own existence and with it all the well-being that mankind can expect from what Mill calls 'received truths'.[102] According to Mill, the liveliest example of this is the decay of Christian faith. He claims that what distinguishes early Christians from the Christians of his times is the strength with which the former held their opinions and the force with which their practices were guided by their beliefs. By contrast, according to Mill, the Christians of his own era were completely disengaged from their Christian beliefs, which were subordinated to their *nation, class or religious profession*.[103] Mill sees here an inherent weakness that explains the cause of why 'Christianity now makes so little progress in extending its domain'.[104] Vital belief is an indispensable requirement for the maintenance of a particular doctrine and not necessarily an end in itself: *in the*

---

[99] Gray, above n 79, 104–05.
[100] Mill, above n 16, 46.
[101] ibid 48.
[102] ibid 53.
[103] ibid 50.
[104] ibid 51.

absence of discussion, the meaning of the opinion itself is forgotten, and with it the relevance and strength of any received truth.[105]

The last argument (iv) given by Mill in his defence is best known as the theory of half-truths. The argument starts from the assumption that popular opinions often contain the truth, but seldom or never the whole of the truth.[106] A diversity of opinions is thus advantageous, because when conflicting doctrines share part of the truth, the non-conforming opinion provides the remainder that the other opinion contains only in part and vice versa. Consequently, as every opinion is likely to contain a portion of truth, the wider and freer the debate, the likelier would be its discovery.[107] This part of the defence has been traditionally presented as the one that contains, in its most clear way, Mill's conception of truth.[108] It is a conception that, as will be shown, is not so different from Milton's: a truth that, in the form of a jigsaw puzzle, has been cut apart from its very centre and spread throughout the world for men to put it back together.

The importance of the epistemological dimension in Mill's defence of the freedom of thought and discussion is undeniable. Having shown this, I now want to demonstrate that the way in which Mill depicted the nature of the conflict, although altered by the political circumstances of his time, is not so different from the way in which Milton portrayed it in his *Areopagitica*. As a point of fact, in both there is an agent that represents an obstacle to the exercise of this freedom. While in Milton the agent is government, Mill adds to it the threat of public opinion. Moreover, the threat of silencing opinions is identical, and in both cases amounts to the preclusion of the discovery of truth and the advancement of knowledge. But the coincidences between Mill and Milton do not stop here. Like Milton, Mill cultivates a theocentric mode of knowledge in which truth is a correspondence with the thing in itself. Like Milton, Mill believes that this truth might be advanced through open discussion and the debate of ideas. This is why in Mill, just as in Milton, the affirmation of the epistemological dimension is also constitutive of the *illusion of the free press*. The question is how this illusion is still possible in a secularised context, so different from the religious one prevalent in Milton's time. In order to answer this question, it is necessary to explore Mill's conception of truth in more detail.

B. The Meaning of Truth

The ambiguities (some authors use the word inconsistencies) of some of the arguments deployed in *On Liberty* were identified in the early critiques made of the

---

[105] ibid 48.

[106] ibid 56.

[107] ibid.

[108] According to Gray, this argument protects 'the value of the truth': see Gray, above n 79, 104; see also I Berlin, 'John Stuart Mill and the Ends of Life' in *Liberty*, ed H Hardy (Oxford, Oxford University Press, 2002) above n 1, 233.

book, and have been repeated ever since.[109] One thing that has helped produce controversy is Mill's conception of truth. The question is whether Mill is defending the idea of an objective and single truth, which might be discovered if the right mechanisms are in place, or, contrarily, arguing for a notion in which the *truth* of any single man or any particular nation is as valid as that of any other if only it is held rationally.

It will be argued in this section that Mill's ambiguous conception of truth is a symptom of tensions existing between truth and freedom (which will be explored in further detail in the next chapter) and a manifestation of the 'illusion of the free press'. On the one hand, his theory seems to be grounded in a theocentric mode of knowledge, where truth is correspondence with the thing in itself. This truth, although not available to human beings in their current state of mental development, functions as a measuring rod that defines the standard of objectivity in knowledge. While this conception of truth is a consequence of Mill's theoretical commitments, there is another conception identifiable in the text, which plays a practical role. This second version speaks of a perspectival or multidimensional truth, and its role is to make the discovery of truth compatible with the liberty of discussion. Indeed, as will be explained, while the notion of truth derived from a theocentric mode of knowledge is not attuned to the liberty of discussion, a perspectival version of it is. Mill's ambiguous approach to truth reveals the illusion of the free press, because while his theocentric mode of knowledge reaffirms his commitment to truth, his perspectival approach recognises the value of liberty. Truth and freedom are blended at the expense of ambiguity. And this ambiguity is a manifestation of the illusion of the free press: it keeps alive the hope that *if there is a better truth*, it might be advanced by the liberty of the press and discussion.

---

[109] One of the central problems identified in the early critiques of *On Liberty* is that at certain points Mill grounds his arguments on the principle of liberty, at others on the principle of utility. The problem is that these principles are at odds with each other. Indeed, while the principle of liberty is in harmony with the value of freedom, the principle of utility tallies with a contradictory value, which is the accumulation of happiness. In human affairs huge losses of happiness could be the result of a consistent application of the principle of liberty and vice versa. By recognising and applying both set of principles in *On Liberty*, Mill was caught up in an inconsistency from which he could not escape. For early critiques of *On Liberty*, see JC Rees, *John Stuart Mill's On Liberty* (Oxford, Clarendon Press, 1995) 78–106. The ambiguity of his theory of free speech consists in that, while the main goal of freedom of speech is the social utility derived from the discovery of truth, there are also some aspects of human liberty identifiable as justifications for its protection. Those who defend the priority of human liberty over the discovery of truth claim that this is the only way in which his theory can be read consistently. Otherwise, they warn that all speech that is not conducive to the discovery of the truth will fall outside its ambit of protection. Any trivial speech, any discourse that lacks the necessary qualities or attributes required to build a consistent truth would not be considered valuable. That would be inconsistent with Mill's attempt to bring absolute protection to the liberty of discussion. Although these positions might save Mill's theory from its inconsistencies, as we have already seen, they are asking more than what the text is able to offer. For a defence to the second chapter of 'On Liberty', see Gray, above n 79, 103–10.

i. Objective Truth and the Theocentric Mode of Knowledge

According to Isaiah Berlin, the source of Mill's ambiguity is the fact that he does not express the assumptions upon which his notion of truth rests.[110] Therefore, in order to examine this problem, those assumptions need to be inferred from the text. This is not, however, an easy task, because sometimes Mill seems to be referring to an objective and single truth: when, for example, comparing the opinions of his time with those of the eighteenth century, he says '[n]ot that the current opinions were on the whole farther from the truth than Rousseau's were; on the contrary they were nearer to it'.[111] However, on other occasions Mill seems to be referring to subjective or perspectival truths: when, for example, he promotes 'fair play to all sides of the truth'.[112] According to Berlin, Mill's theory is plausible only if it is grounded on the latter conception of truth. Berlin claims that whether Mill knew it or not, he obviously assumed that

> human knowledge was in principle never complete, and always fallible; that there was no single, universally visible, truth; ... that consequently the conviction, common to Aristotelians and a good many Christian scholastics and atheistical materialists alike, that there exists a basic knowable human nature, one and the same, at all times, in all places, in all men—a static, unchanging substance underneath the altering appearances, with permanent needs, dictated by a single, discoverable goal, or pattern of goals, the same for all mankind—is mistaken; and so, too, is the notion that is bound with it, of a single true doctrine carrying salvation to all men everywhere.[113]

Berlin's claim starts from Mill's argument of infallibility, according to which human beings cannot gain cognitive access to an ultimate, single truth. Human fallibility, in other words, implies that human beings lack intellectual intuition. Mill refers to this in several passages of the essay, such as when he claims, for example, that 'in an imperfect state of the human mind the interests of truth require a diversity of opinions'.[114] From this basic assumption in Mill's argument, Berlin seems to derive the inexistence of a *single true doctrine*. This interpretation, according to Berlin, makes Mill's theory productive, because as it supposes a multidimensional conception of truth in which every opinion counts as a contribution to the only possible truth available in our limited state of mental development, freedom of speech and a free press play a fundamental role in its discovery.

However productive this interpretation of Mill's conception of truth may be, a denial of an objective and single truth does not necessarily follow from the assumption of human fallibility. Like other empiricists who downgrade conceptual representations or believe that ideas are inadequate to apprehend the object as it is in itself, Mill does not necessarily deny intellectual intuition itself. And this

---

[110] Berlin, above n 1, 233.
[111] Mill, above n 16, 57.
[112] ibid 58.
[113] Berlin, above n 1, 233–34.
[114] Mill, above n 16, 62.

is so because, against all appearances, empiricists too are implicitly committed to a 'theocentric model of cognition'.[115] This does not mean that Mill is dedicated to some kind of theological belief, but only that the model of knowledge he is using makes implicit reference to a point of view, the 'god's eye view'. This model, according to Allison is

> a programme or method of epistemological reflection, according to which human knowledge is analyzed and evaluated in terms of its conformity, or lack thereof, to the standard of cognition theoretically achievable by an 'absolute' or 'infinite intellect'. By the latter I understand one that is not encumbered by the limitations of the human intellect, and which, therefore, knows objects 'as they are in themselves'. Such an intellect functions in this model essentially as a regulative idea in the Kantian sense. Thus the appeal to it does not commit one either to the existence of such an intellect or to the assumption that knowledge of this type is actually possessed by the human mind. The point is only that a hypothetical 'God's-eye view' of things is used as a standard in terms of which the 'objectivity' of human knowledge is analyzed.[116]

The 'theocentric model of knowledge' implicitly refers to and makes use of a 'god's-eye view of things', which distinguishes intellectual intuition from sensible intuition. While the former is a way of capturing the essence of things, comparable to a divine understanding of the world, the latter is related to the possibility of forming ideas about the objects of cognition, ideas that are, however, inadequate to grasp those very objects as they are in themselves.[117] Of course, while empiricists, such as Mill, think that their theories do not rely on a theocentric model of knowledge, in reality, they do! As has already been seen, Mill continuously repeated that human beings are ill equipped to receive the whole of the truth, to understand the totality of a subject. Yet at the same time, he does make use of intellectual intuition. After all, intellectual intuition is, in *On Liberty*, the very rod by which human cognition is measured. In fact, implicit in the limitations of human cognoscibility there is a recognition of a superior form of knowledge, a knowledge that although inaccessible to our current state of intellectual development, should not restrain us from its discovery, however unsuccessful our attempts may be:

> The beliefs which we have most warrant for have no safeguard to rest on but a standing invitation to the whole world to prove them unfounded. If the challenge is not accepted, or is accepted and the attempt fails, we are far enough from certainty still, but we have done the best that the existing state of human reason admits of: we have neglected nothing that could give the truth a chance of reaching us; if the lists are kept open, we may hope that, if there be a better truth, it will be found when the human mind is capable of receiving it: and in the meantime we may rely on having attained such approach to truth as is possible in our own day. This is the amount of certainty attainable by a fallible being, and this the sole way of attaining it.[118]

---

[115] See Allison, above n 27, 28.

[116] HE Allison, 'Transcendental Realism and Transcendental Idealism' in P Kitcher (ed), *Kant's Critique of Pure Reason: Critical Essays* (Lanham, MD, Rowman & Littlefield, 1998) 159.

[117] Allison, above n 27, 27.

[118] Mill, above n 16, 26.

Although this better truth, inaccessible to human beings, unreachable in our current state of mind, appears in the previous paragraph as a mere possibility, it is much more than that. This final truth is conceived by Mill as a landmark, a final destination in relation to which the objectivity of knowledge is measured. And Mill is not alone in this. According to Allison, this is a problem shared by empiricists.[119] This is so because empiricists naturally worry about conceptual representations, because for them ideas are always downgraded versions of things: 'representation is at best partial and abstract; and as such, it fails to grasp objects in their full concreteness'.[120] The explanation for this resides in the fact that empiricists deny the human capacity to organize the raw information provided by sensible intuition; they deny that it is the understanding that orders and gives sense to the objects of sensible intuition. This is what Allison refers to as the 'discursivity thesis'.[121] For empiricists, on the contrary, cognition requires that objects be given to the mind as they are in themselves. But the only kind of intuition that is able to grasp things as they are in themselves, independently from its apperception, is divine intuition. In other words, only divine intuition can compare the apperception with the thing. Empiricists implicitly refer to a divine point of view, to a god's-eye view of things, while they deny the possibility of grasping that knowledge. It follows that they are—at the same time—necessarily committed to a theocentric mode of knowledge.

ii. Perspectival Truth and its Practical Value

The fact that Mill denies, but at the same time presupposes, intellectual intuition and the objective truth bound to it affects the consistency of his theory. This is so because another conception of truth is also recognisable in the text. This is a perspectival truth, in which the opinion of every individual is as valuable as the opinion of any other. And this conception of truth is necessary in Mill's theory for two reasons. First, as has been insisted, like other empiricists Mill denies that human beings possess intellectual intuition. However, although human beings are unable to grasp things as they are in themselves, their cognitive capabilities allow them to attain what Locke called the 'conveniences of life'.[122] As he put it in the Introduction to the *Essay Concerning Human Understanding*, 'The candle that is set up in us shines bright enough for all our purposes.'[123] The same holds true for Mill. Indeed, in *On Liberty* he states that although '[t]here is no such thing as absolute certainty ... there is assurance sufficient for the purposes of human life.'[124]

---

[119] See Allison, above n 27, 28.

[120] ibid 27.

[121] This is the discursivity thesis developed by Kant in the *Critique of Pure Reason*, which holds that cognition requires both concepts and sensible intuition. It has been often put in Kant's famous phrase, '[t]houghts without contents are empty, intuitions without concepts are blind'. Kant, above n 29, A51/B76.

[122] J Locke, *An Essay Concerning Human Understanding*, ed AC Fraser (New York, Dover, 1996) 45.

[123] ibid.

[124] Mill, above n 16, 24.

The whole of the truth is unavailable to human beings, not necessarily because there is no such thing, but because we, limited human beings, are still not ready to grasp it. In the meantime, however, we can accept fragmentary representations of it where every portion is as valuable as any other. In this context, liberty of discussion is fundamental, because it guarantees that all the sides or perspectives of truth are exposed. As Mill argues, liberty of discussion is the only way to approach this truth in issues as complex as 'morals, religion, politics, social relations, and the business of life'.[125] Although it does not guarantee access to the whole of the truth, it creates the conditions that are necessary to achieve a higher intellectual state:

> As mankind improve, the number of doctrines which are no longer disputed or doubted will be constantly on the increase; and the well-being of mankind may almost be measured by the number and gravity of the truths which have reached the point of being uncontested.[126]

But there is still another reason why Mill needs a perspectival conception of truth. And this is related to the fact that, as Berlin claimed, only this conception can make Mill's liberty of discussion productive. As a point of fact, the latter might be an adequate tool for the discovery of truth only when the opinion of every individual counts as much as the opinion of any other in attaining the truth. And although Mill was not theoretically committed to this conception of truth—his theoretical commitment is to a theocentric mode of knowledge—he still needs it for practical reasons.

One of these reasons, according to Habermas, is that only this version of truth provides a defence of the expression of the best educated who were threatened by the *tyranny of majorities*.[127] This is why Mill would have defended with such vigour the liberty of discussion in *On Liberty*, although in previous works he was sceptical about the benefits of this liberty in the pursuit of truth. In fact, Mill gave huge importance to the opinions and doctrines of the educated and their relevance in informing and teaching the uneducated classes. This position is eloquently expressed in Mill's article 'The Spirit of the Age', where he distinguishes a natural state of society, in which 'the opinions and feelings of the people are, with their voluntary acquiescence, formed *for* them, by the most cultivated minds which the intelligence and morality of the times call into existence',[123] from a transitional period, in which 'there are no persons to whom the mass of the uninstructed habitually defer, and in whom they trust for finding the right, and for pointing it out'.[129] By the time this essay was written, Mill claimed that England

---

[125] ibid 44.

[126] ibid 53.

[127] J Habermas, *The Structural Transformation of the Public Sphere: An Inquiry into a Category of Bourgeois Society*, tr T Burger (Cambridge, MA, MIT Press, 1989) 135.

[128] JS Mill, 'The Spirit of the Age, V [Part 1]' in AP Robson and JM Robson (eds), *Newspaper Writings: Collected Works of John Stuart Mill*, vol XXII (Toronto, University of Toronto Press; London, Routledge & Kegan Paul, 1986) 304.

[129] ibid.

was in a transitional phase in which traditional institutions and doctrines had fallen into disrespect without any new authority having arisen to replace them. In such times the knowledge of the educated was the one that needed to guide society, and liberty of discussion was not necessarily a way to promote this: 'Reason itself will teach most men that they must, in the last resort, fall back upon the authority of still more cultivated minds, as the ultimate sanction of the convictions of their reason itself.'[130] Himmelfarb shows that this position is reiterated and reinforced by Mill in different articles and essays written after 'The Spirit of the Age'.[131] In many of them, Mill claims that the people were not ready for the liberty of discussion because they were not ready to discern by their own means what was true from what was false, and what was right from what was wrong.

The question that arises is if in some of his previous writings Mill rejected the utility of the liberty of discussion as a proper means for the discovery of truth, why he decided to defend it in *On Liberty* with such a strength and putting forward the same reasons he had previously used to oppose it. Some authors have argued that Mill's change of strategy is the consequence of the more advanced intellectual state of English society in the second half of the nineteenth century. O'Rourke, for example, claims that given this state of intellectual development, Mill was ready to defend the benefits of the liberty of discussion.[132] It is also possible to argue that the conditions of the time did not allow an opposition to a liberty that had been so hard to achieve and which was openly recognised among politicians and intellectuals.

According to Habermas, Mill's change of strategy was a mechanism designed to solve rationally the competition of interests in the public sphere.[133] What Mill demands in *On Liberty* is tolerance,[134] and he does so in order to secure a space in the public sphere for those enlightened views that were succumbing to the overwhelming weight of the opinions of a majority reduced to an ignorant mass. As Mill himself claims in *On Liberty*:

> It is not too much to require that what the wisest of mankind, those who are best entitled to trust their own judgement, find necessary to warrant their relying on it, should be submitted to by that miscellaneous collection of a few wise and many foolish individuals called the public.[135]

As Habermas argues in *The Structural Transformation of the Public Sphere*, the enlargement of the public sphere in the nineteenth century led to the disintegration of the principles by which public opinion used to be formed. The order of things is broken, a public opinion built on the basis of principles that are rationally deduced from natural laws is replaced by one which is the product of struggling

---

[130] Himmelfarb, above n 84, 40–41.
[131] See ibid 37–56.
[132] O'Rourke, above n 40, 65–70.
[133] Habermas, above n 127, 135.
[134] ibid 135.
[135] Mill, above n 16, 26.

forces emerging in the public arena. Violence replaced order; unity was transformed into ambiguity; coercion undermined the compulsion of reason.[136] It is against these forces that Mill directed his attacks in *On Liberty*. A public opinion dominated by the 'tyranny of the majorities' is his central enemy. His main goal is to prevent this new public opinion, which is mainly formed by groups of uneducated, unskilled labourers, imposing its view on the rest.

Perspectival epistemology or a multidimensional face of the truth was, according to Habermas, Mill's solution to this threat.[137] In a public sphere that was no longer able to solve the competition of interests rationally, perspectival epistemology at least secured some space for the voices that opposed those of the majority. Perspectival epistemology, in other words, guaranteed a final breath for reason in a breathless public sphere.

Regardless of the intentions behind Mill's decision to defend the liberty of discussion as he did in *On Liberty*, his ambiguous conception of truth is crucial for this investigation because it provides the theoretical basis for the emergence of what was defined in the previous chapter as the *illusion of the free press*. Indeed, Mill's denial of intellectual intuition, and at the same time his need to presuppose it for the sake of the theory, produces an ambivalence that is manifested in his two versions of truth. These different versions can be identified in different passages of the text. As has been explained, Mill's presupposition of intellectual intuition and of objective truth has theoretical causes. It is grounded in his empiricism and appeals to a theocentric mode of knowledge in which a god's-eye view of things is the very measure of knowledge and truth. This mode of knowledge is fundamental for a correspondence theory of truth in which apperception is compared to the thing as it is in itself. And it is fundamental in Mill, because it allows him to defend the liberty of discussion on the grounds of an objective truth, a truth that is independent from apperception, a truth existing in itself. This defence configures part of the illusion of the free press. And it does so because, as has been argued, only a divine intellect is able of knowing things as they are in themselves, and only such an intellect can thus compare them with the apperception and delimit what is true and what is not. Access to this truth is hence a mere illusion.

But there is something more. In fact, although there are theoretical reasons to explain why Mill presupposes a theocentric mode of knowledge and an objective truth associated with it, there are also practical reasons to explain why there is another version of truth pullulating in the text. The point is that Mill needs a perspectival truth as much as he needs an objective one. And this is so because the relationship between the liberty of discussion and truth is problematic. As Mill himself identified prior to *On Liberty*, truth does not always benefit from this freedom. And this is so because truth (at least an objective version of it) requires a systematic construction of arguments and ideas and an adequate use of reason,

---

[136] Habermas, n 127, 132–33.
[137] ibid 135.

which are not conditions that are necessarily present in a free debate of ideas. However, if truth is perspectival, if it depends on different points of view, freedom of discussion is essential for its discovery. In fact, the more positions are shown, the more likely we are to obtain the full picture that a perspectival notion of truth requires.

Mill's ambiguity in relation to the notion of truth is constitutive of the *illusion of the free press*. This is so because the theocentric mode of knowledge presupposed in his theory keeps alive the idea that truth is correspondence with the thing in itself. Although inaccessible in our current state of mental development, this truth is still there functioning as a measuring rod, as a standard of objectiveness in knowledge; its mere presupposition keeps alive the hope of advancing towards it. However, as this notion of truth is not necessarily compatible with liberty of discussion, Mill also needs a perspectival conception of truth that vindicates this liberty. In consequence, the illusion is the product of an ambiguity; an ambiguity that merges the liberty of discussion with truth without necessarily annihilating one for the sake of the other.

V. Conclusions

Although the political, social and intellectual conditions in England had changed substantially in the period that separated Milton's *Areopagitica* from Mill's *On Liberty*, the structure and form of the defence of the liberty of discussion remained very similar. First, this liberty has always been defended against an entity that threatens to repress it. While in Milton's time and in the time of the Philosophical Radicals this liberty was defended against governments, Mill adds the tyranny of the majorities to the censuring threat of government. Secondly, the epistemological dimension of this liberty remained a central concern in the struggle for the freedom of the press. Although it lost some strength in favour of the political freedoms associated with the press in the eighteenth century and at the beginning of the nineteenth century, Mill's theory of truth resuscitates it in *On Liberty* with admirable strength. Finally, although Mill's theory is a secularised version of Milton's argument and his purpose is not to defend a theological belief, there is a theocentric remainder in his theory that he has to presuppose for the sake of the theory. This residue manifests itself in his theoretical commitment to a theocentric mode of knowledge where truth is correspondence with the thing in itself. However, parallel to this conception of truth, it is possible to identify a subjective or perspectival one that is necessary to reaffirm the relevance of the liberty of discussion. Mill's ambiguity, as has been argued, is a symptom of the tension between freedom and truth (which will be explored in further detail in the next chapter) and a manifestation of the illusion of the free press.

Although this chapter has analysed the conditions of the illusion of the free press and how they emerged in England between the seventeenth and the nineteenth centuries, it has not assessed how these conditions apply to the press itself. The next chapter will explore the reception of Mill's theory of the truth and its application to the press through what has been traditionally known as the theory of the 'marketplace of ideas'. This theory develops an issue left untouched by Mill in *On Liberty*. This issue is the conditions of production required from the press in order to fulfil its truth-seeking purpose. The 'marketplace of ideas', in other words, translates Mill's abstract conditions for the discovery of truth to the concrete requirements of the press. As will be seen, however, this connection faces a double problem. The first is the problem of Mill's own theory. The second is the assumption that a market-orientated press would be able to produce or discover truth. This theory has provided a central justification for the role of the press in liberal democracies, and is central to understanding later developments of the illusion of the free press.

3

Truth and Politics: Democratic Justifications of a Free Press

I. Introduction

John Stuart Mill did not prescribe how the press should be organised and structured in order to fulfil its truth-seeking purpose in a democratic society. Arguably, the most successful interpretation of how the classic defence of freedom of speech should be applied to the press came much later, in a judicial opinion on the other side of the Atlantic in 1919. Many of the principles articulated in Mill's 'theory of the truth' gained traction in the judiciary of the United States in the form of a theory which became known as the *marketplace of ideas*, first articulated by Oliver Wendell Holmes Jr in his dissenting opinion in *Abrams v United States*.[1] Considered by some to be an almost canonical interpretation of the First Amendment,[2] the marketplace of ideas not only conceived of the advancement of knowledge and the discovery of truth as fundamental aims of a free press, it also provided the normative framework in which public discussion should be organised in order to achieve these aims.

The marketplace of ideas was created as a metaphorical device designed to provide standards adequate to assess the truth of an opinion in a democratic society. These standards suppose unrestrained debate and competition of ideas. Just as laissez-faire economic theory assumes that goods and services will be allocated in a manner that maximises efficiency if markets are left to their own devices, the marketplace of ideas assumes that unrestrained freedom of speech will permit the emergence of the best ideas. For the marketplace is—according to Holmes—the best test of truth. Originally conceived as a metaphor, the marketplace of ideas became much more than that. With a press already transformed in a giant industry in the first half of the twentieth century, the marketplace of ideas was a powerful device for legitimising a laissez-faire system of speech.

---

[1] See CE Baker, *Human Liberty and Freedom of Speech* (Oxford, Oxford University Press, 1989) 8.
[2] V Blasi, 'Holmes and the Marketplace of Ideas' 2004 *The Supreme Court Review* 1.

Holmes's theory was subjected to several critiques that questioned the relationship between expressive freedoms and the discovery of truth in a democratic society. Some of them criticised Holmes's conception of truth and proposed an alternative that would be compatible with democratic values. Others went further and claimed absolute incompatibility between truth and freedom of speech in a democratic society. Underlying all these critiques and Holmes's theory itself is the question of the relationship between politics and truth. Is the truth-seeking purpose of expressive freedoms consistent with democratic principles? If so, is the marketplace of ideas a proper standard of truth? More generally, are political modes of communication compatible with truth-seeking modes of communication? Lastly, how do these questions relate to the 'illusion of the free press'?

Democratic theories of free speech have provided answers to these questions, and the purpose of this chapter is to analyse them. It will commence by analysing the theoretical problems generally associated with the relationship between truth and politics. It will be seen that Burke and Arendt reach the same conclusion, even if they do so from opposite perspectives: the incompatibility of politics and truth. Section III will address how Holmes's theorising of the First Amendment— the marketplace of ideas—has rejected this incompatibility. Some authors have argued that Holmes is able to do this because he is a sceptic, and when he speaks of truth he is just referring to subjective belief or unanimous consent.[3] Others believe that Holmes's conception of truth is wider than that and hence able to accommodate sceptical conceptions of truth as well as objective ones.[4] Regardless of Holmes's conception of truth, it will be argued that his marketplace of ideas is an ideological device that has nourished the illusion of the free press. Moreover, Holmes's metaphor is incompatible with democratic values, and it is precisely this incompatibility that stimulated the emergence of Alexander Meiklejohn's theory, which is the first of a number of influential defences known as democratic theories of free speech.

Section IV will explore the complex role that truth plays in Meiklejohn's theory. On the one hand, Meiklejohn recognises the 'truth-seeking purpose' of expressive freedoms so far as these truths are functional to the political system itself. On the other, he derives this purpose from a 'political truth', a particular conception of democracy, which for him is reducible to the idea of collective self-government. Section V will analyse a democratic theory developed by Robert Post. Although this theory denies the truth-seeking purpose of free speech and shows why expressive freedoms should not be seen as a mechanism of truth-discovery, it follows the same methodological framework as Meiklejohn's theory. In fact, Post also starts from a particular conception of democracy or a 'political truth' (based on political autonomy) that defines the scope of protected speech and the role of expressive

---

[3] See AW Alschuler, *Law Without Values: The Life, Work, and Legacy of Justice Holmes* (Chicago, IL, University of Chicago Press, 2000) 80.
[4] See Blasi, above n 2, 16.

freedoms in his theory. Section VI will explore the practical consequences of the application of these theories. It will be seen that they have constitutive effects, because prevalent conceptions of democracy tend to define both the form of the democratic public sphere and what the public is entitled to know.

II. Politics and Truth

It is important to start this chapter by analysing the relationship between truth and politics, because a free press has fundamental political functions in democratic societies.[5] As a matter of fact, the press is the forum in which the different forces of the political arena express themselves and show the public their views, ideas and projects. But the purpose of this confrontation of ideas, as has been argued in this book, is not merely to expose the different views available in a political community. According to a line of influential authors from Milton to Holmes, the advancement of knowledge and the discovery of truth that follows from this confrontation of ideas are also relevant political functions, because they stimulate the intellectual progress of society. This is why, before analysing the relationship between freedom and truth in democratic theories, it is important to take a step back and explore the relationship between politics and truth.

According to Fernando Atria, there are two widely held positions on the relationship between politics and truth.[6] The first rejects the idea of an objective truth in the realm of politics. This rejection is a consequence of the recognition of politics as a sphere of discussion where different positions meet in order to arrive at a final decision. The political sphere, accordingly, cannot accept objective truths because they preclude debate and discussion, which are essential for the survival of politics itself. The second position, by contrast, clings to objective (moral) truths and argues that the only fair political decisions are those which reflect such truths. According to this theory, it is the content of those decisions and not the process of decision making which is relevant in a political community. Democratic decisions only express the number of people that support them, but not their validity. The first position is sceptical with respect to truths in the political sphere, and assigns value only to decisions that have been politically decided, independent of their content; the second recognises value in political decisions only as far as they reflect valid moral axioms. Although there is a sharp contrast between these two positions, they coincide on a fundamental point: politics and truth cannot be

[5] Kathleen Sullivan argues that there are two positions on the political function of freedom of speech. The first one is political equality and the second one political liberty. See generally KM Sullivan, 'Two Concepts of Freedom of Speech' (2010) 124 *Harvard Law Review* 143.

[6] See F Atria, 'La verdad y lo político (I) La verdad y su dimensión constitutiva' (2009) 23 *Persona y Sociedad/Universidad Alberto Hurtado* 21.

mixed and must remain independent of each other. In both positions, according to Atria, there is no internal connection between what is (morally) fair and what has been politically decided. While the first position devalues the objectivity of truth (only democratic decisions are valid), the second devalues the political (only moral truths are valid).[7]

Edmund Burke is a good proponent of the second position, for which correct political decisions are the reflection of valid (moral) truths. In his 'Reflections on the Revolution in France', Burke compared the British political system of the late eighteenth century with the new republic formed in France after the Revolution. The former, according to Burke, was 'placed in a just correspondence and symmetry with the order of the world'.[8] This was so because it paid due respect to ancient institutions inherited from the forefathers, in which 'a stupendous wisdom, moulding together the great mysterious incorporation of the human race, the whole, at one time, is never old, or middle-aged, or young, but in a condition of unchangeable constancy'.[9] This system, according to Burke, was 'the result of profound reflection; or rather the happy effect of following nature, which is wisdom without reflection, and above it'.[10] Burke firmly believes in the values and principles gathered in ancient institutions. Only time, he argues, would guarantee a political system that mirrors the 'order of things' and enable a system to adjust itself to that nature and design. Time has crafted the wisdom and truth that according to Burke could be found in the British institutions of the late eighteenth century.

To the rationality and stability of the English political system Burke opposed the newly formed French Republic, which he did not even dare to call a 'system'.[11] His main criticism is that those who designed it had the '[p]ersonal self-sufficiency and arrogance' of those who had 'never experienced a wisdom greater than their own' but believed that they could imagine and create a new political order based solely on abstract reason. Those individuals, according to Burke,

> act as if they were the entire masters ... by destroying at their pleasure the whole original fabric of their society: hazarding to leave to those who come after them a ruin instead of an habitation, and teaching these successors as little to respect their contrivances as they had themselves respected the institutions of their forefathers.[12]

Burke's central criticism is directed against the revolutionaries' contempt for the wisdom embedded in ancient institutions. He contends that they 'began ill, because [they] began by despising everything that belonged to [them]'.[13] Burke's

---

[7] For a systematic version of this argument see ibid.
[8] E Burke, 'Reflections on the Revolution in France' in *The Works of the Right Honorable Edmund Burke*, vol 2 (London, Henry G Bohn, 1855) 307.
[9] ibid.
[10] ibid.
[11] ibid 403.
[12] ibid 367.
[13] ibid 309.

attack on the radicalism of the French revolutionaries is not necessarily a rejection of change and improvement of political institutions. He does not claim that institutions are perfect or that they could not be corrupted. Change and transformation, he believed, are indeed necessary, but they should be carried out without perverting the order of things, maintaining due respect for the truth and wisdom contained in them. As the state is for Burke a partnership 'of eternal society, linking the lower with the higher natures, connecting the visible and invisible world', it should always be looked at 'with reverence', just as a man approaches 'to the wounds of [his] father, with pious awe and trembling solicitude'.[14] Deliberation and change, accordingly, need to be subordinated to this higher order and not the other way around. Burke was indeed no fan of democracy; for him the decisions of the many were an arithmetical fact, which had nothing to do with the reasonableness of decisions themselves.[15] If a 'purely democratic form' became necessary and changes were to be brought about through the deliberation of the many, this would only be good, according to Burke, as long as it '[preserved] the method of nature in the conduct of the state'.[16] Deliberation and judgement, the fundamental tools of politics, would be acceptable for Burke as long as they mirrored the deeper truth and wisdom contained in the institutions above it.[17] In this sense, Burke downgraded politics in favour of truth.

The idea of a relationship between truth and politics has also been criticised from another side. This time, the critique is not based on the protection of inherited institutions but on the idea that truth and politics belong to two conflicting spheres that deal with different modes of communication and legitimation. According to Hannah Arendt, truth precludes politics because

> [t]he modes of thought and communication that deal with truth, if seen from the political perspective, are necessarily domineering; they don't take into account other people's opinions, and taking these into account is the hallmark of all strictly political thinking.[18]

Arendt argues that every truth, rational or factual, shares a degree of compulsion or coercion in its mode of affirmation: 'once perceived as true and pronounced to be so, they have in common that they are beyond agreement, dispute, opinion or consent.'[19] Persuasion and dissuasion are not rhetorical strategies that may alter the fact that the earth orbits around the sun, that two plus two is four or that the Holocaust did happen. Similarly, the number of people supporting or rejecting

---

[14] ibid 368.

[15] ibid 325.

[16] ibid 307.

[17] For a different perspective on Burke's position on the relationship between truth and politics, see J Elkins, 'Concerning Practices of Truth' in J Elkins and A Norris (eds), *Truth and Democracy* (Philadelphia, PA, University of Pennsylvania Press, 2012) 23–24.

[18] H Arendt, 'Truth and Politics' in *Between Past and Future: Eight Exercises in Political Thought* (New York, Penguin Books, 1977) 241.

[19] ibid 240.

those statements would not change the fact that they are true. These statements have a coercive nature that does not allow for alterations. They have a despotic force that radically contrasts with the modes of communication prevalent in the political realm. They are 'beyond' and even in contradiction with them. And they must remain beyond that realm, Arendt claims, if they are to be secured.[20] If the discovery of truths were left to the political realm, truth would succumb to the interests and power struggles proper to that domain.[21]

But just as politics is a threat to truth; truth is, according to this position, a threat to politics. Political thought is, according to Arendt, representative. Forming an opinion about an issue requires taking into consideration the views of multiple persons, persons who occupy different positions and hold different interests in the social body. Arendt argues that the more viewpoints are considered in pondering an issue and the better one can imagine how the persons holding those viewpoints would feel and think about the issue, the better the capacity for representative thought.[22] Political thought is thus radically different from rational or factual truths. It is eminently discursive, it integrates views collected from different places, agglutinates a series of positions containing different interests, experiences and so on. Hence, while the political process of communication supposes that through a collection of particularities it is possible to arrive at some impartial generality, truth seems to follow the opposite road. While rational truth enlightens human understanding and factual truths inform opinions, they do so on the basis of the authoritativeness and coercion proper to the nature of their statements. From this perspective, the language of truth is the end of politics, because it precludes discussion, persuasion and dissuasion, which are fundamental modes of political communication.

According to this position, politics should be isolated from truth if it is to remain loyal to its discursive modes. A political community that values plurality and diversity, it is said, cannot impose particular versions of the good life or certain truth discourses. On the contrary, it should be neutral and permit the expression of the widest range of perspectives available. Otherwise, as Elkins observes, it will be tempted 'to mandate for others a particular way of life and too often end up restraining political dialogue by privileging those who are thought to have special access to truth', favouring the educated over the uneducated, the rational over the emotional, the articulate argument over the clumsy attempt to give form to novel ideas, and so on.[23]

---

[20] Arendt reminds us that Plato was a privileged witness of what Athenians were likely to do to those, like Socrates, who dared to expose the truth: ibid 230–31.

[21] ibid 230.

[22] ibid 241.

[23] See Elkins, above n 17, 25.

III. Holmes and the Marketplace of Ideas

The idea that an open and free exchange of ideas is an adequate means for the discovery of truth and the intellectual progress of democratic societies has not lost its influence, despite the ill-defined relationship between truth and politics. During the twentieth century, defences of free speech emphasising the importance of unrestrained discussion to citizen knowledge, informed decision making, effective self-government and the discovery of political truths developed strongly on the other side of the Atlantic. The classic argument of free speech was transplanted to the United States through the Supreme Court-designed tests of the scope and limits of this freedom. After a period known as the *First Red Scare* in the early 1920s, during which free speech suffered restrictions as fears spread of a Bolshevik revolution in the United States, Justices Brandeis and Holmes raised their voices in the Supreme Court in defence of free speech. Much of reasoning behind their decisions resembles the arguments developed by Mill and Milton before them. Articulating the doctrine of clear and present danger to test the limits of speech, they claimed that 'if there be time to expose through discussion the falsehood and fallacies, to avert the evil by the processes of education, the remedy to be applied is more speech, not enforced silence'.[24] Similarly, they argued that 'freedom to think as you will and to speak as you think are means indispensable to the discovery and spread of political truth'.[25]

Although the classic argument was grafted onto the Supreme Court's conception of free speech, the thinking of the Court changed the graft itself. Baker notes that a 'marketplace imagery ("competition of ideas," the value of "robust debate") pervades judicial opinions and provides justification for the courts' first amendment "tests"'.[26] This imagery is best captured by Holmes in his famous dissenting opinion in *Abrams v United States*, where he claimed that the competition in the marketplace is the best test of truth to which an idea can be subject. The marketplace imagery has not been a harmless metaphor used only by courts to justify unrestrained speech. It has also pervaded, as Napoli claimed at the end of the 1990s, the Federal Communications Commission's (FCC's) regulatory decisions. Accordingly, the FCC 'has increasingly focused on the criteria of efficiency, competition, and consumer satisfaction that characterize traditional economic regulation [...] and found deregulatory policies to be the best method of achieving these objectives'.[27] The marketplace metaphor provides the opening for the introduction of economic theory into a realm that was previously sole dominion

---

[24] *Whitney v California*, 274 US 378 (1927).
[25] ibid 377.
[26] CE Baker, *Human Liberty and Freedom of Speech* (Oxford, Oxford University Press, 1989) 7.
[27] See PM Napoli, 'The Marketplace of Ideas Metaphor in Communication Regulation' (1999) 49 *Journal of Communication* 151, 166.

of political theory.[28] This approach has been criticised on different levels, but there are two types of critique relevant for the purposes of this book. The first is the critique of political economy, according to which the marketplace metaphor reaffirms the illusion that a market-orientated press is a proper means for the discovery of truths and the intellectual progress of the body politic. The second attacks the concept of truth contained in the argument. It stresses the point that the marketplace of ideas is a source of intellectual degradation where the capacity of the people to think and act as a self-governing community is stifled. Before examining these critiques, I shall briefly lay out the central argument and the context in which it emerged.

In 1919, when Holmes provides his famous dissenting opinion in *Abrams v United States*, the press was radically different from the one known by John Stuart Mill less than a century before. The process of industrialisation of the press in the United States transformed the local, small and partisan newspapers of the nineteenth century into a 'concentrated site of massive profit generation'.[29] By the same process, the Harmsworth brothers in Britain obtained control by 1921 of a chain of newspapers with an aggregate circulation of more than six million, the largest in the world at that time.[30] The emergence of large-scale corporations, controlled by a few men, and the increasing invisibility of the expression of dissident views produced an early crisis of legitimacy of the press.[31] This crisis arose, according to Curran, due to the fact that the accelerated process of industrialisation in the press did not dilute the strict control that newspapers' owners historically had over editorial decisions.[32] While this form of administration had been tolerable in a partisan press environment characterised by multiple newspapers with diverse owners reflecting the views of different portions of society, it was no longer permissible in a system in which press ownership was concentrated in a few hands.

The system responded to this crisis. According to McChesney, the emergence and consolidation of professional journalism at the beginning of the twentieth century was one response to it.[33] Professional journalism gave the press a new aura of independence, as it limited both the intervention of owners and the increasing intervention of advertisers in editorial decisions. Moreover, it privileged an objective, impartial and non-partisan recounting of events and ideas. The emergence of professional journalists strengthened the sense of a press committed first and foremost to facts and to an objective and neutral depiction of reality. In addition to this, the idea promoted by laissez-faire ideologists, that the processing of

---

[28] ibid 154.

[29] R McChesney, *The Political Economy of Media: Enduring Issues, Emerging Dilemmas* (New York, Monthly Review Press, 2008) 309.

[30] See J Curran and J Seaton, *Power without Responsibility*, 7th edn (Oxford, Routledge, 2010) 39.

[31] For the crises in the US, see McChesney, above n 29, 309; in Britain, see Curran and Seaton, above n 30, 24–29.

[32] Curran and Seaton, above n 30, 42–43.

[33] See McChesney, above n 29, 309.

communications by markets as commodities contributes to the objectification of ideas, gained momentum at the beginning of the twentieth century.[34] Objectification supposes that in the marketplace, ideas are conceptually detached from the people who hold them. It is, according to Margaret Radin, the belief that '[a]s long as ideas that meet the demand of the audience are produced, it doesn't matter how (if at all) committed to them their producers are, or how (if at all) the ideas are connected with the self-constitution of their producers'.[35] Objectification of ideas or the allocative efficiency of the market was supposed to contribute to achieving higher levels of editorial independence, and thus to separating the work of the journalist from the interests of proprietors and advertisers. Therefore free market apologists might argue that the market is the best form, or at least the most democratic way, of distributing ideas in the public sphere.

A professionally-led press in a market-based system provided ideological conditions favourable to the affirmation of the idea that the press was properly equipped for the search for truth and for advancing knowledge about social reality. Indeed, with independent professionals managing communications aimed at satisfying the objective requirements of the market, and not the mere caprice of media moguls, conditions seemed to be optimal for attaining these purposes. Such ideas gained momentum in the United States in the early twentieth century and were synthesised with great eloquence by Holmes in his dissenting opinion in *Abrams v United States*. Using the metaphor of the *marketplace of ideas*, Holmes articulated the idea that a free market of speech was the best means for searching for and discovering the truth. In a vivid statement, he claimed:

> [W]hen men have realized that time has upset many fighting faiths, they may come to believe even more than they believe the very foundations of their own conduct that the ultimate good desired is better reached by free trade in ideas—that the best test of truth is the power of the thought itself accepted in the competition of the market, and that truth is the only ground upon which their wishes safely can be carried out.[36]

If early theorists provided abstract arguments to justify the relationship between truth and a free press, Holmes provided arguments related to the conditions under which that relationship could sprout. His famous dissenting opinion in *Abrams* established a causal link between efficient, unrestrained markets and informed decision-making processes. This is why Holmes's economic approach to the marketplace of ideas opened the door for more strictly neoclassical economic interpretations of the function and role of the press in liberal societies. For indeed, according to this marketplace logic, the conditions required for the press to advance and discover truth are the conditions of the market. Applied to the press this means that speakers are transformed into producers, citizens into consumers, and speech is turned into a commodity.

---

[34] See MJ Radin, *Contested Commodities* (Cambridge, MA, Harvard University Press, 1996) 166.
[35] ibid 166–67.
[36] *Abrams v United States*, 250 US 616 (1919), 630.

Holmes's marketplace of ideas is deeply troubling and has been criticised from different angles. Seen from the critique of political economy perspective, the marketplace of ideas metaphor perverts the public sphere, because when speech is produced for the market as a commodity, it gets entangled in market logics and necessities, it becomes a fetish, in the Marxist sense of the word. According to Marx, the fetishism of commodities is 'nothing but the definite social relation between men themselves which assumes here, for them, the fantastic form of a relation between things'.[37] The fetishism is related to Marx's theory of value. The value of commodities appears to be an expression of an inherent property of the commodity itself, but the fact is, according to Marx, that exchange value expresses the socially necessary labour-time. According to Žižek, the fetish is a misrecognition: 'what is really a structural effect, an effect of the network of relations between elements, appears as an immediate property of one of the elements, as if the property also belongs to it outside its elements'.[38] The exchange value of a commodity is not to be identified in a property that belongs to the commodity itself. It is a consequence of the work of men and women who transform a given element into something that is useful for other men and women.

The distorting effect of the fetishism leads to an essential confusion, which consists in identifying exchange value with something that belongs to the commodity itself, independent of the social relations of production in which it is immersed, when the fact is that value is precisely a consequence of those relations. When speech is commoditised, when it is produced for the market as a commodity, its value is as its market appeal. As Holmes put it, *the best test of truth is the power of thought itself accepted in the competition of the market.* From this point of view, the strongest ideas will succeed and see the light of publicity, while the weakest will perish. What makes an idea strong or weak is conceived, under this logic, as an inherent quality of the idea itself; it is a quality that the market can identify and rewards with visibility when the idea passes muster. And this particular quality is, according to Holmes, the truth, something that is best tested by means of the competition in the market.

However, when speech is transformed into a commodity, the profit-maximising goal of the producer is not necessarily compatible with truth-seeking purposes. An idea receives wide publicity not because of its quality but rather due to the conditions in which it is produced. News providers will favour content that attracts massive audiences to increase their advertisement revenues. Hyperbole, scandal, exposure of private life of celebrities and so on abound in the market of speech and do not necessarily enhance any truth-seeking purpose of the press. The emergence of the Internet and the explosion of social media have exacerbated the deficit in truth-seeking practices of the press, as will be analysed in more detail in Chapter 5. Dogged by the extreme competition introduced into the market by

<hr/>

[37] ibid.
[38] S Žižek, *The Sublime Object of Ideology*, 2nd edn (London, Verso Books, 2008) 19.

the Internet, newspapers have been forced to reduce their costs. The number of journalists working in newsrooms has been drastically reduced, severely affecting the process of news gathering, checking and publishing. Newspapers no longer have the resources to do responsible investigative journalism. According to Davies, intense market competition has made contemporary journalists incapable of 'perform[ing] the simple basic functions of their profession; quite unable to tell their readers the truth about what is happening on their patch'.[39]

Holmes is a victim of the misrecognition identified by Marx. Ideas do not necessarily become accepted in the market thanks to some intrinsic quality that the market can identify in the process of exchange. Behind the sphere of appearances, behind the content offered by the media, there is a logic of production that defines what will and will not be offered to the public. And these definitions are not necessarily the consequence of the intrinsic properties of speech but of the logics and the interests governing the market. The influence that Holmes's misrecognition has had not only on First Amendment theorising but also on communication regulation has contributed to reinforcing the negative aspect of the illusion of the free press, that is, the belief that a market-structured press is a proper mechanism for the advancement of truth. It has done so because this misrecognition has eroded any plausible notion of truth by equating it to competition in the market. Alexander Meiklejohn, who saw Holmes's marketplace as an 'intellectual degradation' of the American people, proposed a sophisticated challenge to the theory. This challenge offered a different way of combining the truth-seeking purpose of the press with the needs of a self-governing society.

IV. Truth and Politics: Alexander Meiklejohn and the Critique of the Marketplace of Ideas

Meiklejohn's famous essay *Free Speech and its Relation to Self-Government*, first published in 1948, contains one of the most influential theories of the First Amendment. Although it is not currently accepted as an adequate interpretation of the free speech clause, it is still acknowledged as having inaugurated a novel approach to the topic, with the principle of collective self-determination at its very core.[40] This theory and its derivations are widely known today as democratic theories of free speech.[41] They are not only held by a number of influential First

---

[39] N Davies, *Flat Earth News* (London, Vintage, 2009) 59.

[40] See E Barendt, *Freedom of Speech*, 2nd edn (Oxford, Oxford University Press, 2007) 18.

[41] Current proponents of this theory in the United States are Owen Fiss, Cass Sunstein and Robert Post, among others. See O Fiss, *The Irony of Free Speech* (Cambridge, MA, Harvard University, 1996); C Sunstein, *Democracy and the Problem of Free Speech* (New York, The Free Press, 1995); R Post, 'Participatory Democracy and Free Speech' (2011) 97 *Virginia Law Review* 477.

Amendment scholars in the United States, but they are also important in other countries,[42] where they have been consistently used by courts in a wide number of jurisdictions.[43]

Meiklejohn's theory emerged as a critique of Holmes's marketplace logic and its philosophical assumptions. He not only attacked Holmes's views on the meaning and goals of the First Amendment, he also challenged his 'Darwinian individualism', his social atomism and his moral scepticism.[44] According to Meiklejohn, Holmes's marketplace of ideas was 'a fruitful source of intellectual irresponsibility' where

> the 'competition of the market' principle [means] that as separate thinkers, we have no obligation to test our thinking, to make sure that it is worthy of a citizen who is one of the 'rulers of the nation.' That testing is to be done, we believe, not by us, but by 'the competition of the market.' Each one of us, therefore, feels free to think as he pleases, to believe whatever will serve his own private interests. We think, not as members of the body politic ... but as farmers, as trade-union workers, as employers, as investors ... And our aim, as we debate in those capacities, is not that of finding the truth. The competition of the market will take care of that. Our aim is to 'make a case,' to win a fight, to make our plea plausible, to keep the pressure on. And the intellectual degradation which that interpretation of truth-testing has brought upon the minds of our people is almost unbelievable.[45]

Meiklejohn's central complaint about the marketplace of ideas is that it offers no adequate standards to distinguish what is true from what is false; it only provides options from which audiences can pick according to their best interests. Truth is thus the outcome of a savage struggle where everyone fights to impose their own views on others. Meiklejohn asserts that 'dependence upon intellectual laissez-faire ... has destroyed the foundations of our national education, has robbed of their meaning such terms as "reasonableness" and "intelligence," and "devotion to the general welfare."'[46] Against this chaotic scenario, Meiklejohn proposes a theory of free speech grounded on the principle of collective self-determination. This theory is designed not to protect the rights of individuals to express their interests in the public sphere, but rather to protect the interests of the body politic as a whole. It conceives of the First Amendment as an instrument that guarantees an informed process of decision making, where all citizens should be able to understand the issues bearing upon common life and to decide for themselves how to deal with them, the type of society they want to form and the way they want to live their lives in common.

---

[42] Barendt shows that the German Constitutional Court has recognised the importance of freedom of speech in the formation of public opinion on political questions since the early 1960s. See Barendt, above n 40, 18.

[43] See ibid, 18–21.

[44] A Meiklejohn, 'Free Speech and its Relation to Self-Government' in *Political Freedom: The Constitutional Powers of the People* (New York, Oxford University Press, 1965) 60–66.

[45] ibid 73–74.

[46] ibid 74.

Central to the purpose of this book is the fact that although Meiklejohn's theory focuses essentially on the political aspects of the First Amendment, it always shows, at the same time, a robust concern for its truth-seeking function. And this is so because for Meiklejohn, politics and truth are intrinsically connected. According to him, '[f]ree men need the truth as they need nothing else. In the last resort, it is only the search for and the dissemination of truth that can keep our country safe'.[47] The truth-seeking function of speech takes a complex form in this theory. Truth is not about a blind Miltonian faith that unabridged freedom of discussion will necessarily lead to its discovery.[48] Nor is it exclusively about approaching objective truths, which are somewhere out there waiting to be discovered, as in John Stuart Mill's account. On the contrary, according to Meiklejohn, truth is contained in the normative framework that orients the behaviour and reasoning of citizens that have freely decided to govern themselves. Therefore, truth cannot be found in the competition of the market but in the bond that holds together a self-governing people, that is, in the nation's constitution. The latter contains a 'political truth' in the sense of a central premise that shapes the meaning and functions of the political system in general and of the First Amendment in particular.

Meiklejohn's interpretation of the First Amendment is informed by this political truth, derived from his understanding of the political program contained in the Constitution of the United States: 'The principle of freedom of speech springs from the necessities of the program of self-government.'[49] The program of self-government as defined by Meiklejohn is diametrically opposed to a political system in which men and women are governed by others. Its basic feature is a single entity of people who are, at the same time, their own masters and their own subjects; they are people governed by themselves, the self-governing people.[50] This conception of 'political truth' appears vividly in Meiklejohn's critique of Holmes's moral scepticism. Indeed, Meiklejohn agrees with Holmes, to a certain extent, when the latter states that 'I don't believe that it is an absolute principle or even a human ultimate that man is always an end in himself—that his dignity must be respected, etc'.[51] Meiklejohn's point is that if by an 'absolute principle' Holmes means 'a principle of the universe', the statement is unproblematic.[52] He accepts that the non-human universe has no moral principles and does not care about human dignity or anything else.[53] However, when the statement is assessed under the terms of the Constitution, things are radically different, as he observes. Indeed, if someone's dignity is negated in the face of the Constitution, whoever does so

---

[47] ibid 59.
[48] See A Meiklejohn, 'The First Amendment Is an Absolute' 1961 *The Supreme Court Review* 245.
[49] See Meiklejohn, above n 44, 27.
[50] ibid 12.
[51] ibid.
[52] ibid.
[53] ibid.

'flatly repudiates the moral *compact* on which our plan of self-government rests. And, especially, he breaks down the basic principle of the First Amendment'.[54] Following Jefferson, Meiklejohn claims that at the bottom of the American plan of government there is a *compact*, there is a profound truth to which all provisions of the Constitution, laws, statutes and decrees are subsidiary and on which they are dependent. And the nature of this compact, according to Meiklejohn, can be traced back to the meeting of the Pilgrims in the *Mayflower*, where they agreed on the following:

> Do by these Presents solemnly and mutually, in the presence of God, and one another, Covenant and Combine ourselves together into a Civil Body Politik, for our better ordering and preservation, and furtherance of the ends aforesaid; and by virtue hereof do enact, constitute, and frame such just and equal Laws, Ordinances, Acts, Constitutions, and Offices, from time to time, as shall be thought most meet and convenient for the general good of the Colony; unto which we promise all due submission and obedience ...[55]

As Meiklejohn argues, the same idea was subsequently re-enacted in the Declaration of Independence and then in the Preamble to the American Constitution.[56] This central idea is that the people of the United States should govern themselves. To this 'political truth' the First Amendment, according to Meiklejohn, gives breath and substance. The First Amendment's aim is to contribute to this fundamental purpose. In order to do so, it has two central functions.

The first function of the free speech clause is to stimulate what will be called here the 'creative power of the people'. A self-governing people need to define themselves the way in which they want to live their lives in common. To do so, they require an active capacity to collectively define and interpret the scope and meaning of the principles contained in the Constitution. The validity of the text, according to Meiklejohn, derives precisely from this interpretative exercise:

> [The] Constitution derives whatever validity, whatever meaning, it has, not from its acceptance by our forefathers one hundred and sixty years ago, but from its acceptance by us, now. Clearly, however, we cannot, in any valid sense, 'accept' the Constitution unless we know what it says. And, for that reason, every loyal citizen of the nation must join with his fellows in the attempt to interpret, in principle and in action, that provision of the Constitution which is rightly regarded as its most vital assertion, its most significant contribution to political wisdom.[57]

This is no easy job. 'The voting of wise decisions', to borrow Meiklejohn's phrase, and knowledge of the Constitution require a highly capable and educated people. This is the first fundamental function of freedom of speech in a political

---

[54] ibid 70 (emphasis added).
[55] Mayflower Compact, HS Commanger (ed), *Documents of American History* (New York, Appleton-Century Crofts, 1968).
[56] Meiklejohn, above n 44, 18.
[57] ibid 3.

community.[58] Meiklejohn argues that just as absolute privileges or immunities of speech are required in parliamentary debates in order to reach the best and most informed decisions, so does the self-governing people require the most open and free debate of ideas so that they can be properly informed and make equally good decisions in matters of public interest. However, Meiklejohn claims that speech needs to be organised to fulfil this goal. To define the limits of speech and the rationality of the debate, Meiklejohn uses the town hall model.[59] Discussion needs to be moderated and abridged to achieve the goal of the meeting, which is getting things done. In this context, two issues are fundamental. The first one is that the people gather to decide things that are in their common interest, that is, to decide matters of public policy. The second is a consequence of the first. The ultimate aim of the meeting is the voting of wise decisions, and in order to achieve this aim, voters must be made as wise as possible. They need to know everything about the objects under scrutiny, the whole truth that is available about them. Nothing should be hindered; nothing should be abridged if the people are to make the best possible decisions. This is why the First Amendment, according to Meiklejohn, is not primarily concerned with the needs of men to express their opinions but with the common needs of all the members of the body politic.[60] In his words, '[w]hat is essential is not that everyone shall speak, but that everything worth saying should be said'.[61]

The completion of the program of self-government is not reduced, according to Meiklejohn, to the voting of wise decisions. As a point of fact, just as the self-governing people are their own masters, they are also their own subjects. Just as they give to themselves the laws under which they regulate their lives in common, they also need to respect and follow these laws. Without compliance with the law, a political community is not possible. Therefore, the second purpose of the truth-seeking function of the First Amendment is, according to Meiklejohn, to secure what we might call a 'self-restraining power' of the people. This function is fundamental to Meiklejohn's system because it guarantees compliance with and obedience to the law. For in fact, compliance with the law requires a legitimate authority, and the latter is obtained, among other things, when government exercise of power is subject to constant scrutiny by the people. The truth-seeking function of the First Amendment consists here in unveiling who the representatives *really* are and the *real* motives behind their actions. The checking function of expressive freedoms also unveils the *real* functioning of the political machinery by exposing scandal and corruption. By facilitating a permanent and rigorous scrutiny of government authorities, expressive freedoms are a guarantee against government corruption. As such, they provide democratic legitimacy and enable the self-restraining power of the people by making compliance with the law easier.

---

[58] ibid 26.
[59] See ibid 24–28.
[60] See ibid 55.
[61] ibid 26.

As Meiklejohn argues, 'political self-government comes into being only insofar as the common judgement, the available intelligence, of the community takes control over all interests, only insofar as its authority over them is recognized and effective'.[62]

Meiklejohn provides a solution to the intellectual poverty he identified in Holmes's marketplace of ideas. Truth cannot be, according to him, reduced to choice and interest. There is instead a political truth that is grounded in the programme of self-government, which shapes the functions and aims of the political body in coherence with it. This truth requires a citizenry that is intellectually prepared to know and understand the plan of self-government contained in the Constitution. To this 'political truth' the First Amendment, according to Meiklejohn, pays tribute. As has been seen, it does so in two ways. First, it allows an informed process of decision-making, where the people can make the wisest decisions possible. Secondly, it enables the checking function of the press, which contributes to the observance of the law. Meiklejohn inaugurated a new way of justifying the importance of free speech, which is inherently connected to the motives of a self-governing people. And although many authors have followed the democratic core of Meiklejohn's argument, not all of them have agreed on its epistemological side. That is the case of Robert Post, to whom we now direct our attention.

V. Robert Post's Participatory Democracy: Politics without Truth

Within the democratic tradition, Post emphatically rejects the truth-seeking purpose of expressive freedoms. For him, the advancement of new knowledge, which he identifies with the marketplace model, is not fitted to the First Amendment's purposes, because this function requires 'both freedom of thought and disciplined application of existing standards'.[63] While free speech guarantees the former, it does not guarantee the latter. This is so, argues Post, because new knowledge is formed only when thought is framed by certain practices that define what knowledge is, practices which discriminate between what is true and what is false, an activity that is essential to advancing knowledge and human understanding in a wide range of disciplines.[64] Many institutions—from universities to scientific journals—perform these practices in contemporary societies. However, the First Amendment, according to Post, is not designed to fulfil that purpose,[65] because

---

[62] Meiklejohn, above n 44, 60.

[63] Post, above n 41, 478.

[64] ibid 479.

[65] Marketplace of ideas theorists would agree with Post's argument that the advancement of knowledge requires distinctions between true and false statements. They would also agree with him that freedom of speech prevents the state from making such distinctions. However, they would disagree with his

governments cannot decide for the rest what is true and what is false in a free debate of ideas and opinions. In such a context, 'there is no such thing as a false idea'.[66]

Like Arendt, Post believes that discussion in the public sphere is antinomic to the advancement of truth and knowledge, because they depend on modes of communication that completely differ from each other.[67] Post also shares with Arendt the belief that these spheres must be kept separate if they are to be secured. There are, however, certain differences in their perspectives. These differences are related to the fact that when Arendt speaks of political modes of communication, she is referring broadly to the sphere of decision making, while Post, for his part, is referring to the broader concept of 'public discourse'. This includes all 'those speech acts and media of communication that are socially regarded as necessary and proper means in the formation of public opinion'.[68] This distinction explains why Arendt argues that if left to the modes of political communication, truth will succumb to the interest and power struggles proper to this domain, while Post thinks that the result will just be anarchy, as public discourse is unable to provide the discipline required to advance any form of knowledge.[69] Now, if the reversal procedure is applied, that is, if the modes of communication proper to the formation of knowledge are taken to the political realm, both agree that politics itself is threatened. Indeed, while for Arendt the nature of truth statements precludes discussion and deliberation, Post argues that they impose forms of discrimination (content and viewpoint) that are unacceptable in a democratic society.[70]

In this way, Post develops an interpretation of the First Amendment that, although framed in the model of democratic justifications, distances itself from its truth-seeking purpose. His conception of democracy allows him to do so. Indeed, by contrast with Meiklejohn, whose conception of collective self-government makes the discovery of truths necessary to enabling the creative and the restraining powers of the people, Post's conception of democracy does not need this function. His conception is grounded in a particular relationship between the will of individuals and the general will of the community.[71]

---

conclusions. The truth, they would claim, is still discoverable, because individuals who are exposed to an open debate of ideas, and not the state, will be able to make those distinctions. This same point was made by John Stuart Mill in *On Liberty*, when he defended the truth-seeking purpose of free speech through the argument of rationality. See E Volokh, 'In Defense of the Marketplace of Ideas/Search for Truth as a Theory of Free Speech Protection' (2011) 97 *Virginia Law Review* 595.

[66] Post, above n 41, 479.
[67] Although Post uses the language of 'new knowledge' rather than the more common notion of 'political truths', he is making an explicit reference to the latter when he claims that 'the creation of new knowledge often goes under the appellation of the "marketplace of ideas"'. See ibid 478.
[68] ibid 483.
[69] ibid 478; Arendt, above n 18, 230.
[70] Arendt, above n 18, 241; Post, above n 41, 479.
[71] Post makes this point clear in a previous paper, where he claims that '[i]t is a grave mistake to confuse democracy with particular decision making procedures, and to fail to identify the core values that democracy as a form of government seek to instantiate'. R Post, 'Democracy and Equality' (2005) 1 *Law, Culture and the Humanities* 142.

According to Post, 'democracy is achieved when those who are subject to law *believe* that they are also potential authors of the law'.[72] And his understanding of the speech clause corresponds to this conception of democracy. Its purpose is to reinforce this state of mind in individual citizens, that is, a certain conviction that the law, in some way or another, reflects their own voices. Post's main concern is thus to strengthen a particular dimension of individual autonomy. This is something that might be denominated 'political autonomy': a sense of being, as active citizens, potential authors of the law. And this purpose, at first sight, has nothing to do with the advancement of political truths.

Post's focus on political autonomy presents a compelling alternative to democratic theories aimed at discovering political truths, such as Meiklejohn's. It is an alternative that seems to surmount the difficulties we have already identified in the relationship between truth and politics, without abandoning the political significance of the First Amendment. However, as will be shown, although Post's theory distances itself from this conflictive relationship, it does so only (and partially) in relation to the truth-seeking functions of the First Amendment, that is, to the idea that expressive freedoms are adequate means of advancing truths that are out there, waiting to be discovered. But Post does not and cannot avoid reflecting the other 'political truth' that has been described throughout this chapter.[73] This other truth is supposed to be inherent in the political system itself, and shape institutions and practices in coherence with it.

A. The Unavoidability of Truth

As has been argued during this chapter, the meaning and functions of free speech in democratic theories are derived from a political truth or a central premise that consists of particular conceptions of democracy. The meaning of the free speech clause is thus shaped in accordance with that conception, and its functions are a way of legitimising the conception by reinforcing what are supposed to be its central values. In Meiklejohn's case, the truth-seeking function of the First Amendment is essential to legitimising a democratic system understood as collective self-government. First, it contributes to advancing knowledge about the issues that are subject to the deliberation of the self-governing people. Secondly, it makes compliance with the law easier because, by enabling government accountability, expressive freedoms contribute to the recognition and the effectiveness of authority.[74] Post, by contrast, rejects the truth-seeking purpose of the First Amendment. However, it will be shown that his theory has two problems. First, it cannot completely deny the importance of the truth-seeking function of free speech, because this function

---

[72] Post, above n 41, 482 (emphasis added).
[73] See ibid 478 and 487.
[74] Meiklejohn, above n 44, 60.

is fundamental to his conception of democracy. The second problem is related to the first. Indeed, as in Meiklejohn's theory, the meaning and function of the First Amendment in Post's theory is shaped in coherence with a higher political truth, that is, a particular conception of democracy that moulds the institutions and practices subordinated to it. Let us start with the first problem.

i. The Truth-seeking Purpose

Post's model of democratic legitimation, which he borrows from Habermas, and which guides his understanding of the First Amendment, depends on two things.[75] The first is that government decisions need to be accountable to the public (just as in Meiklejohn's theory).[76] The second depends on access to the public sphere. Government accountability is tightly connected to the discovery and dissemination of truths the discovery of which is functional to the political system as a whole, as Greenawalt has rightly observed.[77] In fact, the purpose of government accountability is to reveal the detailed operation of governments, to illuminate why and how decisions are made, if there are better alternatives and so on. Its purpose is to lift the curtain of political appearances to expose politics as it 'really is'. And sometimes it goes even further, questioning the *real* intentions or motivations of politicians, unveiling hypocrisy and contradictions. The aim of government accountability, in other words, is to make the political process transparent to the vigilant eye of the public by unveiling facts that are functional to the system itself.

Although Post denies the truth-seeking purpose of free speech and gives good reasons for doing so, he nevertheless ends up invoking the discovery of political truths as a form of legitimating the democratic system. This is because by recognising the checking function of the First Amendment, Post is necessarily committed to the discovery of the types of truths described in the previous paragraph. The point is that Post cannot avoid the fact that it would be very difficult, if not impossible, to conceive of a legitimate democracy without an adequate system of government accountability. Post, however, might defend himself by arguing that his theory protects government accountability not because it reveals any truth but because it contributes to the formation of public discourse. He might even add that government accountability is concerned with factual truths whose discovery is not necessarily associated with the disciplined methods and practices required for the advancement of knowledge but with the mere exposition of nude facts.

Although these arguments might help defend Post's position, problems associated with the second element in his model of democratic legitimation are more difficult to overcome.[78] This element is access to the public sphere, and it is

---

[75] Post, above n 41, 482.
[76] See ibid.
[77] See K Greenawalt, 'Free Speech Justifications' (1989) 89 *Columbia Law Review* 119.
[78] Post, above n 41, 482.

essential to Post's theory. Indeed, without it, the value of authorship (a person's belief that he or she is a potential author of the law) is unrealisable. If citizens are not able to express their ideas in the public sphere, it is impossible for them to believe that they are contributing to the formation of public opinion. However, access to the public sphere is a common problem even in the most advanced liberal democracies (despite the opportunities brought by the Internet),[79] where the structural limitations of the press tend to reproduce the status quo, as was argued in Chapter 1. So, if access is a fundamental element of Post's theory, what are his solutions to structural disadvantages? How is access to the public sphere guaranteed in his theory? What mechanisms does he deploy to secure fair participation in the formation of public opinion?

The persuasiveness of Post's answers to these questions falls short, especially given the importance that the second element of democratic legitimacy plays in his theory. In fact, according to him, everyone *within* public discourse should have equal autonomy, 'which reflects the political equality that all citizens enjoy within a democracy'.[80] This does not mean that the state should guarantee fair access to the public sphere. Quite to the contrary, Post is just arguing for equal autonomy for those who have already gained access to it. In other words, the state should treat with equal respect the ideas and opinions of those who are already engaged in the formation of public opinion, but cannot introduce mechanisms designed to assure fair participation in it. As he argues in another context:

> [T]he state can equalize influence on public debate only if it controls the intimate and independent processes by which citizens evaluate the idea of others. Such efforts are intrinsically undesirable when performed by the state, both because ideas are not equal and because any such government efforts likely would verge on the tyrannical.[81]

Post's theory might work well in a society where participation in the public sphere is merely a matter of personal choice. However, when there are structural disadvantages, when certain groups or individuals cannot gain or have difficulties gaining access to public debates as a consequence of economic, political, social, ethnic, educational or any other disadvantage, Post's theory will tend to reproduce the inequality, benefiting dominant groups and individuals to the detriment of weaker ones. Indeed, as his focus is on equality *within* public discourse and not on fair or equal access, his scope of protection reduces to those who are actually contributing to the formation of public opinion rather than to those who are excluded from it. Although Post admits certain exceptions, these only go as far as to recognise that '[d]emocracy requires only that inequities that undermine democratic

---

[79] Although the Internet has substantially increased participation in the formation of public opinion, studies have shown that side-effects, such as concentration of audiences and colonization of the Web by big media providers, have reduced the effectiveness of such participation. For a compelling analysis of the problems of the Internet in the formation of public opinion, see CE Baker, *Media Concentration and Democracy* (Cambridge, Cambridge University Press, 2007) 98–123.

[80] Post, above n 41, 484.

[81] Post, above n 71, 148.

legitimation be ameliorated'.[82] But this solution is a circular trap, as the elements of democratic legitimation recognised by Post himself are reduced to government accountability to and equal autonomy for those who are *already* engaged in public discourse.

The problem is that if expressive freedoms are *a priori* discarded as means of advancing knowledge about matters of public interest, the political autonomy that Post defends and the democratic mode of legitimation on which it rests might be seriously impaired. In fact, as some authors suggest, there is a relationship between access to the public sphere and knowledge about those participating in the formation of public opinion.[83] Those who have specialised knowledge about topics that are discussed in the public sphere increase exponentially their chances not only of gaining access to debates but also, more importantly, of influencing their outcome. Accordingly, knowledge about the central issues and discussions developed in our political communities should be fundamental to a democracy if its central value is, as Post suggests, political autonomy. A good example of this was the student movement in Chile in 2011. One reason for its importance and influence was the level of knowledge of its leaders about the problems of the educational system, and their capacity to communicate them to the general public.[84] When confronted with ministers, members of parliament, vice-chancellors of universities and other relevant actors in the debate, they articulated with remarkable accuracy and consistency the problems of the educational laws in matters as complex as subsidies, funding, access and quality, among many others. Their knowledge helped them not only to gain access to the public debate, but also, more importantly, to persuade an important segment of the population of the legitimacy of their claims.[85] The leaders of the student movement raised awareness and increased knowledge in the population about the state of educational institutions in Chile through the press. They contributed to building a critical citizenry from whom they received ample support. This support was fundamental to pushing for changes in the law.[86]

---

[82] ibid 153.

[83] Pippa Norris shows that knowledge is fundamental to raising awareness about specific problems and to stimulating a participative and critical citizenry. See P Norris, *Democratic Deficit: Critical Citizens Revisited* (Cambridge, Cambridge University Press, 2011) 121.

[84] According to Sehnbruch and Donoso, the Chilean student movement is part of the emergence of a critical citizenry associated with rising levels of education. This, and the way they communicated the structural problems of the educational system in Chile, contributed to raising awareness of the problem, to getting access to the public sphere and to effectively pushing for changes in the law. K Sehnbruch and S Donoso, 'Chilean Winter of Discontent: Are Protests Here to Stay?' (2011) *Open Democracy*, available at https://www.opendemocracy.net/kirsten-sehnbruch-sofia-donoso/chilean-winter-of-discontent-are-protests-here-to-stay.

[85] For the relationship between higher levels of education and the emergence of a critical citizenry, see Norris, above n 83, 121.

[86] In September 2011, 79% of the Chilean population supported the demands for educational reforms advocated by the student movement. See Adimark, *Encuesta: Evaluacion Gestion Del Gobierno* (September 2011) 62.

As Post assigns the advancement of knowledge exclusively to universities and research institutions, and denies *a priori* the role that a free press might have in its development, he is limiting the very political autonomy he wants to defend. The student movement shows the relevance that knowledge and the ability to communicate it has for enabling access to the public sphere and for affecting the outcome of the political process. Without this knowledge, an important part of the population would have been left poorly informed, or perhaps would not have even been aware of the problems of the Chilean educational system, and consequently, modifications to the law would probably not have occurred. The existence of an informed citizenry enables the emergence of a critical mass able to affect the public sphere and to press for changes in the law. And when this happens, all of those who have participated, in plural, are equally responsible for those transformations and can collectively claim to have increased their autonomy. Political autonomy, in other words, would benefit from a conception of free speech in which the advancement of knowledge and the construction of a critical citizenry are central.

ii. The Truth of Democracy

There is yet another dimension in which Post's theory cannot avoid the conflict signalled at the beginning of this chapter, that is, the conflict between politics and truth. As has been argued throughout this chapter, the meaning of the free speech clause in democratic theories is functional to particular conceptions of democracy, to what has been defined in this chapter as 'political truths'. These truths circumscribe the meaning, functions and scope of expressive freedoms. Moreover, when the free speech clause embodies these political truths through court or regulatory decisions, the decisions define the communicative practices that are adequate for the enhancement and reproduction of the truths. In other words, these 'political truths' function as an umbrella that informs an overall system of judgements and practices. All those who conform with them will be tolerated, and all those who do not will be silenced.

This is the political truth from which Post cannot escape. It performs a constitutive function in the discursive practices of a society, as it defines the form, limits and value of speech in the public sphere. It is a truth that discriminates between what might be revealed to the public and what should be kept obscure. Although the criterion of discrimination, as Post rightly observes, is not necessarily based on 'practices that continually separate the true from the false and the better from the worse'[87] in the light of an objective and independent truth, it still makes those distinctions. Only in this case, discrimination is based on a truth that is supposed to be internal to the system itself, and on which depends its subsistence and its reproduction. As Post's conception of democracy is founded on the value of authorship, the meaning and form of the First Amendment in his theory is also framed in

---

[87] Post, above n 41, 479.

those terms. Accordingly, Post circumscribes protection to all speech and modes of communication that contribute to the formation of *public discourse*. He adds that '[s]peech is typically categorised as within or outside of public discourse according to whether it occurs within social relationships that are regarded as requiring autonomy or interdependence'.[88] Since Post is protecting a particular dimension of individual autonomy, one which is limited to the political realm, the types of social relationships that would deserve protection are only those which occur in that sphere.[89] And although Post manages to provide protection to a broad range of discourses,[90] in comparison with other democratic theories, this protection is still framed within and reduced to his particular conception of democracy.[91]

Regardless of how broad or narrow the scope of protected speech, what is important here is that, as happens with other democratic theories, Post bases his protections on his particular understanding of democracy. It is his substantive conception of democracy, based on the value of authorship, which he cannot avoid when defining the practices or speech that are admissible in his theory. This substantive conception or this 'political truth' not only contributes to Post's interpretation of the meaning of the free speech clause; more importantly, it helps him to define what the clause should do to preserve the values that he considers are constitutive of the democratic system he defends.[92] This is the political truth that Post cannot abandon. The problem, as David Richards acknowledges, is that conceptions of democracy are essentially contested: 'views differ about what is and what is not essential to a well functioning democracy, or, conversely, what counts as democratic "pathology" for purposes of determining the legitimate scope of free speech'.[93] The point is that although democratic procedures of deliberation might provide, in appearance, a fair basis with which to delimit the realm of protected speech, this field depends, ultimately, on substantive conceptions of democracy.

But what is the most adequate theory of democracy? Is it a programme of collective self-determination centred on the process of decision making, as Meiklejohn claims, or is it a rights-based scheme, which requires a principled system of adjudication, as Bork argues, or is it perhaps a programme of self-governance where

---

[88] ibid 483.

[89] ibid.

[90] For Post, anything that might contribute to the formation of public discourse, including the arts as well as 'other forms of non cognitive' and even non-political speech, might fall within the scope of the First Amendment. See ibid 486.

[91] Robert Bork, for example, whose conception of democracy was reduced to a principled and neutral process of decision making, only recognised First Amendment protection in a very restricted form of political speech, limited to 'speech concerned with government behavior, policy or personnel, whether the government unit involved is executive, legislative, judicial or administrative'. See R Bork, 'Neutral Principles and Some First Amendment Problems' (1971) 47 *Indiana Law Journal* 1.

[92] This is why although Post opens his paper by warning readers that his purpose is not to determine his theory of free speech 'in the abstract' but through the method of reflective equilibrium where history is examined through the best ideals and those ideals are reordered in the light of history, his interpretation of the First Amendment is still the reflection of a set of values which define what an ideal democracy is supposed to be. Post, above n 41, 477.

[93] DAJ Richards, *Free Speech and the Politics of Identity* (Oxford, Oxford University Press, 1999) 19.

the crucial thing is the right to be an author in the process of communication in the public sphere, as some contemporary versions of the theory suggest?[94] The purpose here is not to answer these questions; it is simply to show that on their answer depends the meaning and function of expressive freedoms in democratic theories of free speech. These freedoms, in other words, depend on the identification of a *political truth*, which is not external to the system but which is supposed to reside in the programme of a given constitution. The purpose of the free speech clause is thus dependent on how the programme of the constitution is conceived. If that programme is conceived as of a collective enterprise, the purpose of the free speech clause would be radically different from the purpose of a free speech clause in a programme conceived of as one of autonomous self-government. The next section will analyse the practical consequences of the unavoidability of this political truth in democratic theories.

VI. Free Press and the Politics of Truth

To understand better how truth and politics coexist in democratic theories despite the obstacles that Arendt and others have identified in this relationship, it is necessary to re-examine some of the concepts developed in this chapter. The first is 'objective truth'. Its discovery follows the patterns of science and rectifies itself according to its rules and principles.[95] As has already been seen, this notion is incompatible with Post's system of free speech, or with Arendt's political sphere, because it contains modes of communication irreconcilable with those of the political realm. Opposed to it is a second version of truth, which has usually been referred to in this chapter as 'political truth'. This truth is not independent of or external to the political process but is precisely a consequence or a product of it. In the context of democratic theories of free speech, this truth takes the form of a particular conception of democracy, and it has a constitutive effect because this conception defines and shapes the institutions that are subordinated to it. In other words, while the objective conception of truth necessarily supposes the possibility of a correspondence, a symmetry between the *world*, as an object of knowledge, and our knowledge about it, the second version of truth is based on the coherence between a prevalent 'political truth' and a number of practices, institutions and judgements that are shaped in accordance to it.

In the political realm, prevalent conceptions of democracy in a particular time and place are the necessary consequence of political struggles. These conceptions are disputed, and those which prevail do so having emerged from conflict and opposition. At the centre of this struggle, as Foucault argues, 'lies the problem of

---

[94] See Post, above n 41, 483.
[95] See M Foucault, 'Truth and Juridical Forms' in JD Faubion (ed), *Power: Essential Works of Foucault 1954–1984*, vol 3 (R Hurley tr, London, Penguin, 2002) 4.

the formation of a certain number of domains of knowledge formed on the basis of ... political relations in society'.[96] And these domains engender what he calls the 'politics of truth':

> Each society has its regime of truth, its 'general politics' of truth—that is, the types of discourse it accepts and makes function as true; the mechanisms and instances that enable one to distinguish true and false statements; the means by which each is sanctioned; the techniques and procedures accorded value in the acquisition of truth; the status of those who are charged with saying what counts as true.[97]

Substantive conceptions of democracy or political truths, it has been argued, function as one of the mechanisms used in our societies to make such distinctions. They are the points of reference not in deciding what is true or false in relation to some objective reality, but in relation to a political system designed to reproduce itself through the means of democratic legitimation. What is true or what is false, accordingly, corresponds to the internal coherence of the system itself. Whatever enables its reproduction is coherent with it, and is thus sanctioned and accorded value. Now, when distinctions about what is acceptable or unacceptable speech (the system of free speech) are defined on the basis of substantive conceptions of democracy, the scope of possible discourses and the knowledge associated with them will depend on those conceptions prevailing in a particular place and time. In this context, the 'illusion of the free press' is that a free press is the expression of a political truth inherent to the political system itself. Under this illusion, Meiklejohn claims that whatever the words of the First Amendment mean, 'they go directly to the heart of our American plan of government. If we understand them we can know what, as a self-governing nation, we are trying to be and to do.'[98] The fact, however, is that democratic values are contested and disputed, and the press, at best, only reflects prevalent versions of democracy at a particular time and place. In other words, it is not the case—as Meiklejohn thought it was—that expressive freedoms reflect permanent values of a democratic society (or 'political truths'). On the contrary, these freedoms vary with prevalent conceptions of democracy, which in turn define admissible discourse in the public sphere.

Wikileaks, which has leaked of hundreds of thousands of classified documents, unveiled a vast and under-explored political reality that reopened a number of questions about the relationship between politics, truth and free speech. Among these questions are how much knowledge about the real making of politics is possible before politics turns against itself? Which issues ought to be disclosed and which (if any) ought to remain hidden for the sake of democratic legitimacy, and who is to define those boundaries? These are difficult questions. Their mere formulation suggests that democratic systems need certain safeguards against

---

[96] ibid 15.

[97] M Foucault, 'Truth and Power' in Faubion (ed), above n 95, 131.

[98] A Meiklejohn, 'The Freedom of the Electorate' in *Political Freedom: The Constitutional Powers of the People* (New York, Oxford University Press, 1965) 107.

complete disclosure; they require a degree of secrecy in order to assure their survival. They also suggest that the answers given by democratic systems to these problems shape the limits of what the people ought to know at all in democratic societies.

Systems of government accountability provide answers to some of these questions. While they tend to stimulate control of government actions, at the same time they set limits to this control. These systems play a fundamental role in liberal democracies because they enable public scrutiny of the real functioning of politics. According to Vincent Blasi, the relevance of accountability lies in the serious evils that the misuse of public power might produce for private individuals and in the administration of common resources.[99] Mechanisms of control, he argues, empower a vigilant citizenry, attentive to government use of power and ready to react against any form of abuse.[100] Moreover, they not only permit corrective action against politicians or public officials who have actually violated rights or exceeded their powers, they also diminish the likelihood of future abuses of power. However, the system itself does not seem to tolerate absolute and unrestrictive scrutiny. Although the need for government accountability is undeniable, there is a question as to how far demands for such accountability can go without undermining democracy itself. The problem is that if the system is completely transparent and absolutely open, democracy might be endangered, since such transparency might bring to the surface contradictions and struggles that are inscribed in the system itself, contradictions which might not survive exposure.

Access to government information, or the 'public's right to know', is one of the current systems of accountability. Consistently and widely recognised in western democracies, this right has been defended as a form of government control available to common citizens.[101] This right usually extends to all records of government and public institutions covered by the statutes, subject to the exemptions prescribed by them.[102] It promotes government transparency and openness, although these principles are usually weakened by the quantity and magnitude of the exemptions prescribed in some systems. In the United Kingdom, for example, the Freedom of Information Act 2000 contains exemptions (subject to the conditions prescribed in it) to issues as broad as national security, international relations, the economy, court records, formulation of government policy, communications with Her Majesty, environmental information and commercial interests, among many others.[103] Access to information related to these topics might be denied simply because it falls into a particular category that cannot be disclosed in

---

[99] V Blasi, 'The Checking Value in First Amendment Theory' (1977) 2 *American Bar Foundation Research Journal* 521.
[100] ibid.
[101] See H Fenwick and G Phillipson, *Media Freedom Under the Human Rights Act* (Oxford, Oxford University Press, 2006) 958.
[102] ibid 967.
[103] Freedom of Information Act 2000, pt II.

any circumstances (class exemptions), or if disclosure could be prejudicial to one of the interests protected in the Act (harm-based exemptions).[104]

The sphere of accountability and the public's right to know is thus constrained and shaped by these exemptions. When the mere nature of the information is sufficient to deny disclosure, as is the case with class exemptions, the public will never have access to it.[105] When disclosure is subject to harm-based exemptions, publicity will depend on the criteria used by the authority to define 'harm'. While extending the public's right to know about the workings of the government, this system of accountability also delimits the scope of that very knowledge. It determines which issues can enter the public sphere and which should be permanently excluded from it. By placing limits on government accountability, the system of *freedom of information* determines the ambit of possible truths tolerated by a democratic system. And the overall level of tolerance will finally depend on the substantial notion of democracy that orients the system itself. The notion of democracy in Meiklejohn's theory, for example, would be much more tolerant of the public's right to know than the conception prevalent in Bork's system, where his principled and neutral conception of democracy reduces protected speech to strictly political issues.[106] The democratic conception used by Post, in turn, would define admissible levels of disclosure by how they might contribute to the formation of public discourse. The same is true for libel laws or the protection of privacy. The way in which the tensions between the protection of one's reputation and free speech are solved in particular jurisdictions, depends on the conception of democracy in which those systems are grounded.[107] Boundaries of knowledge, limits of what the people are allowed to know are thus defined and shaped by prevailing conceptions of democracy, which are in themselves an object of dispute in the political arena.

VII. Conclusions

The relationship between truth and freedom of speech takes a different form in this chapter. Truth, in the context of democratic theories, is not simply correspondence between reality and its descriptions. Although in Meiklejohn's theory the discovery of objective truths is still fundamental to the materialisation of the program of collective self-government, it is no longer important for Post's theory, which follows a conception of democracy based on political autonomy. However, despite Post's rejection of the truth-seeking purpose of the First Amendment, his theory,

---

[104] Fenwick and Phillipson, above n 101, 972.
[105] Freedom of Information Act 2000, s 24.
[106] See Bork, above n 91, 27–28.
[107] See J Charney, 'The Tensions Between Free Speech and the Protection to One's Reputation: Importance and Limits of the Exceptio Veritatis' (2016) 29 *Revista de Derecho (Valdivia)* 175.

like Meiklejohn's, is committed to another 'political truth'. This truth consists in the particular conception of democracy upon which his theory is grounded. It has the form of coherence between a central judgement and the ones subordinated to it. Moreover, it has constitutive effects, because it defines the meaning, scope and functions of the First Amendment and of the communicative practices dependent on it, or on any other free speech clause. Indeed, whenever democratic theories are applied through courts' decisions or statutes (as in the case of libel laws or freedom of information regimes), they have constitutive effects because they shape the form of a democratic public sphere according to their conceptions of democracy. If those conceptions are generous enough to encompass the expression of the multiplicity of visions existent in a political community and to stimulate a discussion that incorporates a broad range of speech, and not merely those reduced to a strictly political dimension, the public sphere will be nurtured with a generous debate. On the contrary, if the public sphere is designed based on a conception of democracy that values speech as far as it is the reflection of the relevant issues of a political community defined according to those who have political representation, the debate will be meagre.

The central point here is that the limits and scope of what the public is entitled to know is, in the context of democratic theories, defined by a political truth or, what is the same, by prevailing conceptions of democracy. It is not—as Meiklejohn thinks—that a free press is the expression of an ultimate truth embedded in the constitution itself.[108] On the contrary, the idea of a free press is merely the reflection of prevailing conceptions of democracy in a particular time and place, conceptions that are the consequence of conflict and struggle between differing parts of the body politic. And those that prevail tend to reproduce themselves by shaping the form of expressive practices and discourses in the democratic public sphere.

---

[108] See Meiklejohn, above n 98, 107.

4

Freedom of Speech
and Autonomy: Towards
the Discovery of the True Self

I. Introduction

Milton and Mill conceived of expressive freedoms as means to the discovery of truth, where truth is something existing in the outer world and its discovery achieved through correspondence with its depictions. In democratic theories, in contrast, truth is internal to the political system itself. Contained in the central plan of a constitution, truth is the fundamental normative framework that defines what a community is supposed to be and how it is supposed to behave. Central to a self-governing people is its capacity to speak freely about the issues that define life in common. Defences of expressive freedoms on autonomy grounds, as will be shown in this chapter, are also committed to the discovery of truth. Truth, however, here assumes a different form. It is no longer something existing outside the subject but is located within the subject himself, and can be discovered through expressive means.

The central purpose of this chapter is to show the connection between autonomy defences of expressive freedoms and truth. In order to do that, a number of steps must be taken. It is necessary to show, first, how truth is internalised so that an agent no longer needs to look for it outside himself but can find truth within himself. Secondly, it is necessary to show that there is a relationship between autonomy and self-discovery (the discovery of the *true self*) that is mediated by self-reflection. Only if this link is established could it be argued that theories of free speech based on autonomy grounds are also truth-seeking theories. Lastly, it is necessary to show the function played by expressive freedoms in the process of self-reflection. Early Christians already saw in confession a fundamental step in the introspective process leading to the contemplation of God and the discovery of truth. Since the use of confession by Christianity, expression has played different roles in processes of self-discovery throughout history. A contemporary use, as will be seen here, is the one given by autonomy theories of free speech that see in public portrayals of certain forms or styles of life a way of validating one's own identity.

Section II of this chapter will explore the relationship between autonomy and the discovery of the true self through Kant's notion of moral autonomy. It will be seen that the philosopher supposes the 'capacity to subject oneself to (objective) moral principles'[1] and that the use of this capacity allows access to one's true self.[2] Although the notion of personal autonomy in which liberal theories of free speech are grounded is substantially different from moral autonomy, it will be shown that there is a relevant connection between them. Indeed, the sounder notions of personal autonomy also emphasise capacities of self-reflection that involve the idea of a true self: the idea of *who I am*. Sections III and IV will analyse a number of theories of freedom of speech grounded in different conceptions of autonomy, and will conclude that the strongest[3] are precisely those that stimulate capacities of self-reflection. Section V will apply this analysis to the free press, in order to see how it might illuminate our notion of the illusion of the free press.

II. Early Techniques of Self-discovery

If Kant is responsible for connecting moral discourse to laws that moral agents give to themselves, Christianity is responsible for the internalisation of divine law.[4] According to Christianity, as Christ had inscribed the law *deep in everyone's heart*, revelation was no longer to be obtained through an external audible message. The believer's duty, accordingly, is not to go outside to look for evidence of the divine promise but 'to discover within himself the present disposition of which Christ is the model, the inner signs of the "true life"'.[5] Christianity not only internalises the law, it also provides the means through which that law can be discovered. Interestingly enough, expression in the form of confession plays a fundamental role in this process of self-discovery. This may sound paradoxical. Indeed, the discovery of the 'true self' and expression seem to follow opposite directions. While the former seems to pre-suppose an introspective movement, a *journey* into oneself which requires a certain isolation from the outside world, speech, or any other expressive form, by contrast, requires contact with the external world, since communication presupposes a movement from the inside to the outside, from individuals to others in their environment. Despite this tension, there is an inherent connection between both, and the purpose of this section is to explore it.

---

[1] See J Christman and J Anderson (eds), 'Introduction' in *Autonomy and the Challenges to Liberalism* (Cambridge, Cambridge University Press, 2005) 2.

[2] This argument is developed by Jeremy Waldron in J Waldron, 'Moral Autonomy and Personal Autonomy' in J Christman and J Anderson (eds), *Autonomy and the Challenges to Liberalism* (Cambridge, Cambridge University Press, 2005) 317.

[3] Mainly J Raz, 'Free Expression and Personal Identification' (1991) 11 *OJLS* 303; T Scanlon, 'Freedom of Expression and Categories of Expression' (1979) 40 *University of Pittsburgh Law Review* 519.

[4] See É Balibar, *Spinoza and Politics*, tr P Snowdon (London, Verso, 1998) 42.

[5] ibid.

In his 'First Conference of Abbot Moses', written in the fifth century, John Cassian describes a procedure of self-discovery designed to help monks contemplate God.[6] Cassian argues that monks should examine the origin or authorship of their own thoughts, just as the good money-changer tests the genuineness of traded coins. They need to identify the materials of which they are made, and distinguish those made of pure gold from those that have been coloured so as to look like gold. They need to weigh them and recognise if their shape and inscriptions are authentic. Only by examining their thoughts would monks be able to expel sinister or extraneous influences and improve their character.

In order to show how this is supposed to work, Cassian tells a story about the young monk Serapion, who acquired the bad habit of every day stealing a biscuit, hiding it in his clothes and eating it after supper. He was discovered by his prior, who decided to speak about the vice of gluttony during mass without mentioning Serapion's deeds. While listening to the sermon, Serapion burst into tears, lay on the ground and produced from his pocket the biscuit he had stolen that day. Immediately after that, he publicly confessed his daily practice, and then, and only then, in the moment of confession, a flood of light emerged from his body accompanied by a deep sulphurous smell that pervaded the whole room.[7]

Thoughts are for Cassian an object of distrust. Behind them, an alien presence, indeed the presence of the devil, is always possible. Consequently, the monk must be ready to identify what is false and illusory in order to reject it and admit into his heart only what is authentic, that is, only thoughts that have a divine or earthly origin. By examining the origin, cause and authorship of their thoughts, monks can prevent deception. This will help them to discriminate between good and evil, and purify themselves in order to contemplate the divine grace of God. But in order to do so monks need to transform their thoughts into words. Observation is not enough to unveil their origin; they need to verbalise them. It is interesting to note, as Foucault points out,[8] that the moment of revelation does not occur when Serapion takes the stolen biscuit from his clothes and shows it as proof of his vice; it occurs with the verbal confession of his sin. Only through expression did the truth appear in all its magnitude, only then did a stream of light emerge from Serapion's body, along with the sulphuric odour that revealed his misconduct's diabolic source, its evil origin.

Kant's thoughts on the matter could be understood as a secularised version of Cassian's. In Kant, the moral law is located within the moral agent himself, and its discovery requires a process of self-reflection that provides access to the true self.[9] From a theoretical perspective this statement is problematic, and its

---

[6] J Cassian, 'First Conference of Abbot Moses' in H Wace and P Schaff (eds), *A Select Library of Nicene and Post-Nicene Fathers of the Christian Church*, vol 11 (Oxford, Parker, 1893) 302.

[7] ibid 312.

[8] See M Foucault, *The Politics of Truth* (Los Angeles, CA, Semiotext(e), 2007) 185.

[9] Waldron, above n 2, 317.

problem lies in identifying the meaning of the *true self* in Kant. In fact, when describing paralogisms in *Critique of Pure Reason*, Kant criticises rational psychology or the rational doctrine of the soul, which attempts to derive a *thinking substance* or a soul with determinate characteristics (permanence, incorruptibility and personality) from the proposition *I think*.[10] This I of pure apperception, this thinking substance, equivalent to the thing in itself, would not be a possible object of cognition according to Kant's transcendental deduction.[11] Indeed, according to Kant, as our knowledge is reduced to the sphere of appearances and it cannot overstep this boundary, there is nothing we can cognise about the thinking substance or of any other being as it is in itself. Consequently, from a Kantian point of view, there is no access to a *true self* in these terms. Kant puts this in the following words:

> Through this I, or He, or It (the thing) which thinks, nothing further is represented than a transcendental subject of thoughts ... which is recognized only through the thoughts that are its predicates, and about which, in abstraction, we can never have even the least concept.[12]

But if there is no cognitive access to this substantial self in Kant's theory, how can his moral philosophy be associated with the discovery of the true self?[13] This question can be answered in two ways. The first is to refer to the distinction between the phenomenal I and the I of pure apperception in order to claim that since we can only acquire knowledge of the former, the *true self* associated with Kantian morality cannot be anything but the phenomenal I. This answer simply shifts the meaning of the *true self* from the I of pure apperception to the empirical subject in order to claim that self-knowledge is merely knowledge of appearances. 'I represent myself to myself neither as I am nor as I appear to myself, but rather I think myself only as I do every object'.[14] However, in the *Groundwork of the Metaphysics of Morals*, Kant answers the question in a second way when he claims that 'when moral worth is at issue, what counts is not actions, which one sees, but those inner principles of actions that one does not see'.[15] Morality is not concerned with things as they are or as they appear to us, which corresponds to the realm of physics, but with things as they ought to be. Morality is concerned with the autonomous subject, with the capacity to give to herself the moral law and to act accordingly.

---

[10] I Kant, *Critique of Pure Reason*, trs P Guyer and A Wood (Cambridge, Cambridge University Press, 1998) B403.

[11] See J Wuerth, 'The Paralogisms of Pure Reason' in P Guyer (ed), *The Cambridge Companion to Kant's Critique of Pure Reason* (Cambridge, Cambridge University Press, 2010) 211.

[12] Kant, above n 10, B404.

[13] See Waldron, above n 2, 317.

[14] Kant, above n 10, B429.

[15] I Kant, *Groundwork of the Metaphysics of Morals*, tr M Gregor (Cambridge Cambridge University Press, 1998) 4:407.

To prove the existence of the moral law, which is the purpose of the *Groundwork*, cognition of the phenomenal self is thus not enough.[16] This is so because that self is governed by laws of nature and as such is determined by them. The moral law, on the contrary, requires that human beings give to themselves the laws by which they are bound, laws that are, nevertheless, universal.[17] This point is crucial for the purposes of our analysis, because this is the point where the notion of autonomy emerges in Kant's moral theory. Kant, for the first time, argues that the moral law resides within rational beings and, as such, is inseparable from them. It is this unity that marks a point of departure from his predecessors who, according to Kant, failed to notice

> that [the human being] is subject *only to laws given by himself but still universal* and that he is bound only to act in conformity with his own will, which, however, in accordance with nature's ends is a will giving universal law.[18]

Kant's conception of moral autonomy basically supposes 'the capacity to subject oneself to (objective) moral principles'.[19] Several elements emerge from this definition. It is important to mention them because they will be useful in analysing, by way of contrast, the conceptions of personal autonomy and the theories of freedom of speech which are grounded in them. First of all, this conception supposes the existence of 'objective moral principles'. Such principles are inscribed in every rational being and serve them as guides for action regardless of time and place. These principles are, in other words, *universal*.[20] Directly connected to the universality of the moral law lies a second element of moral autonomy, which has been defined as the *criterion of reciprocity*.[21] Assuming that rational agents share a universal moral law, if this law is to prevail, a sense of reciprocity and commitment to it is necessary. This *reciprocity* is derived from the fact that the moral law is *a law* and, as such, is a common source of normativity that all must observe equally.[22] A final element in conceptions of moral autonomy, and one that is fundamental to our analysis, is connected to the question raised at the beginning of this section, that is, to forms of deliberation that allow access to the true self. The type of deliberation associated with Kantian morality involves an inner reflection that allows rational beings to derive from within themselves universal

---

[16] ibid 4:392.

[17] ibid 4:432.

[18] ibid.

[19] Christman and Anderson (eds), above n 1, 2.

[20] According to Korsgaard, their universality is not simply related to the idea that every rational agent has access to them, but also to the idea that rational agents should will to have them universalised, that is, to see them as reasons for action in each and every human being. For further analysis of the universalisation of the moral law, see CM Korsgaard, *Creating the Kingdom of Ends* (Cambridge, Cambridge University Press, 1996) 14.

[21] See R Forst, 'Political Liberty: Integrating Five Conceptions of Autonomy' in Christman and Anderson (eds), above n 1, 230.

[22] For further analysis of the criterion of reciprocity, see D Johnston, *The Idea of a Liberal Theory: A Critique and Reconstruction* (Princeton, NJ, Princeton University Press, 1994) 72–73.

principles of action. This form of deliberation is, in other words, a necessary step in subjecting oneself to objective moral principles. Or to put it in other terms, rational capabilities are a necessary condition of moral autonomy. According to Kant, 'all moral concepts have their seat and origin completely a priori in reason, and indeed in the most common reason just as in reason that is speculative in the highest degree'.[23] Every rational being has the capacity to act in conformity with the law, that is, to derive duties out of the law. And this capacity presupposes a process of self-reflection, an exploration of the self in which rational beings are supposed to identify within themselves the maxims that according to the moral law should guide their actions.[24]

Just as in Cassian's method monks had to explore within themselves the authorship of their thoughts, in Kant, rational human beings need to question themselves so as to identify the moral worth of their actions. Both are procedures of self-examination in which the answers to the questions raised (*what is the origin of my thoughts?* and *is my action according to duty?*) are already contained in the individual himself. Additionally, both procedures have a similar purpose: the transformation of the subject, although they conceive of this transformation in completely different ways. In the case of Cassian, the purpose is to purify the subject in order to permit the proper contemplation of God.[25] In the case of Kant, the practical reason of the agent reveals the moral worth of his or her actions. Through such reasoning the individual may make moral progress. As Kant puts it, 'the true vocation of reason must be to produce a will that is good, not perhaps *as a means* to other purposes, but *good in itself*, for which reason was absolutely necessary'.[26]

There is another similarity between both procedures. This similarity is crucial for the purposes of this research because it points to the tension identified at the very beginning of this chapter. This is the tension between procedures of self-examination, which presuppose an inner movement (of the subject), on the one hand, and, on the other, expressive manifestations, which presuppose an outward movement (toward the world). Cassian's example of Serapion reveals how this tension is dissolved through confession, which became a crucial and final step in Christian procedures of self-discovery. Although the process of self-exploration per Kant (at least in the *Groundwork*) is, in principle, independent of expressive

---

[23] Kant, above n 15, 4:411.

[24] A procedure has been identified in the *Groundwork* that is defined as the 'contradiction test', in which the use of practical reason allows the identification of the maxims that should guide our conduct according to the moral law. The first step in this procedure is to identify the maxim (subjective principle of action) that guides a particular action, then turn that maxim into a universal law and finally analyse whether any contradiction emerges from the universalised maxim. If no contradictions emerge, the action is in accordance with duty; if contradictions emerge, the action is against duty. For different interpretations of the meaning, types and forms of contradictions derived from this procedure, see Korsgaard, above n 20, 77–102.

[25] Cassian, above n 6, 302.

[26] Kant, above n 15, 4:396.

manifestations, a relationship between both appears in his later work, 'Perpetual Peace', in the form of the 'principle of publicity'.[27]

The purpose of Kant's principle of publicity is to identify the relationship between politics and morality, to discover where these two spheres meet. Kant proposes a particular test, defined as the 'transcendental formula of public right', in order to show this relationship. According to this test, 'all actions affecting the rights of other human beings are wrong if their maxim is not compatible with their being made public'.[28] The gist of Kant's test, as he acknowledges, is that if maxims cannot be openly declared without frustrating their purposes, or cannot be publicly communicated without arousing everyone's resistance, it is because they are unjust and constitute a threat to everyone.[29] All actions derived from non-communicable maxims will thus be unjust. Although this test is negative[30] and only applies to political actions, it reveals the importance of expression (or its lack thereof) in the process of moral deliberation to Kant's theory. In fact, just as a flood of light emerged from Serapion's body at the moment of confessing his sin, the moral quality of political actions emerges when they are subjected to a test of publicity. While, on the one side, evil actions resist verbalization, on the other, actions whose maxims are, in principle, concordant with the moral law are capable of being made public. Kant thus resolves the tension between the inner movement implied in procedures of self-reflection and the external movement proper to expressive manifestations through the principle of publicity. He shows us that they are not incompatible with each other but that the latter works in the political realm as an auxiliary tool that helps us to evaluate the moral quality of political actions.

Regardless of the similarities between Cassian's procedure of self-discovery and the type of deliberation associated with Kantian morality, there are also radical differences between them. Although both procedures presuppose a subject that 'looks into herself' for an answer to her questions, the selves looked at are radically different from each other. In Cassian, the 'true self' is that which remains after the violent eviction of extraneous thoughts. The process of purification is hence, in part, a form of self-destruction, which, as with Serapion, involves a sacrificial rejection of that which is deemed evil. After this procedure, what remains are thoughts that have a pure origin. And this origin is related to a determinate God with a determinate law and a determinate purpose.

The Kantian 'true self', in contrast, is characterised by its opaqueness, by its inaccessibility as an object of cognition. Kant's process of deliberation does not advance any knowledge about the properties of the I of pure apperception.

---

[27] See I Kant, 'Perpetual Peace: A Philosophical Sketch' in H Reiss (ed), *Kant Political Writings*, 2nd edn (HB Nisbet tr, Cambridge, Cambridge University Press, 1991) 125–30.

[28] See ibid 126.

[29] ibid.

[30] Kant says that this test can only identify what is wrong in relation to others and not necessarily what is right. See ibid.

Nevertheless, it reflects a fundamental capacity of rational beings, the capacity for autonomy, that is, of giving to themselves the universal moral law. This law, contrary to Cassian, belongs *to them*, precisely because no one else (God, the Devil, the Church, the state) has made it mandatory. And this marks a crucial difference between both procedures of self-examination. Indeed, Cassian's procedure is sacrificial because it requires the expulsion of extraneous forces governing the self. Kant's procedure, by contrast, is not sacrificial. It simply requires a reasoned assessment of the maxims that govern our actions.

One might conclude that Kant's procedure of self-examination is in some respects a secularised version of Cassian's. In this version, reason has replaced God and rational reflection has replaced a sacrificial-mystical procedure. Exploring this conclusion further would take us beyond the bounds of the present inquiry; however, for present purposes it is enough to highlight three points:

1.   The internalisation of the divine and the moral law contributes to the development of the idea that truth is not necessarily a relation with something outside us, but that it might be located inside us.
2.   That just as with Christian procedures of self-discovery, Kantian morality contains a type of deliberation that allows access to the true self.
3.   Expressive manifestations are not incompatible with these procedures; on the contrary, expression is a relevant condition of their fulfilment.

III. Personal Autonomy and Freedom of Speech

Now that the connection between autonomy and self-discovery has been established, it is possible to begin our exploration of relevant theories of freedom of speech and to analyse to what extent these theories conceive of this freedom as a modern instrument of self-discovery. To begin this inquiry, it is necessary to say that these theories are generally grounded in conceptions of personal or individual autonomy,[31] and that these conceptions are overtly different from the Kantian conception of moral autonomy just analysed.[32] While the latter, as has been seen, is related to the capacity to give to oneself the moral law, the former have been identified with a trait that individuals can exhibit in any aspect of their lives, not only the moral.[33] According to Waldron, personal autonomy 'evokes the image of a person in charge of his life', and although it is not an immoral idea, 'it has relatively

---

[31] See SJ Brison, 'The Autonomy Defense of Free Speech' (1998) 108 *Ethics* 312.
[32] See Forst, above n 21, 230–31; Christman and Anderson (eds), above n 1, 2–3; Johnston, above n 22, 72–79.
[33] See G Dworkin, *The Theory and Practice of Autonomy* (Cambridge, Cambridge University Press, 1988) 34–47.

little to do with morality'. He adds that those who value it 'see it as a particular way of understanding what each person's interest consists in'.[34] Similarly, for Raz, a fundamental aspect of personal autonomy is to be the author of one's own life.[35] To analyse the differences between personal and moral autonomy, it will help to start with a general reassessment of the elements of moral autonomy (universality, reciprocity and self-examination) and compare them with those of personal autonomy.

First of all—as was seen in the previous section—although moral autonomy presupposes the capacity to give to oneself the moral law, the moral law is still universal. Universality, on the other hand, seems to be at odds with conceptions of personal autonomy that centre on the uniqueness of each individual's interests, choices and decisions. Similarly, if those who value personal autonomy do so as way of valuing the unique character of each and every individual, as Waldron suggests,[36] those who value moral autonomy recognise that each person's interests must be reconciled with the interests of others. This is why Johnston states that while moral autonomy involves certain conceptions of justice, personal autonomy involves only conceptions of the good.[37] Hence, while the element of reciprocity is essential for conceptions of moral autonomy, it is not so for conceptions of personal autonomy. Accordingly, moral reflection leads to a universal law that any rational agent should be capable of identifying and applying to a particular circumstance; this is a law that enjoins one to consider all those who might be affected by one's actions. The exercise of personal autonomy, by contrast, might produce a number of varied responses potentially equal to the number of autonomous individuals making decisions on their own; this is why, for example, a person who renounces her talents and decides to dedicate her life to self-indulgence might do so as an exercise of personal autonomy.[38] However, this would certainly count as a failure to exercise moral autonomy.[39]

Despite these differences and the sharpness with which proponents of personal autonomy separate their conceptions from those of moral autonomy,[40] they share a crucial feature: they both emphasise the ability of self-reflection to provide access to the true self. According to Christman, central to any conception of autonomy is the capacity to be a self-legislating agent, that is, to 'act, reflect and choose on the basis of factors that are somehow [one's] own (authentic in some sense)'.[41]

---

[34] Waldron, above n 2, 307.
[35] J Raz, *The Morality of Freedom* (Oxford, Clarendon, 1986) 204.
[36] See Waldron, above n 2, 307.
[37] Johnston, above n 22, 75.
[38] Although this generous conception of the good life is not generally accepted in liberal political theory, it has been defended as a valid one by Ronald Dworkin. See R Dworkin, *A Matter of Principle* (Oxford, Clarendon, 1986) 191.
[39] See Kant, above n 15, 4:423.
[40] See Raz, above n 35, 370.
[41] J Christman, 'Autonomy in Moral and Political Philosophy' in EN Zalta (ed), *The Stanford Encyclopedia of Philosophy* (2011), available at plato.stanford.edu/archives/spr2011/entries/autonomy-moral/.

Similarly, Waldron argues that the capacities of self-reflection implied in conceptions of moral autonomy are also implied in conceptions of personal autonomy.[42] Now, a condition of self-discovery is the exercise of the capacities of self-reflection. In order to know who I am, I need to look into myself and find the answer. Whether I want to know the quality of my thoughts—as was the case with Cassian—or the moral nature of political actions—as in Kant—I need to make use of the type of deliberation that provides access to my true self, that involves the idea of *who I am*. This is a type of deliberation that is common to both moral and personal autonomy.

Although moral autonomy and personal autonomy suppose similar capacities of self-reflection, not all theories of freedom of speech are grounded in conceptions of personal autonomy that acknowledge the relevance of such capacities. In this section, two of these theories will be analysed (Dworkin and Scanlon). According to them, autonomy is the liberty to think and to act without undue interference from external agents. They see in governments the main threat to the exercise of individual autonomy, and they have thus identified as their main purpose preventing any form of government interference in the sphere of speech. However, in order to do so, they need to ground their theories in extremely weak conceptions of autonomy. This is because the looser the requirements to qualify an action as autonomous, the greater the number of actions which can be deemed autonomous. And the wider the range of autonomous actions, the smaller the capacity of governments to act without harming individual autonomy. The problem, as will be seen, is that rather than defending freedom of speech on the basis of autonomy, these theories end up defending it on the basis of negative liberty, and on this basis they threaten the very autonomy they are supposed to protect. As will be argued in section IV, the theories that are better able to defend freedom of speech on autonomy grounds are those that in their conceptions of autonomy incorporate capacities of self-reflection, that is, capacities that provide access to the 'true self'.[43] But before taking up this task, two theories that identify autonomy with negative liberty will first be assessed.

A. Ronald Dworkin and the Good Life

According to Ronald Dworkin, 'a constitutive feature of a just political society [is] that government treat all its adult members ... as responsible moral agents'.[44] This conception of agency, argues Dworkin, has two dimensions. First, responsible

---

[42] Waldron, above n 2, 307–8.

[43] In the former category are Scanlon, above n 3, and Raz, above n 3; in the latter category, R Dworkin, 'The Coming Battles over Free Speech', *The New York Review of Books* (11 June 1992); T Scanlon, 'A Theory of Freedom of Expression' (1972) 1 *Philosophy & Public Affairs* 204.

[44] Dworkin, above n 43.

moral agents decide for themselves what is good or bad in life or politics, or what is true or false in matters of faith and justice.[45] The second dimension is an active one. Responsible moral agents not only form their own convictions about the good life, but they also express these convictions as a manifestation of their personality, as an expression of who they are. Freedom of speech, according to Dworkin, is essential to realising this basic feature of a just political society. According to these presuppositions, governments would violate the respect agents deserve if they abridged the expression of certain opinions because they might lead to dangerous or offensive convictions. Governments would also frustrate responsible moral agency if they disqualified people from entering public debate when they considered their convictions unworthy.[46]

Dworkin's conception of autonomy (and his defence of free speech) is intimately connected to the individual's capacity to define for herself what the good life is, and to the ability to express this in the public realm. He contends that in deciding what is good or bad for their lives, and in weighing up different reasons for action, citizens should be free to hear and express all opinions or ideas. In this context, Dworkin claims that the censoring powers of government represent the gravest menace to the exercise of this capacity. He argues that whenever governments intervene in what citizens should or should not hear or say, it insults those citizens by reducing them to the condition of children.[47] But what exactly counts as a *good life* within Dworkin's conception of responsible moral agency? And what is so valuable about it that no government intervention should be allowed? The answer to the first question is that almost anything would fall within the range of possible good lives:

> Each person follows a more-or-less articulate conception of what gives value to life. The scholar who values a life of contemplation has such a conception; so does the television-watching beer-drinking citizen who is fond of saying 'This is the life', though he has thought less about the issue and is less able to describe or defend his conception.[48]

This broad understanding of what counts as the good life shows the particularity of Dworkin's conception of autonomy. Indeed, the process of self-reflection that characterises the autonomous individual is absent or severely diminished, as Dworkin himself recognises, in someone who devotes his life to watching television and drinking beer. The problem of this conception is that it is difficult to assess whether this 'autonomous agent' is or is not in charge of his life, and whether his life decisions represent a rational response to his possibilities, interests and tastes. It seems that his so-called 'life decisions' should not even count as such, but should rather be considered the unchosen consequences of his circumstances. Accordingly, if self-reflection, construed as one of the fundamental characteristics

---

[45] ibid.
[46] ibid.
[47] ibid.
[48] Dworkin, above n 38, 191.

of autonomous activity, might be completely absent from someone's definition of the 'good life', what remains is simply the form of his actions, his behaviour. If, in other words, self-reflection is irrelevant for the purpose of defining autonomous actions, then the sphere of autonomy is extended to any form of behaviour, regardless of whether it is the consequence of an inner assessment. Whatever the agent does, regardless of why he does it, counts as a good life and ought to be valued and respected by governments.[49]

Accordingly, if Dworkin's justification of free speech can be construed as protecting the capacity to exercise individual autonomy, surely the conception of autonomy at issue is so broad as to be virtually meaningless. Indeed, if autonomy is identified with the capacity to act without inhibitions from external agents, it is difficult to distinguish its differences from a principle of liberty. Dworkin's defence is thus closer to a principle of negative freedom, in which any intervention from government, regardless of its content or purpose, is seen as a violation of someone's capacity to decide or to act freely. As has been anticipated, the problem with Dworkin's theory is that government decisions aimed at fostering certain forms of speech that might stimulate capacities to think for oneself would be as undesirable as those aimed at restricting other forms of speech that might limit this same capacity. Any intervention would be seen, in other words, as paternalistic government interference.[50] According to Owen Fiss, free speech, if completely unregulated, produces a silencing effect that erodes the autonomy of all those who are victims of violent or degrading forms of speech. Dworkin's theory does not consider the autonomy of these victims who restrain themselves from participating in the public sphere as a consequence of the latter forms of speech. This is because as any government regulation of speech is seen as an unacceptable paternalistic imposition, governments cannot restrict that speech.[51] Hence, free speech—so construed—may inhibit the very autonomy it was supposed to protect. Some government intervention is required to prevent degrading forms of speech, in order to stimulate everyone's capacity to decide for themselves what the good life is and to express those decisions as a manifestation of their own personalities.

B. The First Scanlon

Dworkin is not the only author who builds a theory of freedom of speech grounded in such a weak conception of autonomy. In his influential 'A Theory of Freedom of Expression', Thomas Scanlon proposes a similar approach. His deeper insight

---

[49] This argument is used by Waldron to show the difference between autonomy and negative liberty in 'Moral Autonomy and Personal Autonomy', above n 2.

[50] This paradox is the content of O Fiss, *The Irony of Free Speech* (Cambridge, MA, Harvard University Press, 1996).

[51] See ibid.

into the conception of autonomy at play brings new problems.[52] These problems, as will be analysed, stem from the feeble link he draws between autonomy and responsibility, and the type of justifications given for restricting government intervention in the sphere of speech. Scanlon's purpose is to demonstrate that almost all government restrictions on acts of expression, even when those expressions are inevitably the cause of harmful consequences, are illegitimate encroachments on someone's autonomy. In order to delimit the ambit of admissible restrictions, he develops what he called the Millian principle:

> There are certain harms which, although they would not occur but for certain acts of expression, nonetheless cannot be taken as part of a justification for legal restrictions on these acts. These harms are: (a) harms to certain individuals which consist in their coming to have false beliefs as a result of those acts of expression; (b) harmful consequences of acts performed as a result of those acts of expression, where the connection between the acts of expression and the subsequent harmful acts consists merely in the fact that the act of expression led the agents to believe (or increased their tendency to believe) these acts to be worth performing.[53]

The Millian principle identifies the limits of legitimate government intervention in the field of speech. Regulation is inadmissible when it affects personal autonomy.[54] Scanlon rejects government regulation of acts of expressions when they might cause the type of harms described in the principle. This is because in those cases, regulation is seen as diminishing someone's capacity to judge for herself and to act according to her own judgement. Scanlon, on the other hand, accepts government regulation of speech as long as it is compatible with the exercise of personal autonomy.[55] However, due to the extremely weak conception of autonomy used by Scanlon, government intervention will almost never be acceptable.[56] But what makes Scanlon's conception of autonomy weak, and what precisely is the difference between weak and strong conceptions of autonomy? Also, why do strong conceptions admit more government restrictions on acts of expression than weaker ones?

Scanlon identifies as a strong conception of autonomy the one developed by Kant in *Groundwork*.[57] What makes it strong is the nature of the requirements upon which an autonomous being should act (universality, reciprocity,

---

[52] According to Scanlon, a person is autonomous as long as he 'see[s] himself as sovereign in deciding what to believe and in weighing competing reasons for action'. Scanlon, 'A Theory of Freedom of Expression', above n 43, 215.

[53] ibid 213.

[54] According to Robert Amdur, Scanlon was the first author to offer a defence of freedom of expression based exclusively on autonomy. R Amdur, 'Scanlon on Freedom of Expression' (1980) 9 *Philosophy & Public Affairs* 287.

[55] Scanlon, 'A Theory of Freedom of Expression', above n 43, 215.

[56] ibid.

[57] Scanlon refers to Kant's conception of autonomy developed in the *Groundwork* as one containing strong requirements regarding the reasons on which an autonomous being can act, in opposition to his own conception, which is similar to Hobbes's notion of freedom. See ibid 216.

self-examination). The strength of the requirements incorporated in Kantian morality are such that, according to Scanlon, most of our daily actions and decisions lie outside the realm of (Kantian) autonomy. Indeed, for Kant, only actions that are executed out of duty, that is, out of obedience to the moral law, are autonomous actions. Consequently, anything that is done to attain a goal that is different from subjection to the moral law, such as pursuing my own happiness or the happiness of others, will not necessarily be an autonomous action in the Kantian sense. As a consequence, autonomous actions in the Kantian sense are extremely limited. They are more an exception than a general principle of action. Such a conception of autonomy would have completely defeated the purpose of Scanlon's theory, which is to restrict government intervention in the sphere of speech to its maximum. Indeed, if autonomous action is such an exceptional thing, governments could legitimately interfere in the wide sphere of expressions uttered outside the limited realm of Kantian autonomy.

Scanlon's conception of autonomy in 'A Theory of Freedom of Expression' is remarkably weaker than Kant's. The point is that Scanlon is not concerned with crafting a theory of autonomy; he is not concerned with what makes a decision autonomous, nor with the capacities involved in the process of decision-making. On the contrary, his main concern is with limiting the authority of the state to interfere with acts of expression, whatever they are and whatever harms might be associated with them. As Scanlon puts it, 'the argument for the Millian principle rests on a limitation of the authority of states to command their subjects rather than on a right of individuals'.[58] Autonomy is, in the context of his theory, an instrument used to justify restrictions on state intervention. And for this instrument to be useful, he needs to make a number of dubious assumptions.[59]

The first lies in the relationship between autonomy and responsibility. According to it, autonomous agents are fully and exclusively responsible for their harmful actions, regardless of their motives or causes:

> A person who acts on reasons he has acquired from another's act of expression acts on what *he* has come to believe and has judged to be a sufficient basis for action. The contribution to the genesis of his action made by the act of expression is, so to speak, superseded by the agent's own judgement.[60]

The nature of the expressions and the circumstances in which they are uttered or the conditions in which they are received are completely irrelevant for the purpose of determining responsibility. The problem with this, as Scanlon later recognised, is that an absolute denial of the speaker's responsibility for the potentially harmful consequence of her speech might serve to justify speech deliberately designed to deceive or damage others, such as fraudulent advertising.[61] Furthermore, as Brison claims, for the argument to make sense, it needs to assume that all speech

---

[58] ibid 221.
[59] For a good critique of Scanlon's theory, see Amdur, above n 54.
[60] Scanlon, 'A Theory of Freedom of Expression', above n 43, 212.
[61] Scanlon, above n 3, 532.

is rationally processed and that all beliefs are the consequence of considered judgements.[62] However, it has been argued that hate speech might affect our attitudes through non-rational mechanisms.[63] If this is true, it would be difficult to claim that the harmful consequences derived from hate speech will always be superseded by the agent's *own judgement* and that, as a consequence, the state will never be allowed to restrict that form of speech.

The second problematic assumption in Scanlon's theory is related to the first component of the Millian principle, which is that 'an autonomous person cannot accept without independent consideration the judgement of others as to what he should believe or what he should do'.[64] When, according to Scanlon, governments prohibit expressions because they might lead citizens to form false beliefs, they are not only deciding for others what is true and what is false, they are also assuming that individual agents are not able to make such distinctions for themselves. This is certainly a strong argument to justify protection of, for example, potentially harmful speech. However, Scanlon derives this conclusion from a hypothetical contractual situation in which autonomous individuals would accord no restrictions of speech on these grounds. But it is far from clear that individuals in a hypothetical situation would have reached such conclusions. As Amdur argues, rational autonomous individuals could perfectly agree to accept some restrictions, even if this caused them a degree of sacrifice, if those restrictions were to prevent the harm of others. Moreover, rational individuals are not limited to thinking of themselves only as potential speakers or listeners who are deprived of certain forms of speech; they can also logically think of themselves as potential victims of the consequences brought by certain forms of expression.[65]

Scanlon's 'A Theory of Freedom of Expression' shares the problems identified in Dworkin's theory. Indeed, both theories are fixated on the threats that government intervention in speech can cause to autonomous deliberation. Although it is clear that governments are and always have been a threat to free speech, there are problems associated with this defence. First, it does not recognise that there are other entities able to limit or restrict our capacities as autonomous agents in the sphere of speech. In Chapter 1, it was argued that the press, depending on the structural conditions in which it functions, can foreclose discourses and limit access to information necessary for autonomous thought in ways that might be as severe as government restrictions on speech. The second problem with these theories, as was seen, is that although they are quick to reject any form of government regulation that might reduce autonomy, they are not able to accept restriction of expression even where that restriction could strengthen autonomy, such as prohibitions on fraudulent advertising.

A complementary problem has to do with the conception of autonomy that Dworkin and Scanlon use in order to justify their theories. In order to justify

---

[62] Brison, above n 31, 328.

[63] ibid.

[64] Scanlon, 'A Theory of Freedom of Expression', above n 43, 216.

[65] Amdur, above n 54, 299.

limiting the government's capacity to restrict speech, both ground their theories in weak conceptions of autonomy. We saw that Dworkin is almost indifferent to the rational capacities involved in the process of decision-making. In his theory, an autonomous decision does not require a thoughtful analysis of the circumstances in which it is taken, of the influences or motives that guide it and so on. His notion of autonomy is thus, as I have argued, equivalent to a principle of negative liberty.[66] Something very similar holds true of Scanlon's theory. In order to defend the Millian principle 'as an exceptionless restriction on government authority',[67] he needs to ground his theory on a weak conception of autonomy in order to justify the view that almost any choice, decision or action is autonomous. The consequence is that although these theories claim that their free speech justifications are rooted in autonomy, they end up being justified on principles of negative liberty.

In these theories the government represents the only serious threat to autonomy in the ambit of speech. Consequently, the requirements of autonomy are limited to the absence of government intervention. If the state does not interfere in the free flow of ideas, autonomy is safeguarded; if the state interferes, autonomy is threatened. These are indeed weak specifications for what is to count as an exercise of autonomy. Scanlon later recognised that a notion of autonomy based on restrictions on state intervention (or, to say the same thing, on a conception of negative liberty) is not adequate.[68] This is because not every restriction of liberty is necessarily a restriction on autonomy. Moreover, absolute liberty might diminish rather than stimulate capacities for autonomous thought and action. Accordingly, there must be distinctions between negative freedom and autonomy. Such distinctions are not easy to identify in Dworkin or in the *first* Scanlon. The next section will analyse justifications of free speech based on stronger conceptions of autonomy, conceptions which incorporate a reflection on the inner self.[69] The importance of this analysis is that these theories (contrary to the theories just covered) recognise that capacities of self-reflection are a fundamental aspect of individual autonomy. And, as has been argued throughout this chapter, these capacities provide access to the true self.

IV. Autonomy and Authenticity: Back to the True Self

This section's purpose is to explore the extent to which autonomy theories of freedom of speech conceive of expressive freedoms as modern mechanisms of

---

[66] Brison makes a similar claim in 'The Autonomy Defense of Free Speech', above n 31, 324.
[67] Scanlon, 'A Theory of Freedom of Expression', above n 43, 215.
[68] In Scanlon, above n 3.
[69] The theories that will be analysed are ibid and Raz, above n 3.

self-discovery. Two theories will be analysed. The first is Scanlon's second theory and the other is Joseph Raz's theory of 'personal identification'. As will be seen, both are grounded in conceptions of personal autonomy that recognise the relevance of self-reflecting capacities. These are capacities that, as has been repeated throughout this chapter, provide access to the true self. These theories borrow their conception of autonomy from the influential model developed by Gerald Dworkin, which is in turn inspired by the work of Harry Frankfurt. Hence, before analysing these theories, a short explanation of this model will be given.

According to Gerald Dworkin, autonomy is 'more than just a matter of what the agent does; it is also a matter of why he does it'.[70] The autonomous agent not only needs to be free to choose and define his plan of life, that plan of life must also be *his own*. This requires a process of self-reflection, a capacity for self-evaluation in which decisions and choices are examined and tested upon what Frankfurt defines as *second order desires*, that is, the desires about one's desires.[71] To be a self-legislating agent, or in other words an autonomous individual, decisions and choices, plans and actions need to be constantly scrutinised. According to Gerald Dworkin this scrutiny, or process of self-reflection, consists in analysing whether or not second order desires are consistent with first order motivations: 'It is the attitude a person takes towards the influences motivating him which determines whether or not they are to be considered "his"'.[72] If someone identifies with them, assimilates them as their own or wants to be motivated in that way, then those motivations belong to him.[73] Dworkin designates this form of identification as authenticity[74] and claims that it is a necessary condition of autonomy.[75] That part of the individual who wishes his first order desires to be (or not be) fulfilled, Dworkin calls the *true self*.[76] This is why the exercise of individual autonomy in the Dworkin-Frankfurt model, necessarily contains an exploration of the true self.

Although authenticity is a necessary condition of autonomy in this model, it is not a sufficient one. Authenticity, according to Gerald Dworkin, can only be

---

[70] G Dworkin, 'Autonomy and Behavior Control' (1976) 6 *Hastings Center Report* 23.

[71] HG Frankfurt, 'Freedom of the Will and the Concept of a Person' in *The Importance of What We Care About: Philosophical Essays* (Cambridge, Cambridge University Press, 1988) 11–25.

[72] Dworkin, above n 70, 23.

[73] In Frankfurt's account, what defines a person is not simply his capacity to identify his actions with second order desires, it is also his capacity to have second order volitions, that is, wanting those desires to constitute his will. For example, the physician engaged in psychotherapy with narcotic addicts might want to have the desire to desire drugs in order to understand his patients better. However, his desire to have a desire for drugs is not a desire to change his will. Frankfurt designates this as a truncated second order desire. See Frankfurt, above n 71, 16.

[74] Dworkin, above n 70, 25.

[75] Gerald Dworkin, in *Theory and Practice of Autonomy*, modified his thoughts about authenticity to claim that it is not identification or lack of identification that is crucial in his conception of autonomy but the 'capacity to raise the question of whether I will identify with or reject the reasons for which I now act'. Despite this, the mere fact of raising an inner question supposes an answering agent and a capacity of self-introspection. There is still, in other words, a true self involved in his theory. See Dworkin, above n 33, 15.

[76] Dworkin, above n 70, 28.

guaranteed if the adequate conditions for its exercise are secured: 'A person is autonomous if he identifies with his desires, goals, and values, and such identification is not itself influenced in ways which make the process of identification in some way alien to the individual.'[77] Identification, in other words, also requires certain conditions of independence that prevent unwarranted interference from external agents.[78] This model contains a procedure of self-identification that resembles the type of deliberation not only proper to Kantian morality, but also to Cassian's procedure of self-examination. Indeed, as in Cassian and in Kant, the autonomous individual needs to distance herself from her desires (or thoughts) in order to analyse them and decide whether they are the sorts of things with which she ought to identify. Waldron, when comparing this conception of personal autonomy with moral autonomy, concludes that 'in both cases there is an achievement of critical distance, in both cases there is reflection, and in both cases this reflection involves the idea of "who I really am"'.[79] The Frankfurt-Dworkin model has been influential in liberal theories of autonomy, and therefore in theories of free speech defended on autonomy grounds. The latter are the theories we shall now proceed to analyse.[80]

A. The Second Scanlon

After accepting a number of criticisms made of his Millian principle, Scanlon recognised the limitations of his previous conception of autonomy and adjusted it to something closer to the Frankfurt-Dworkin model just described.[81] In fact, in his new theory, Scanlon not only identifies the relevance of authenticity as an element of autonomy, he also acknowledges that it requires an adequate environment for its exercise. This new approach is inscribed in his definition of autonomy as 'the actual ability to exercise independent rational judgement, as a good to be promoted'.[82] The element of authenticity appears in the value he assigns to expression. According to him, exposure to expressions is valuable if 'it affects our future decisions and attitudes by making us aware of good reasons for them, so long as it does not interfere with our ability to weigh these reasons against others'.[83] On the other hand, expressions are undesirable when they make us believe that we have good *reasons to act* when in fact we have no such reasons, as in the case of subliminal advertising, for example.[84] In order to identify what good reasons to act are, in

---

[77] G Dworkin, 'The Concept of Autonomy' in J Christman (ed), *The Inner Citadel: Essays on Individual Autonomy* (New York, Oxford University Press, 1989) 61.

[78] See Dworkin, above n 70.

[79] Waldron, above n 2, 317.

[80] See Christman and Anderson (eds), above n 1, 3.

[81] See Scanlon, above n 3, 532. Here Scanlon modifies his conception of autonomy, acknowledging the criticisms of his theory made by Gerald Dworkin and Robert Amdur.

[82] ibid 533.

[83] ibid 525.

[84] ibid.

Scanlon's theory, it is necessary to distinguish between beliefs and desires, on the one side, and actions, on the other. The latter are the consequence of the former; they are motivated by them. I do X or Y because I have a desire to do X or Y, or because my beliefs motivated me to do X or Y. Reasons to act are good, or they are autonomous reasons, according to Scanlon, when I have given them to myself as a product of the exercise of independent rational judgement. Accordingly, as in the Frankfurt-Dworkin model, Scanlon's second theory acknowledges the element of authenticity in its conception of autonomy: autonomous action requires identification with second order desires; and, as in the model it follows, in Scanlon's theory the *part of the individual who wishes his first order desires to be or not to be fulfilled* is the *true self.*

The type of deliberation emphasised in Scanlon's conception of autonomy resembles, to a certain extent, the Kantian procedure of moral deliberation described previously. Both stimulate critical distance and a type of reflection that provides access to the self. In fact, at a certain point Scanlon criticises subliminal advertising, not because we are unaware of its influence, but because it makes us think that we have reasons to do something when in fact we do not.[85] Autonomy is affected in this case because our capacity to reflect upon second order considerations is itself affected. Accordingly, rational procedures of self-reflection acquire in his second theory an importance they were denied in his first one. By recognising the relevance of conditions of authenticity, the second Scanlon acknowledges that (at least from audiences' perspective) freedom of speech is valuable as long as it does not block procedures of self-reflection, procedures which, following Waldron, allow access to one's true self.

Furthermore, Scanlon's theory resembles the Frankfurt-Dworkin model because it recognises as crucial an adequate environment for the exercise of rational independent judgement: 'What we should want in general is to have our beliefs and desires produced by processes that are reliable—processes whose effectiveness depends on the grounds for the beliefs and on the goodness of the desires it produces.'[86] Although governments are still in his theory a major threat to free speech, and thus to the exercise of personal autonomy, he now recognises that they might actively contribute—in exceptional cases—to the formation of an adequate environment for the exercise of rational judgement. This environment, as has been seen, is one that permits individuals to assess different reasons for action and to identify with them. Freedom of speech is, nevertheless, in Scanlon's theory still the main engine for guaranteeing this adequate environment. And as this environment is supposed to secure conditions of authenticity, conditions that provide access to the true self, Scanlon's second theory necessarily conceives of freedom of speech as a mechanism of self-discovery.

---

[85] ibid 525–26.
[86] ibid 526.

B. Joseph Raz: Integrity and Personal Identification

Joseph Raz, more than anyone else, proposes a conception of personal autonomy that emphasises capacities of self-reflection at both a procedural and a
substantive level. From a procedural point of view Raz, like Scanlon, follows the
Frankfurt-Dworkin model, acknowledging that autonomy requires a process of
self-reflection through which first order desires are identified with second order
considerations. But he goes further, because from a substantive point of view the
admissible outcome of this procedure of self-reflection is reduced in his theory to
a moral dimension. As will be argued, this dimension limits individual decisions
to some ultimate truths that can only be found in the ethical sphere. In this section, it will be argued that his conception of autonomy, which is the ground for his
theory of freedom of speech, stresses the relevance of free speech in the discovery
of the true self to a greater extent than is the case in any other theory. As a consequence, just as we have seen in other truth-seeking theories of free speech analysed in this book, an ambiguity emerges between the strictures that truth-seeking
activities suppose, on the one hand, and the flexibility that free speech requires, on
the other. According to Raz:

> The ruling idea behind the ideal of personal autonomy is that people should make their
> own lives. The autonomous person is a (part) author of his own life. The ideal of per-
> sonal autonomy is the vision of people controlling, to some degree, their own destiny,
> fashioning it through successive decisions throughout their lives.[87]

In principle, this conception of personal autonomy does not sound very different from the one provided by Scanlon, and even from the one given by Ronald
Dworkin. All of them share the idea that personal autonomy reflects the capacity
to be to a certain extent the author of one's own life. For Raz, however, autonomy
is not simply the capacity to decide or to plan one's life free from external forces,
as in Dworkin, or in an environment which allows the exercise of rational capabilities, as in the second Scanlon. Although he follows the Frankfurt-Dworkin model,
Raz takes his conception of autonomy much further at a procedural level, because
he demands higher levels of self-awareness from the autonomous individual. At
a substantive level, moreover, his conception of autonomy not only requires the
ability to choose rationally and independently (a project, a plan of life or a future
partner) from a range of multiple options; those options are reduced to *morally
acceptable ones.*[88]

Raz's image of the autonomous individual as an author, as a self-creating
agent who designs a plan and follows it throughout his life, is not the image of a
Hollywood film actor, say, who in order to play his role must stick firmly to a script.
The autonomous individual does not need to give herself a detailed life plan that

---

[87] Raz, above n 35, 369.
[88] See ibid 381.

she will follow strictly until her death.[89] Rather, the ideal of self-creation proper to Raz's conception of autonomy is more flexible; a person can either change or abandon plans without necessarily compromising her autonomy. However, there are limits to this flexibility, limits that are much stricter than the ones required by conceptions of personal autonomy previously analysed. This is why, according to Raz, an autonomous individual requires certain control over his projects: '[O]ne who drifts through life unawares is not leading an autonomous life'.[90]

The way in which Raz proposes to find an adequate balance between control and flexibility in the design of our life plans is through the 'principle of integrity'. Integrity in his theory works as a measuring rod, something that allows the identification of acceptable or unacceptable deviations from a project. The connections between his idea of integrity and Gerald Dworkin's notion of authenticity derived from Frankfurt's work are evident. Integrity in Razian language supposes identification with one's choices.[91] According to Raz, individuals can identify with their choices when they have given them to themselves, when they are their own.[92] Accordingly, the Razian plan of life amounts to a set of second order desires that provide a self-legislated corpus to autonomous agents from which they can derive principles for action. Their choices are going to be *their own*; in other words, they are going to be true to themselves when those choices are compatible with their life projects. Likewise, choices that are contradictory to the plan of life are considered to be the product of an alienated self, of someone who does not respond to himself, someone who has failed to carry out his own projects.

Raz's notion of integrity, the identification with a higher project, is not intended simply to evaluate the quality of particular choices. It is not a matter of having choices and advancing them. On the contrary, his purpose is to provide elements to evaluate oneself through a broader picture, through the identification of a wider project which he calls the 'character of a way of life'.[93] According to Raz, a *good life* requires loyalty to one's plan, that is, a sustained commitment throughout time to one's true desires. Failure is, in turn, a betrayal of one's plan of life, and its effect is that '[t]he more failures one accumulates in one's important pursuit the more of a failure one's life becomes'.[94] This idea is extremely important because the *good life* is not simply assessed in relation to the comfort of the moment, as it might be the case with Ronald Dworkin's television-watching, beer-drinking subject who claims 'this is the life'. The good life is assessed in terms of the consistency of actions with a broader picture, with something that shapes and gives meaning to someone's existence as a whole. And here a moral element emerges, an element that permits assessing admissible and inadmissible deviations from the plan of life.

[89] See ibid 370.
[90] ibid 382.
[91] ibid.
[92] At this point Raz expressly rests his argument on Frankfurt's ideas. See ibid fn 1.
[93] Raz, above n 3, 319.
[94] Raz, above n 35, 383.

If the principle of integrity strengthens self-awareness at a procedural level, that is at the level of identification between first and second order desires, at a substantive level it reduces the range of options available to autonomous subjects to morally acceptable ones.[95] Raz explicitly remarks that an autonomous individual 'requires only the availability of morally acceptable options'.[96] According to Waldron, this conception of personal autonomy 'evokes the idea of the subjection of a[n] individual's life to the discipline of objectively appropriate or inappropriate responses to the presence or absence of value'.[97] In other words, the formal procedure of deliberation in which the autonomous subject looks into herself in order to identify principles for action is complemented by a narrower vision of the self into which the subject looks. Although there are multiple valuable options an individual might choose (and that makes Raz's theory consistent with liberal thought), the reduction of acceptable options to morally valuable ones is important, for our purposes, for two reasons. First, if, as has been argued, the procedure of self-reflection in Raz's theory provides access to the true self, the reduction of possible options to *morally acceptable ones* reduces the idea of the true self to a particular realm, namely, that of morality. Secondly, from the previous point it follows that his principle of integrity (and therewith one's loyalty to one's true self) is also defined in moral terms. If the 'true self' of the Frankfurt-Dworkin model[98] is reduced to a number of morally acceptable options, the definition of who one is and the extent to which one can define and modify life projects is, accordingly, seriously reduced. This relevant point will be analysed further later, but before doing so, it is necessary to assess the relevance of freedom of speech to Raz's conception of autonomy.

Freedom of speech is crucial in the Razian system because it serves the fundamental purpose of strengthening individual integrity. Indeed, the main argument developed by Raz in 'Free Expression and Personal Identification' is that

> public portrayal and expression of forms of life validate the styles of life portrayed, and that censoring expression normally expresses authoritative condemnation not merely of the views or opinions censored but of the whole style of life which they are a part.[99]

According to Raz, public portrayal of ways of life serves several functions. First, it familiarises the general public with that form of life. Secondly, it reassures individuals whose ways of life are being portrayed that they are not alone, that there are other people sharing their projects and plans. Thirdly, public portrayal validates the ways of life portrayed; it gives them the 'stamp of *public acceptability*'.[100]

---

[95] See ibid 381.

[96] ibid.

[97] Waldron, above n 2, 315.

[98] The true self, as has been said, is for Dworkin the part of the individual who wishes certain first order desires to be (or not be) fulfilled. See Dworkin, above n 70, 28.

[99] Raz, above n 3, 310.

[100] ibid 311 (emphasis added).

These functions taken together are defined by Raz as 'validation'.[101] On the other hand, censorship is an insult to these ways of life, an open rejection of the plans and projects that certain individuals have given to themselves.[102]

Raz assumes that the chances for individuals to identify with their projects and to remain loyal to them will increase in step with the degree of confidence they have in their validity. On the other hand, strong doubts about the validity of one's projects will affect one's capacity to identify with and be loyal to them. This is equivalent to saying that individual integrity depends on the validity (or value) individuals assign to their projects. Now, integrity depends not only on the strength of someone's will or on the conviction of the correctness of her choices. According to Raz, it also depends on public acceptance of those projects, and here lies the relevance of freedom of speech. Raz claims that through public portrayal and validation of different forms of life, the individual's process of self-identification is strengthened because it gives to the autonomous subject the confidence that her decisions and choices are valid (in so far as they are accepted by other individuals).[103] Freedom of speech is thus crucial in Raz's system, because it improves the chances that individuals can be true to their own selves by identifying with and by remaining loyal to their plans and projects.

But reinforcing individual integrity is not the exclusive purpose of freedom of speech in the Razian system. He adds that by allowing public exposition of different forms of lives, freedom of speech also exposes people to a variety of options with respect to how to design or adjust their own plans of life.[104] As we have seen, these options are not unlimited. Not *anything* would serve as a valid option. Only *valuable* forms of life will qualify, and these are limited, according to Raz, to those that are both rewarding and meaningful for those who live them, that is, those that are morally acceptable.[105] Accordingly, Raz justifies full protection of any form of speech, whatever its content might be, as long as it is a manifestation of a valuable form of life.[106] Only these forms of life deserve public validation and are considered acceptable options for autonomous individuals. The problem is how to determine what counts as a valuable form of life, and who is responsible for doing that? Although Raz does not attempt to solve this problem, at least he recognises that its solution is not simply a matter of individual choice but a central question of ethics.[107]

At this point a paradox emerges in Raz's theory, a paradox that is related to the *true self* that is supposed to be unveiled through freedom of speech. Is Raz defending an immutable conception of the self that remains unchangeable throughout

---

[101] ibid 313.
[102] ibid.
[103] ibid.
[104] ibid 312.
[105] ibid 318.
[106] ibid 319.
[107] ibid.

time and space, or is the Razian self in a constant process of reconfiguration and change? On the one hand, the moral content identifiable in Raz's theory is intrinsically associated with certain immutable, permanent and universal elements from which truths about ourselves can be derived. We are human beings because we share certain things with other human beings that elephants, monkeys and snakes do not share. If the discovery of the true self is pursued through a moral dimension, what is emphasised is what we share with other human beings, our commonalities. In fact, as in Kant's notion of moral autonomy, one of the main characteristics of his conception of autonomy is that it is universal and presupposes 'objective moral principles', inscribed in every rational being independent of time and place.[108] When Raz affirms the value of integrity in the sense of maintaining certain control of who we are, he is appealing precisely to this conception of the self.

On the other hand, however, if freedom of speech is not to be a chimera, the discovery of the true self cannot be reduced to an immutable self, because in that case the types of speech available in the public sphere would be reduced to a limited number of options. Accordingly, a serious commitment to this freedom supposes to value difference rather than commonality. It supposes that rather than being an immutable entity, the self is in a constant process of articulation and transformation, and freedom of speech is hence an important tool that allows individuals to identify different options from which they can choose how to live their lives. If this is true, it needs to be admitted that the *self* is mutable, changeable and in a permanent process of reconfiguration. It needs to be acknowledged that the self is *difference* rather than commonality. As has been seen, Raz's theory, more than any other, expresses this constant tension between commonality and difference, between control and flexibility.

But this tension is not exclusive to Raz's theory. If, as we have been arguing, the strongest autonomy theories of free speech recognise, to a certain extent, that personal autonomy requires reflective capacities, which are common to conceptions of moral autonomy, they are all subject to this tension. This is important for our purposes because it reveals certain clues about the nature of the *self* involved in liberal procedures of self-discovery and the role that free speech plays in these procedures. Throughout this chapter it has been argued that some theories of free speech based on autonomous grounds are means of self-discovery. They are instruments designed 'to know oneself, to tell the truth about oneself, and to constitute oneself as an object of knowledge both for other people and for oneself'.[109] But freedom of speech, as a modern procedure of self-discovery, at least in the way in which it has been analysed until now, is different from the procedures analysed in previous sections. First, it is not sacrificial as in the Christian version, because it does not require renouncing who one is in order to identify a 'pure self' free from extraneous forces.[110] Nor is it a secular version of the latter, where public

---

[108] See Korsgaard, above n 20, 14.
[109] Foucault, above n 8, 151.
[110] See Cassian, above n 6, 312.

expression is a way of testing the moral qualities of certain actions. Freedom of speech (as analysed in this chapter) works the other way around. Instead of revealing the qualities of the speaker or the moral worth of her actions, it feeds the public sphere with discourses that provide options to individuals. These are options that help them to choose how they can live and plan their lives, or validate the lives they have decided to live. In other words, instead of discovering a deep internal essence hidden by a thick layer of appearances, freedom of speech provides options from which individuals can build or construct their own identities. In this sense, autonomy theories of free speech assume that autonomous beings are able to freely define and redefine themselves, and plan their lives according to those definitions.

Consequently, contrary to other procedures of self-discovery, liberal procedures are flexible. They admit the possibility of reinventing and freely constructing oneself, and to build plans of life according to those constructions. Here lies the importance of free speech. It is a tool that allows access to different forms of lives, and which permits individuals to identify and to design their plans in accordance with them. However, the extent to which the latter is true, the extent to which the liberal autonomous individual can transform and redefine herself with total freedom, varies in the different theories analysed. And the more closely these theories are explored, the more it unfolds that that flexibility is not as great as it originally appeared to be. Ronald Dworkin and the first Scanlon were able to offer high levels of flexibility at the expense of vitiating the meaning of autonomy. Indeed, as was concluded, they were not defending free speech on grounds of autonomy but rather on the basis of the principle of negative liberty. The second Scanlon takes a crucial step in identifying autonomy with authenticity, and by doing so he incorporates into the liberal framework the types of capacities required by moral deliberation. Finally, Raz goes further, not simply because he reduces the typical liberal flexibility to the principle of integrity, but also because he gives a proper moral content to the type of deliberation of autonomous individuals. The paradox seems to be that the further they go, the more they stimulate the discovery of the self, while reducing, at the same time, the possible range of admissible options to a moral dimension.

V. The Free Press and Self-discovery

In this chapter it has been argued that autonomy theories of free speech implicitly conceive of freedom of speech as a mechanism of self-discovery, to the extent that their conceptions of autonomy favour certain capacities of self-reflection which in the Frankfurt-Dworkin model are called 'authenticity conditions'.[111]

---

[111] See Dworkin, above n 70, 25.

Although this is an important discovery for the purpose of the book—because it shows that the truth-seeking purpose of freedom of speech is not reduced to truth as correspondence with an external reality or to coherence with particular conceptions of democracy—it is still necessary to take a final step in the argument. It is still necessary to assess to what extent what has been examined illuminates the general discussion of the free press. In other words, what still needs to be assessed is whether the theories of free speech analysed in this chapter are also applicable to the idea of a free press, so as to claim that the free press is also for these theories an adequate tool for the discovery of the true self. And if this is so, how might this possibly affect our understanding of the 'illusion of the free press'?

The process of self-reflection, fundamental to some of the free speech theories analysed,[112] is affected and determined by environmental conditions. In fact, it has already been mentioned that according to Gerald Dworkin, '[a] person is autonomous if he identifies with his desires, goals, and values, and such identification is not itself influenced in ways which make the process of identification in some way alien to the individual'. If I live an isolated life and my knowledge about poverty, war and global exploitation is built exclusively upon the information provided by Fox News, for example, it would be difficult for me to express *my* ideas about those issues, because it would be difficult for me to form ideas on these issues that are indeed my own. The environmental conditions that are relevant for the purpose of this analysis are the conditions of the press. This leads us to the following questions that will be examined in what remains of this chapter. The first is whether the free press can be justified, in principle, as a mechanism designed to strengthen individual autonomy in the sense that we have understood it until now, this is, as a mechanism of self-discovery? If it can, we should raise a further question, which is whether the discovery of the true self is in fact compatible with a free press?

To answer the first question, it is necessary to ask whether the justifications used by autonomy theories of free speech are extensible to conceptions of the free press. To approach this, it is important to mention first that it is possible to distinguish—broadly—two types of justifications within autonomy theories of free speech. On the one hand, there are those theories that value the interests of listeners and not exclusively the interest of speakers. Ronald Dworkin, Scanlon and Raz all value freedom of speech, to a certain extent, because it provides options that help individuals to enhance their rational capabilities, to design life plans and to validate themselves by identifying with the ways of life portrayed in the public realm. As will be argued, these justifications are extensible to notions of the free press. On the other hand, there are a number of autonomy theories of freedom of speech, which have not been mentioned in this chapter, that value this freedom because they view it as an extension of individual autonomy. Freedom of speech, according to these

---

[112] Specifically, Scanlon, above n 3, and Raz, above n 3.

theories, allows individuals to express themselves, and through those expressions to reveal to the world who they are.[113] For these theories, freedom of speech is a means of self-realisation or self-fulfilment. This is why, instead of focussing on the interests of listeners, these theories centre on the interest of speakers. Although they have contributed extensively to the free speech literature, they have not contributed in the same way to debates about the free press. And this is because their justifications are not extensible to it.

First of all, there are different activities that are self-expressive, or that might enhance personal autonomy (understood as a form of self-realisation) without being themselves forms of *speech* in a strict sense. The way we dress, the places we tend to go, the music we listen to and even the use of drugs might be considered self-expressive activities without necessarily being forms of speech. Although some of these activities might possibly contribute to self-expression, and might be even welcomed for the way they justify the expansion of expressive freedoms, they are, insufficient to justify press freedoms.[114] This is because the press is not in the business of self-expression and should not get into that business.[115] The standards of communication appropriate to the press are totally different from, if not contradictory with, the standards involved in self-expressive manifestations. In fact, we expect the press to communicate information that is relevant to our common life, and we expect that communication to happen in a way that is intelligible, that is, provides the resources we need in order to make adequate judgements about it. Self-expressive communication, on the other hand, does not need to be, and should not be, subjected to such requirements. On the contrary, some might argue, the more flexible the standards of communication are, the better the environment for self-expressive manifestations. Great artists, poets and filmmakers have explored the depths and mysteries of the self through works that are sometimes deceptive, ambiguous and irrational. Breaking the rules, including the standards of conventional communication, has often been crucial for many of them not only to express themselves, but also to reveal to their audiences aspects of themselves and of the world that would have otherwise remained obscure. Those forms of communication deserve protection—there is no question about that. However, with all their richness and potentiality for self-discovery, these communicative forms are simply not consistent with the aims of the press.

---

[113] For theories centred on self-fulfilment and the development of personality, see mainly CE Baker, *Human Liberty and Freedom of Speech* (Oxford, Oxford University Press, 1989); MH Redish, *Freedom of Expression: A Critical Analysis* (Charlottesville, VA, Michie Co, 1984). For commentary on theories of self-fulfilment, see K Greenawalt, 'Free Speech Justifications' (1989) 89 *Columbia Law Review* 119, 144; Brison, above n 31, 336.

[114] For an interesting analysis of the communicative/non-communicative dichotomy in free speech, see Baker, n 113, 51–54.

[115] O O'Neill, 'News of This World', *Financial Times* (18 November 2011).

The second problem with extending autonomy theories based on self-fulfilment to the press is that these justifications offer protection only to individual speakers.[116] According to Baker,

> if the speech is not chosen by anyone and is not properly treated as a manifestation of the speaker's values, even though the speech may cause change or advance knowledge, it does not serve this liberty value and is not protected.[117]

Speech deserves protection, according to Baker, as long as it is an individual manifestation. Consequently, speech without a speaker, that is, without an individual who is the source and cause of speech, does not deserve protection. Baker denies protection to commercial speech because it expresses the profit-seeking purpose of corporations and not individual liberty.[118] The same holds true for the press, he argues. Indeed, with some notable exceptions, newspapers, magazines, the broadcasting industry, electronic media and publishing houses almost all operate under the rules of the market. Their decisions, both corporate and editorial, are usually influenced by their desire to obtain profits, and although their speech is not necessarily commercial, most of them are commercial entities. In these circumstances, how can press freedoms possibly be justified by autonomy arguments? It could be said that when individuals speak through the press, their speech deserves protection because it is a manifestation of their individuality. Although this is true to a certain extent, the press cannot be conceived as the sum of the individuals that speak through its platforms. Journalists, editors, and reporters follow orders, and they place their skills and efforts at the service of their employers. Most of the time, they are speaking not for themselves but for the companies for which they work. For Baker, there is no solution to this problem. Just as he cannot justify protection for commercial speech, so too he cannot justify protection of press freedoms, at least not through his theory based on autonomy as self-fulfilment.[119]

There is a further problem with extending to the press autonomy justifications of free speech based on self-fulfilment. The problem is that the few privileged people who are able to use the press as a mechanism of self-expression are precisely that—a few privileged people. Most citizens are little interested themselves in communicating with a larger audience, and many of those who are do not have the means to do so or have limited access to them. Consequently, press freedom

---

[116] For an interesting alternative to the speaker/listener dichotomy, see SV Shiffrin, 'A Thinker-Based Approach to Freedom of Speech' (2011) 27 *Constitutional Comment* 283.

[117] Baker, above n 113, 298, fn 2.

[118] ibid, ch 9.

[119] Of course Baker makes distinctions between commercial speech and speech that has its origin in the press. He claims that any theoretical justification needs to recognise constitutional protection for the press. However, due to the difficulties of justifying protection through autonomy arguments, he simply decides to use what he calls the Fourth State theory of the press to justify protection. This theory is taken from Blasi's paper 'The Checking Value of the First Amendment', which was analysed in the previous chapter. See Baker, above n 113, 230.

is not the proper domain for those theorists who concentrate on the speakers' self-fulfilment, because the press can satisfy this only for the very few.

Despite all these problems, autonomy justifications of free speech can still be used to justify press freedoms. However, for the reasons already mentioned, this is possible only so long as these justifications recognise that not only is the speaker's autonomy at stake in this freedom but also the autonomy of listeners. If free speech is valued as a common good, as something that contributes to the general welfare of a community and not just as something relevant to the individual speaker, there are grounds for extending free speech justifications to the idea of the free press. Therefore, as has been suggested, the theories of free speech analysed in this chapter are, in principle, applicable to the free press. Indeed, in his second justification of free speech, Scanlon gives central importance to audiences' interests 'in having a good environment for the formation of [their] beliefs and desires'.[120] Raz goes further and justifies the protection of free speech as a public good. According to him,

> a person's right to free expression is protected not in order to protect him, but in order to protect a public good, a benefit which respect for the right of free expression brings to all those who live in the society which it is respected ...[121]

Scanlon, Raz and even Ronald Dworkin recognise the relevance of audiences' interests in their justifications of free speech. And all these theorists, as has been seen, justify free speech on autonomy grounds. These theories of freedom of speech are applicable to the free press because they are particularly interested in strengthening audiences' personal autonomy by providing them with an adequate environment for the formation of beliefs and desires, or by increasing the range of options from which they can design their life plans, or by validating those they have already chosen. These theories are thus applicable to the press because the press might advance all these aims. When freedom of speech is valued for the way it supports the interests of audiences, the press necessarily becomes important because, as one of the fundamental conduits of public discourse, it should— at least in principle—contribute to creating an adequate environment for the exercise of personal autonomy.[122]

A. The Free Press and the Discovery of the True Self

Now that the first question raised at the beginning of this section has been answered, and it has been seen that autonomy theories of freedom of speech might

---

[120] Scanlon, above n 3, 527.

[121] Raz, above n 3, 305.

[122] Similarly, justifications of free speech that are centred neither on speakers nor listeners but on integral subjects who are interested in forming true beliefs about themselves, also leave the door open for extending autonomy-based arguments for free speech to the press. For an interesting example, see the thinker-based approach defended by SV Shiffrin in Shiffrin, above n 116.

be extended, in principle, to the freedom of the press, it is time to address the second question. To what extent is the press able to provide an adequate environment for the identification of one's values, beliefs and desires, that is, for the discovery of one's true self? If autonomy theories of free speech based on the Frankfurt-Dworkin model are applicable to the press, the press needs to guarantee conditions of authenticity. Accordingly, the press would need to stimulate the development of capabilities that enable individuals to think and make decisions on their own, and prevent communications that tend to degrade those same capabilities. There are many ways in which these conditions might be unduly affected. However, autonomy theorists of free speech, in line with the way free speech protection has evolved in the West, have consistently identified governments as the major threat to the exercise of this freedom and hence to individual autonomy. Based on their suspicion of governments, they implicitly grant the regulation of speech to the market, but fail, by way of omission, to address the consequences this might have on the value underlying their theories: personal autonomy.[123]

Ronald Dworkin's defence of free speech and his commitment to personal autonomy are equivalent to a principle of negative liberty. Scanlon, similarly, assumes that the fundamental interest of audiences in having an adequate environment for the formation of their beliefs and desires is achieved by keeping government intervention at a minimum: '[W]here political issues are involved governments are notoriously partisan and unreliable. Therefore, giving government the authority to make policy by balancing interests in such cases presents a serious threat to particular important participant and audience interests'.[124] According to Scanlon, government should intervene mainly to restrict expressions that affect rational capabilities to the point of deception. He is very specific about when that is the case. Indeed, he presents subliminal advertising as the paradigmatic form of deception because of its ability to make us believe that we have reasons to buy a particular thing or to do something when those reasons are not *our own*.[125] Deceptive advertising clearly affects our ability to decide for ourselves, but is that the only way in which our autonomy might be affected by others' expressive activities? Do not hegemonic discourses in a press dominated by commercial interests affect our capacity to think for ourselves and to make decisions according to our *own* judgements? Do such discourses and the free rein they enjoy stimulate the types of capacities Scanlon favours in his theory? Should government intervention be limited only to cases of deception, or should other forms of expression affecting personal autonomy also be subject to regulation? Scanlon runs the risk of defeating himself if, on the one hand, he assumes that the audience's interest in having an adequate communicative environment is best served by minimum

---

[123] For a similar line of critique, see CR Sunstein, *Democracy and the Problem of Free Speech* (New York, The Free Press, 1995); Fiss, above n 50.

[124] Scanlon, above n 3, 534.

[125] ibid 532.

state intervention, while at the same time failing to justify why speech that might endanger the very autonomy he is trying to defend should be tolerated.

The failure of a market-orientated press to provide an ideal environment for the identification of one's values, beliefs and desires—that is, for the identification of *who one is*—is even more problematic for Raz's theory. This is also more relevant for the analysis, because Raz's theory, more than any other, contains the idea that free speech is a means of discovering the true self. As was seen, freedom of speech plays a fundamental role in Raz's system because it reaffirms personal identity through public validation of different forms of life.[126] According to Raz, whenever individuals discover that their projects, plans or convictions concerning the good life are publicly portrayed, they are reassured that those plans, projects and convictions are legitimate ones: '[People] depend on finding themselves reflected in the public media for a sense of their own legitimacy, for a feeling that their problems and experience are not freak deviations.'[127] But freedom of speech is also important in his theory because it allows individuals to choose from a diverse range of life options the ones they find most appealing in redefining or even transforming their own lives. This second function, rather than reaffirming personal identity through public validation, provides resources that help individuals to redefine or shape their own identities according to the models offered by the media.

Raz's argument rests on a fragile equilibrium between a *flexible self* that changes or accommodates his life plans according to the options provided by the press and the media in general and, on the other hand, a substantive self who has a clear sense of who he is, control over his character and attachment to basic values that define his identity. This equilibrium requires a press that can offer a diverse range of options from which individuals can improve or even transform their lives. It requires what might be called a *diverse press for a flexible self*. But Raz's equilibrium also needs a press that reflects only a set of valuable life options: options that validate the identities of those who have a substantive conception of their own selves. As has been seen, in Raz these conceptions have a moral content. They are hence limited to a number of admissible valuable options, and thus require a press that is limited to reflecting only those options. The idea of the free press required for this substantive self might be labelled a *limited press for a substantive self*. The last step in the argument is to show that while the former (*the flexible self*) requires a press system that Raz is unable to justify, the latter (*the substantive self*) is incompatible with the promotion of free speech.

B. A Diverse Press for a Flexible Self

It is difficult to conceive of a media system that is able to satisfy the requirements of diversity and plurality implied in the slogan 'a diverse press for a flexible self'.

---

[126] Raz, above n 3, 313.
[127] ibid 312.

Raz sees this problem and recognises, at least at an abstract level, the need for providing access rights to the media to guarantee the expression of various forms of life.[128] However, access regulations, as he sees them, are limited in scope and depth. They are limited in scope because, as Raz himself argues, their application requires making distinctions between publicly owned and privately owned media, where the duties of the former would be much stronger than the duties of the latter.[129] The problem is that if access regulations are not applied widely and systematically to all media platforms, regardless of who owns them, it is difficult to stimulate diversity.[130] Indeed, the market, which is the basic productive platform of the media, rather than promoting a diverse media environment, has a tendency to concentrate in mega corporations that generate the sorts of harmful consequences that were analysed in Chapter 1 and which will be analysed in further detail in the next chapter.[131]

Minimal state interference in the sphere of speech, as suggested by Raz, does not necessarily guarantee the strengthening of personal autonomy.[132] The flexibility to construct one's own identity and plans of life, when left to the market, does not provide the multiplicity of options that Raz needs in order to effectively fulfil the expression of diversity required for his *flexible self*. Much has been said (and more will be said) throughout this book about the fact that the political economy of an unregulated press (one that has been completely left to market logics) stimulates the reproduction of contents, ideas, opinions and ways of life that are generally acceptable and appealing to large audiences. Market-based media, financially driven by advertisement, favour ways and styles of life based on role models to which everyone should aspire. Difference, in contrast, is usually punished by exclusion or by condescending portrayals. Therefore, according to Fiss 'limiting state intervention is likely to reproduce social disadvantages rather than enhancing autonomy'.[133]

C. A Limited Press for a Substantive Self

But Raz's flexible self, the one that is supposed to design and shape his identity and life plans according to the options offered by the media, contrasts with a substantive self that is also recognisable in his theory. The latter, by contrast, has a pretty

---

[128] ibid 313.

[129] ibid, fn 21.

[130] For the broadcasting market, see L Hitchens, *Broadcasting Pluralism and Diversity: A Comparative Study of Policy and Regulation* (Oxford, Hart Publishing, 2006) 65.

[131] See generally CE Baker, *Media Concentration and Democracy* (Cambridge, Cambridge University Press 2007); BH Bagdikian, *The New Media Monopoly*, 7th edn (Boston, MA, Beacon Press, 2004); R McChesney, *The Political Economy of Media: Enduring Issues, Emerging Dilemmas* (New York, Monthly Review Press, 2008); G Doyle, *Understanding Media Economics* (London, Sage Publications Ltd, 2002).

[132] See especially Fiss, above n 50; Sunstein, above n 123.

[133] O Fiss, 'Why the State?' (1987) 100 *Harvard Law Review* 781, 786.

clear idea of who he is, and is not looking for options that help him to define his life plans. On the contrary, for this substantive self, expressive freedoms contribute to validating his identity in the public sphere. What defines this substantive self, according to Raz, is a certain commitment to a character of life, a certain consistency with regard to who one is, which, as was already seen, necessarily involves a moral commitment. And when morality defines the scope of possible options, those options are severely reduced. So the question that emerges here is whether these limited options are compatible with the diversity that expressive freedoms are supposed to stimulate. For Raz, as has been seen, the answers to the questions about who is supposed to decide what is morally admissible are to be found in ethics.[134] Although there might be a number of different responses to this question, depending on the theoretical orientation, whatever this response is, the number of morally available options will always be less than if there are no moral considerations at stake. As a consequence, the substantive self in Raz's theory necessarily reduces the range of admissible discourses tolerated in the public sphere. And the narrower the moral theory used to define what a substantive self is supposed to mean, the more limited the range of discourses that will be considered admissible.

If at one end of Raz's fragile equilibrium there is a flexible self that requires exposure to a wide range of options to define what the good life is and to plan her life accordingly, at the other extreme Raz presents a substantive self that has a strong idea of herself and who validates this idea when she sees it reflected in the media. The problem with his theory is—as has been seen—that his distrust of government intervention in the sphere of speech does not allow him to offer the diverse press that his flexible self requires. From, another point of view, his substantive conception of the self is incompatible with free speech and a free press altogether. Surprisingly, however, Raz needs the flexible self just as much as he needs the substantive self. He needs the former to justify a plural and diverse press that can offer a wide range of options for those who are in search of models that might define their own identity. But he also needs the substantive self if he is not to fall prey to a radical scepticism about the constitution of modern subjectivity. Indeed, if Raz is not to renounce the moral dimension of human subjectivity, he cannot concede that the self is a mere construction based on the models offered in the public sphere.[135]

At this point it is possible to link Raz's theory—and to a lesser extent other autonomy theories of freedom of speech based on the Frankfurt-Dworkin model—with those theories of freedom of speech analysed in previous chapters

---

[134] Raz, above n 3, 319.

[135] Cass Sunstein gives a grim picture of the influence of the Internet on the constitution of subjectivity. He argues that today, with media platforms that are able to predict our tastes, our options and views, we are trapped in what he calls the 'daily me'. This is a mediated world that only appeals to me, an enclosed circuit where I receive only the items of news that fit with my political views and background, where I am offered books that match my intellectual tastes, music that meets my expectations, and so on. C Sunstein, *Republic.com 2.0* (Princeton, NJ, Princeton University Press, 2007).

that also emphasise its truth-seeking function. In fact, the truth of the self, like truth as correspondence with reality or the truth of a political system, needs a point of reference on the basis of which it is possible to make distinctions between what is true and what is false. In the case of the self, it is morality that provides this key reference. Without it, scepticism about the self necessarily ensues, because if there is no reference available, subjectivity becomes a mere social construct, shaped and defined by contingency. However, just as Raz is committed to the enhancement of capacities for self-reflection, he is also committed to freedom of expression and to a free press. And his commitment to the latter requires a looser conception of the self: one that is adaptable to change and transformation, one that is able to construct its own identity according to the options offered by the media and the press. This conception of the self, in opposition to the substantive self, needs a wider number of options from which to choose how to define itself and build its life accordingly. This flexible self, in other words, needs a plural and diverse media environment. Without this flexible self, expressive freedoms would be a chimera.

Raz's theory seems to reveal an ambiguity that is inherent in the system itself. On the one hand, the media, and particularly the press, need the illusion that there is an objective truth. This necessity has manifested itself in the liberal theory in different forms. In John Stuart Mill it took the form of a correspondence between an objective reality and its mediated representations. In democratic theories it took the form of coherence between particular conceptions of democracy and the role of expressive freedoms in the legitimacy or reproduction of those conceptions. In Raz—and in other autonomy theories that recognise the importance of capacities of self-reflection—it takes the form of a substantive self or a true-self, and reaffirms the relevance of free speech and a free press in its discovery. This necessity of a substantive truth keeps the system safe from a destructive scepticism that sees media narratives as mere constructions of realities, or mere discourses that tend to reproduce power formations, or models that define and shape modern subjectivity. But just as they need the truth, these theories need to admit, to a certain extent, that mediated reality is a social construct where every voice is a valuable as any other; they need to recognise that democracy is an open concept that is in a constant process of self-reconfiguration, and that subjectivity is moulded and reshaped according to the prevailing discourses of the time. If they do not accept the latter and remain loyal to truth—in whatever form it presents—then expressive freedoms have no space. They lose their meaning and become servants to the purpose of identifying or validating narrow conceptions of truth—whether of reality, of democracy or of the self. These freedoms, in other words, are in an irresolute or ambiguous dispute with truth. This ambiguity is the basis of the 'illusion of the free press'. It is what makes the free press at one and the same time such a vital and such a fragile institution in liberal theory.

5

Freedom and Truth

I. Introduction

The illusion of the free press is an epistemological necessity. It is the consequence of our desire to understand the world we live in, to grasp our political contingency with all its nuances and subtleties, to enhance our sense of identity and so on. This illusion is powerful enough that it is not thwarted by our knowledge of the actual conditions of the press in capitalist systems. Even if we know that the press is far from being free and independent, even if we know that it is subject to a series of constraints that severely affect how it portrays social reality, we still cling to the illusion of the free press. We do it because we need it. In fact, if we renounce the illusion, we renounce social reality itself. The illusion of the free press is inscribed in the theory of free speech and manifests itself in the importance the latter assigns to the discovery and dissemination of truth. The clearest example is the classic theory, which claims that the purpose of a free press is the intellectual progress of a political community. Championed since the seventeenth century by authors like Milton, and later by Mill and Holmes, it remains one of the central justifications of the free press in liberal democracies. But the theory of truth has been challenged. As seen in Chapters 3 and 4 of this book, democratic theorists have argued that the central purpose of the press is not the discovery of truth but the strengthening of democracy. A free press contributes to a democratic polity, from this point of view, by facilitating an open and broad debate, a discussion and deliberation of political ideas. It also strengthens the system by checking government action, and hence by aligning the interests of representatives with those of the public. Autonomists, on the other hand, believe that the purpose of expressive freedoms is to validate personal identity, promote self-fulfilment, and enhance personal and political autonomy.

Although democratic and autonomy theories have provided persuasive justifications of the free press, they have not been able to oust truth discourse from free speech theory. Whenever it has been challenged as an adequate aim of the press (sometimes more emphatically than others), truth justifications have emerged, albeit in different forms. In democratic theories, truth appears in the form of coherence. What the public is entitled to know, from a democratic perspective, depends on a political truth, what Meiklejohn calls the 'plan of the Constitution'.[1] This truth shapes and defines the communicative practices of a community. Indeed, all forms of speech that are compatible with it should be admissible in the public sphere, while all those that threaten it should be rejected. In autonomy theories, on the other hand, truth takes the form of authenticity. Autonomist theorists conceive expressive freedoms as vehicles of self-discovery. They allow individuals to decide for themselves their plans of life and to remain truthful to them throughout their lives. According to Raz, public portrayals are a stamp of public acceptability or public validation of particular life styles portrayed. They help individuals committed to those forms of life to feel good about themselves, and hence to remain faithful to the form of life they have decided to live. Expressive freedoms are thus a vehicle for the discovery and affirmation of the true self.

Truth is a pervasive theme within free speech literature, and this is problematic. As has been argued throughout this book, truth and freedom are values that are in tension with each other. The modes of communication that characterise truth-seeking practices are coercive and domineering. If applied in the public sphere, they necessarily preclude freedom. On the other hand, the modes of communication that characterise discussion in the public sphere are unrestrained and tolerant. Their purpose is to incorporate different views and opinions into public discussion. Truth, however, is not the necessary consequence of an open and free debate of ideas.[2] Many times, as Marcuse thoughtfully acknowledges, truth is the victim of such debates. So we find ourselves in a conundrum. There are two forces pushing in opposite directions. On the one hand, the epistemological necessity of the illusion of the free press makes the relationship between freedom and truth unavoidable. On the other, we find that freedom and truth are values that exclude one another. Is there a way out of this riddle? Could we think of the relationship between truth and freedom in different ways? Could they be combined in a way that allows the press actually to work as an institution dedicated to broadening our understanding of social reality?

The relationship between truth and freedom has been analysed up to now within free speech theory. It has been seen that regardless of the form truth takes in the theory, it is always in tension with freedom. This chapter will take a different approach. First, it will look at the relationship between truth and freedom in the actually operating press. It will use as references the experiences of the United Kingdom and the United States. Secondly, the analysis will be centred on the notion of freedom. It will be argued that the tension between freedom and truth can be at least partly explained by the influence of a concept of freedom that has been instrumental to the modern understanding of the free press. This is the

---

[1] A Meiklejohn, 'Free Speech and its Relation to Self-Government' in *Political Freedom: The Constitutional Powers of the People* (New York, Oxford University Press, 1965) 70.

[2] See especially H Arendt, 'Truth and Politics' in *Between Past and Future: Eight Exercises in Political Thought* (New York, Penguin Books, 1977).

concept of freedom as non-interference. As will be shown, this concept was not only useful for providing a constitutional guarantee against undue government interference in the function and structure of the press, allowing it to become a fundamental institution in the democratic system; it has also contributed to the formation of a system of communications that is controlled by market logics. As will be shown, these logics have created forms of domination that have eroded not only media freedoms but also the truth-seeking purpose of the press. A republican concept of freedom (freedom as non-domination) will be presented as an alternative. In contrast to the concept of freedom as non-interference, the republican concept of freedom accepts that certain forms of interference can be compatible with freedom. The law, for example, could be a form of interference that is compatible with freedom and could contribute to removing the conditions of domination affecting the market of speech. Now, if those conditions are the ones thwarting the truth-seeking purpose of the press, then interference aimed at removing them could contribute to the existence of a press committed to the discovery of truth. If the tensions between truth and freedom described up to now in the book reduce the illusion of the free press to an empty hope for gaining access to social reality, the republican concept of freedom provides a conceptual basis that reduces the gap between truth and freedom, thus making the illusion of the free press a productive idea.

II. Truth, Freedom and the Political

The work of John Milton—conceptually and historically—shows vividly that a successful combination of truth and freedom is dependent on the political. Written in the midst of an age of political turmoil and constitutional crisis in England, *Areopagitica* made the argument that a free press is a fundamental instrument for the discovery of truth. Framed within a theocentric model of truth, Milton's theory is based on the belief that man—created in God's image—was given reason in order to achieve understanding and truth. However, Milton also acknowledges that certain political conditions are required for the development of human understanding. Milton opens the tract 'The Tenure of Kings and Magistrates', published a fortnight after Charles I's execution, with the following passage:

> If men within themselves would be governed by reason, and not generally give up their understanding to a double tyranny, of custom from without, and blind affections within, they would discern better, what it is to favour and uphold the tyrant of a nation. But being slaves within doors, no wonder that they strive so much to have the public state conformably governed to the inward vicious rule, by which they govern themselves.[3]

---

[3] J Milton, 'The Tenure of Kings and Magistates' in *The Prose Works of John Milton*, vol 1 (London, Methuen, 1905) 142.

This passage shows an interesting relationship between truth, freedom and politics. For indeed, the capacity of common men to make discernments about the rule of kings is dependent on their freedom to think for themselves. Their capacity to think for themselves, on the other hand, is dependent on the political or 'outward conditions' of their time. What Milton suggests is that if truth is the product of free thought and discussion, and the latter is only possible within an adequate political framework, then the discovery of truth is intrinsically connected to the political. There is, in other words, a dialectical relationship between truth and politics, which is nevertheless mediated by freedom. In fact, Milton formidably concludes this passage expressing that 'none can love freedom heartily, but good men; the rest love not freedom but licence; which never hath more scope or more indulgence than under tyrants'.[4] Although Milton's theocentric notion of truth is problematic, as seen in Chapter 2, his notion of freedom remains useful for our purposes. It is this particular notion of freedom that will be explored further to examine whether a free press could be committed to the discovery of truth.

Milton's concept of freedom has been located by recent scholarship within the republican tradition.[5] Quentin Skinner has noted that this tradition was advanced during the period of the English Civil War by a group of authors that he calls neo-Romans, of whom Milton was one of the leading figures.[6] By appropriating the supreme moral value of freedom, this group created a subversive ideology that was used to advocate for radical forms of representative democracy and to oppose different types of oppressive governments, including the English monarchy and the French *ancien régime*.[7] Their notion of freedom had two central characteristics. The first was that a free association of people, which Milton calls 'common liberty' or 'free government', was a fundamental condition for individual freedom.[8] The second was that the liberty of individuals, just like the liberty of the state, is defined as the capacity for self-government. A state is free as long as it gives to itself the laws that govern the realm, just as an individual is free as long as he is able to think and decide for himself what is good and what is wrong, what is just and what is not. Two major consequences follow from this concept of freedom, according to Skinner. The first one is that for a state to qualify as free, its laws have to be the product of the people's consent. Notice that this notion of consent is very different from Locke's understanding of the term. Indeed, while for Locke consent is related to the origin of legitimate government, for republicans consent is the realisation of self-government. As such, in a free government consent becomes a permanent practice by which those who are subject to the law are, at the same

---

[4] ibid.

[5] See generally P Pettit, *Republicanism: A Theory of Freedom and Government* (Oxford, Oxford University Press 1997); Q Skinner, *Liberty before Liberalism* (Cambridge, Cambridge University Press, 1998).

[6] In *Hobbes and Republican Liberty*, Skinner adopts the terminology of 'republicans' which is the one 'in use' to refer to this group. See Q Skinner, *Hobbes and Republican Liberty* (Cambridge, Cambridge University Press, 2008) vii.

[7] Skinner, above n 5, 59.

[8] ibid 23.

time, its authors.[9] The second consequence of the republican notion of freedom, which follows directly from the previous one, is that participation in the political process is crucial. If citizens are to count as free, they must not only submit to laws that are given by them but must also enjoy equal participatory rights in the enactment of those laws.

The republican concept of freedom is thus clearly a political concept. Its most salient characteristic, the capacity for self-government, was crucial to enabling a discourse against oppression and domination. Milton himself engaged in such discourse in his 'Eikonoklastes' and 'The Tenure of Kings and Magistrates', both of which were written soon after Charles I's execution, not only to justify it, but to appease the scruples of remorse among Parliamentarians. This notion of freedom contains an emancipatory force that is also visible in Milton's defence of the freedom of discussion and opinion. *Areopagitica* is in fact a tract that challenges the oppressive conditions of discussion existing in England in the first half of the seventeenth century. And as a manifestation of political freedom, freedom of discussion also requires certain political conditions for its realisation. These are the conditions of a free society, conditions which, according to Milton, would enable the emergence of truth. If there is no freedom under conditions of domination and oppression, and there is no truth without freedom, then truth is possible only in a free society: a society in which citizens give to themselves the laws by which they are governed. And this is crucial to understanding how the tensions between freedom and truth described at the beginning of this chapter can be tackled. Indeed, when freedom is understood politically, it is possible to foresee how, if a society organises its communicative practices towards the advancement of knowledge and the discovery of truth, and that organisation is the product of a free decision given by the community itself, this organisation (aimed at truth) might be compatible with freedom. This point will be developed further in the next section. For now, it is important to acknowledge that Milton provides a concept of freedom that may enable us today to consider the possibility of a truth-seeking press.

If Milton—the first prominent theorist of the free press—provided in the middle of the seventeenth century a concept of freedom that may be complementary to truth-seeking practices in the public sphere, something must have gone terribly wrong at some point. Something must have so radically changed our common understanding of freedom that it produced insurmountable antinomies within the classic defence of free speech itself, on the one hand, or simply the abandonment of truth as a proper justification of the free press, on the other. Interestingly enough, a rival concept of freedom emerged as a consequence of the events that led to the English Civil War and that subsequently unfolded. This concept of freedom was authored by Thomas Hobbes, and one of its central aims was to defeat—theoretically as well as politically—the arguments raised by republicans.

---

[9] ibid 27.

According to Hobbes, all those who were caught in the spell of the Athenian version of liberty—Milton included—and thought of it simply as the absence of arbitrary government, were not only deluded but were also responsible for instigating the ideology that led to civil war and to 'the effusion of so much blood'.[10] In a famous passage of *Leviathan*, Hobbes states:

> There is written on the Turrets of the city of *Luca* in great characters at this day, the word *LIBERTAS*; yet no man can thence inferre, that a particular man has more Libertie, or Immunitie from the service of the Commonwealth there, than in *Constantinople*.[11]

The central critique made by Hobbes against the republican notion of freedom is that the latter has no necessary connection with any particular form of government. Accordingly, freedoms could be curtailed without a problem in a well-organised republic just as they could be perfectly protected in an absolute monarchy. In Hobbes's words, 'whether a Commonwealth be Monarchicall, or Popular, the Freedome is still the same'.[12] It is clear that Hobbes could reach such a conclusion only by radically depoliticising freedom, that is, by removing any conceptual relationship between freedom and the political conditions required for its exercise. This depoliticisation not only contributed to the rejection of the republican claim that freedom could only be achieved in a well-ordered republic. More importantly, it cemented the modern understanding of freedom. What is then so novel about Hobbes's concept of freedom?

According to Hobbes, '[a] FREE-MAN, *is he, that in those things, which by his strength and wit he is able to do, is not hindred to doe what he has a will to*'.[13] Freedom is, accordingly, the absence of external impediments to motion. The first interesting thing about this concept is that it draws a distinction between external and internal impediments. Only external impediments count as restrictions on freedom. In a vivid example Hobbes expresses that

> all living creatures, whilest they are imprisoned, or restrained, with walls, or chayns; and of the water whilest it is kept in by banks, or vessels, that otherwise would spread it selfe into a larger space, we use to say, they are not at Liberty, to move in such manner, as without those externall impediments they would. But when the impediment of motion, is in the constitution of the thing it selfe, we use not to say, it wants the Liberty; but the Power to move; as when a stone lyeth still, or a man is fastned to his bed by sicknesse.[14]

Skinner notes that this was an extraordinary conceptual innovation.[15] In fact, as was shown, the received concept of freedom consisted in the absence of subjection

---

[10] T Hobbes, *Leviathan* (London, Penguin Books, 1985) 267.
[11] ibid 266.
[12] ibid.
[13] ibid 262.
[14] ibid.
[15] In contrast, Arendt traces the concept of freedom as non-interference back to antiquity, where philosophers saw abstention from politics as a condition of the contemplative life, the freest way of life. See H Arendt, 'What is Freedom?' in *Between Past and Future*, rev'd edn (London, Penguin Books, 2006) 149.

to the will of others and, hence, from the *possibility* of arbitrary impediment of their chosen ends.[16] In contrast, Hobbes's novel concept of freedom admits that freedom is compatible with subjection to the will of another so long as this subjection does not revert to impediments to motion. This explains why, among other things, Hobbes's concept of freedom is compatible with fear. Covenants could thus be reached as a consequence of the people's fear without affecting their freedom. This would be something unimaginable for republicans.

Another important aspect of Hobbes's concept of freedom is its relation to law. Laws are seen by Hobbes as external impediments to motion, and hence as limits to freedom: 'Law was brought into the world for nothing else, but to limit the naturall liberty of particular men'.[17] From this point of view, a man could only remain free in the absence of law. However, as all states require laws for their organisation, 'free states', as well as monarchies, necessarily limit men's freedoms. This is why Hobbes claims that it is absurd to believe, as republicans do, that a free state guarantees freedom to its members. This notion of freedom helped Hobbes to dismiss the powerful claim made by republicans that freedom was the consequence of self-government. It was a radical regressive movement that not only contributed to his defence of authoritative government, but was also later used by a group of authors who opposed American independence.[18] If indeed liberty has nothing to do with the organisation of a political community, there is no point in arguing that the subjects of the American colonies were less free than their British counterparts. According to this concept of freedom, 'there is nothing inherently opposed to freedom in a colonial system of law'.[19] The incompatibility between this concept of freedom and the law is also recognised by one of the most eloquent defenders of freedom as non-interference in the twentieth century, Isaiah Berlin, who claimed that '[l]aw is always a fetter, even if it protects you from being bound in chains that are heavier than those of the law'.[20]

A concept of freedom that was supposed to serve the interests of authoritative government proved to be much more than that. For indeed, a concept of freedom that is focused mainly on the absence of interference, and is hence indifferent to political structures or power relations, can be servile not only to the interest of an absolute monarch but to other forms of domination as well. Hobbes provided the conceptual tools needed to contain the transformative forces of the multitude unleashed in the English Civil War. His genius consists in that he did this without completely disenfranchising them from the body politic. The transcendental figure of the Leviathan was the catalyser of these forces. The absolute sovereign received its power and legitimacy from a covenant given by the people to secure peace in the realm and to guarantee their own security. Hobbes went even further

[16] Skinner, above n 6, 157.
[17] Hobbes, above n 10, 315.
[18] See Pettit, above n 5, 42.
[19] ibid.
[20] I Berlin, *Four Essays on Liberty* (Oxford, Oxford University Press, 1969) 3.

to claim that absolute government did not necessarily imply a loss of freedom in its subjects vis-à-vis other forms of government. In fact, Hobbes sees laws as external impediments to motion, and as every state needs them for its organisation, all states necessarily limit human freedom.

Freedom as non-interference, originally designed as a conceptual tool for opposing progressive politics and justifying absolute forms of government, was forgotten for a long period of time. Its revival occurred only at the end of the eighteenth century in the work of Jeremy Bentham. So buried in time was this concept that Bentham thought that it was his own 'discovery'.[21] Although Bentham originally used it to oppose American independence, later, when he became a more reformist and progressive thinker, he used it as a way of reinforcing democracy.[22] The fact that this notion of freedom could be compatible with progressive politics, despite its bleak origins, is explained, according to Pettit, by the radical transformations that occurred in England during the eighteenth and nineteenth centuries.[23] Thinkers like Bentham and John Stuart Mill, immersed in the logics of the Enlightenment, firmly believed in the principle of equality, epitomised in their slogan 'everybody to count for one, nobody for more than one'.[24] This principle, however, was thought to be incompatible with the demanding requirements of freedom as non-domination. For indeed, a society that counts its members as equals has enormous difficulties making all of them the bearers of collective decisions. And from a republican perspective, this is precisely what is required for the realisation of freedom. Bentham and Mill were not ready to defend such an approach. For that reason, a less demanding version of freedom, one that could make their principle of equality compatible with their view of government, was more suitable: freedom as non-interference. As will be seen in the next section, this version of freedom was instrumental for defining the meaning and scope of the free press. Although it was revived in a different political, social and cultural context from the one in which it was created, this concept of freedom carried with it the shadow of its origins.

III. Freedom as Non-Interference: Origins and Consolidation of Market Domination

If Hobbes's formula could secure legitimacy for an absolute form of government, it could certainly legitimise less obvious forms of domination. For domination

---

[21] Pettit, above n 5, 44.
[22] ibid 45.
[23] ibid 46–47.
[24] JS Mill, 'Essays on Ethics, Religion and Society' in *Collected Works*, vol 10 (London, Routledge, 1969) 257.

cannot originate only in the state or, as Weber claims, in 'the actual presence of one person successfully issuing orders to others'.[25] According to Ian Shapiro, this is too narrow a definition of domination, because the latter 'can, and often does, occur without explicit orders emanating from identifiable agents'. Furthermore, it 'can also be the by-product of the distribution of resources and can be embedded in structural relationships'.[26] This section will argue that the concept of freedom as non-interference defined the conditions of the modern press in liberal democracies through a process of liberalisation that began at the end of the seventeenth century, accelerated during the nineteenth century and has continued developing aggressively ever since. Although this concept was fundamental to securing guarantees against undue government interference in the functioning of the press, it also provided a conceptual apparatus that ended up securing domination of the public sphere by the market, under the guise of freedom. The forms of domination introduced by the market of free speech affected not only media freedoms, but also the truth-seeking purpose of the press and the right of citizens to adequately inform themselves about social reality. The purpose of this section is to show how the concept of freedom as non-interference was instrumental in permitting structural domination of the media market in the public sphere. In the next section, how domination has affected the truth-seeking purpose of the press will be explored in more detail.

The concept of freedom as non-interference was fundamental in defining the meaning and scope of the free press in Britain in the nineteenth century, when a section of the press indeed became more independent from government interference. From that time comes the idea that the free press was finally achieved after a series of laws and regulations affecting the press were repealed or amended.[27] Among them especially figure the abolition of the Court of Star Chamber in 1641, the Fox Libel Act of 1792 and the repeal between 1853–1861 of those taxation laws commonly known as taxes on knowledge. This progressive deregulation of the press led John Stuart Mill to claim in the middle of the nineteenth century that the freedom of the press was achieved in England: 'the time, it is to be hoped, is gone by when any defense would be necessary of the "liberty of the press" as one of the securities against corrupt or tyrannical government'.[28] It is important to recall that the liberty of the press is to be welcomed, according to Mill, because it is a necessary condition for the discovery of truth. Among other reasons, Mill argues that government was eminently fallible. As a consequence, if it interfered in the free discussion of ideas and opinions, it could, for the wrong reasons, censure opinions that later could be proved to be true. This argument, which was later circumscribed by the metaphor of the marketplace of ideas, was originally concerned not

[25] M Weber, *Economy and Society*, eds G Roth and C Wittich (Berkeley, CA, University of California Press, 1968) 43.
[26] I Shapiro, *Politics Against Domination* (Cambridge, MA, Belknap/Harvard, 2016) 21.
[27] See J Curran and J Seaton, *Power Without Responsibility*, 7th edn (Oxford, Routledge, 2010) 3.
[28] JS Mill, *On Liberty* (New York, Cosimo Classics, 2005) 19.

with the economic freedom of media agents involved in the formation of public opinion but with their liberty to produce stories, ideas and opinions that when confronted with others would permit a debate to enhance understanding of social reality. The condition necessary to achieve the latter was a free press, that is, the absence of state interference.

The idea of a free press under the concept of freedom as non-interference was originally concerned mainly with the evils associated with a long history of government intervention in the workings of the press, which were analysed in more detail in Chapter 2. However, it ended up providing fundamental theoretical and practical support for a market of free speech that, in the middle of the nineteenth century, was beginning to configure new forms of domination that have radically affected its truth-seeking purposes. This explains why Curran and Seaton argue that '[t]he period around the mid nineteenth century ... did not inaugurate a new era of press freedom and liberty; it established instead a new system of press censorship more effective than anything that had gone before.'[29] Mill cannot be accused of consciously providing the theoretical basis for the formation of a market of free speech designed to control public opinion. However, about the time when *On Liberty* was published, there were those who were purportedly using a defence of the free press on non-interference grounds to justify the creation of a commercial press, which was thought by them to be an adequate means of educating the working classes. As will be argued here, what was emerging at that time was the basis that secured a market-driven press that produced new forms of domination of the public sphere, which were, however, legitimised under the concept of freedom as non-interference.

What is interesting to note is that the new forms of domination that emerged as the consequence of the liberalisation of the press were not an unwanted consequence for many of those who supported deregulation. On the contrary, deregulation was seen by many as a mechanism that could socialise the radical instincts of the multitude, which were controlled—according to them—by a radical and subversive press. This phenomenon is clearly seen in the discussions that took place in Britain in the nineteenth century regarding the abolition of the laws that taxed newspapers (commonly known as taxes on knowledge). Although these laws were correctly seen as a grave restriction of the free press, and their repeal was thus defended by some on higher principles, there were others (the parliamentary repeal lobby) who correctly anticipated that their repeal could attract businessmen into the media market and thus enrol 'more temperate and disinterested friends of the people who would lend themselves to their real instruction'.[30] They were rather conscious that a capitalist-expanded press could be an instrument of political socialisation that could contain radical or progressive movements. According to Alexander Andrews, editor of the first journalists' trade journal and supporter

---

[29] Curran and Seaton, above n 27, 5.
[30] ibid 18.

of the abolition of the taxes on knowledge, the main goal of the free press was to 'educate and enlighten those classes whose political knowledge has been hitherto so little, and by consequence so dangerous'.[31]

According to Curran and Seaton, these reformers combined authoritarian and libertarian arguments in ways that today could sound incongruous. The fact is, however, that there is no incongruity between the concept of freedom defended by these 'reformers' and the authoritarian political socialisation that they promoted and that followed the liberalisation of the press. For indeed, applied to the press, freedom as non-interference consists, basically, in the absence of laws regulating it. The press, in other words, is free so long as the state does not interfere in its structure, organisation and functioning: just like any other business, the press should be left to its own devices for it to thrive. This concept of a free press is compatible with the sort of authoritarian arguments made by defenders of the abolition of taxes on knowledge. It is compatible because preventing government control of the press by abolishing the laws that regulate it does not guarantee the absence of other forms of domination. It only modifies the agent doing the domination. Many of those who defended the abolition of taxes of knowledge were perfectly aware of this. They knew that the absence of taxes would favour a capitalist press that would be owned and controlled by businessmen. One of those activists, Thomas Milner-Gibson, president of the Association for the Promotion of the Repeal of the Taxes on Knowledge, claimed that free trade would 'give to men of capital and respectability the power of gaining access by newspapers, by faithful records of facts, to the minds of the working classes'.[32] The concept of freedom as non-interference was once again used to promote reactionary politics. This time the purpose was not to defend absolute government but to guide public communications towards the reproduction of class interest through the instrument of 'political socialisation'.

Despite the intentions of some of those who supported the repeal of the taxes on knowledge, the fact is that abolition produced a chain reaction that was fundamental not only to the industrialisation of the press, but also to the creation of a media system where market logics commenced dictating the terms of production and the dissemination of news.[33] Indeed, the abolition of taxes on knowledge reduced the cost of production of newspapers; with it, cover costs were also reduced and sales increased. Increased revenues, on the other hand, triggered the development of new print technologies. The rotary press was first introduced in the 1860s and then replaced by web rotary machines. The linotype, introduced at the end of the nineteenth century (and in use for almost a century), accelerated the typesetting and composition processes and made the whole production even more efficient. Innovations were also made in image reproduction. These technological developments improved the quality and circulation of newspapers.

---

[31] ibid 19.
[32] Milner-Gibson, HC Deb 15 April 1850, vol 110, col 378.
[33] Curran and Seaton, above n 27, 26.

Large numbers could be printed at low cost. As a consequence, the prices of individual newspapers dropped sharply: they were halved in the 1850s and then halved again in the 1860s.[34] However, technological developments also increased the fixed costs of newspapers, making it more difficult (though not yet impossible) for new actors to access the market. New technological conditions also increased the costs of running a newspaper. As a consequence, and to make the business profitable, proprietors were forced to reduce internal costs and increase the circulation of newspapers. Capital gained a privileged position in the modern press. Indeed, as Curran and Seaton observe, although in 1837 the *Northern Star*, a national weekly newspaper, could be established for £690 and break even with a circulation of 6,200 copies, in 1918 the *Sunday Express* required more than £2 million to establish and was only able to break even with a circulation of 250,000 copies.[35]

The industrialisation of the press was not completed, however, with the repeal of the taxes on knowledge. A second phenomenon, also conceived under the logics of freedom as non-interference, was fundamental for establishing the economic grounds on which the market of free speech has been governed up to today. This was only possible with the repeal in 1853 of the advertisement duty.[36] The liberalisation of advertisement radically changed the rules of the game, particularly the economic structure of the press. For in fact, the partisan press of the first half of the nineteenth century was replaced by the present industrialist press. The main cause of this transformation was that the press became financially dependent on advertisement. As the prices of individual newspapers dramatically decreased in the middle of the nineteenth century, their net cover prices no longer met their costs.[37] Advertisement was thus needed to fill the financial shortfalls of inexpensive newspapers. This had several effects. First of all, according to Curran, it substantially affected the vitality of the radical press. For although it diminished over time, the political prejudices of advertisers have always affected left-wing newspapers. But more important were the economic considerations of advertisers who, back in the nineteenth century and even at the beginning of the twentieth century, saw no value in advertising in newspapers for the lower classes. As an advertisement handbook of 1851 stated that '[a] journal that circulates a thousand among the upper or middle classes is a better medium than would be one circulating a hundred thousand among the lower classes.'[38] To survive under these conditions, the radical press could only move upmarket to attract advertisement or remain 'in a small working class ghetto with manageable losses that could be offset by donations'.[39] With time, the media became financially dependent on advertisers,

---

[34] ibid 26–29.
[35] ibid 27.
[36] ibid 28.
[37] ibid 49.
[38] ibid 30.
[39] ibid 31.

and advertisement commenced dictating the terms of media production, severely affecting the freedom of the media.

The growth of advertisement exponentially increased the number of local daily and local weekly newspapers. There was also a substantial increase in national dailies and Sunday newspapers. Entrepreneurs launched newspapers that were tailored to the tastes of those markets that were attractive to advertisers and generated substantial profits. The growth in the number of publications was followed by an increase in readership and sales. Over a period of 70 years, sales of newspapers grew from £85 million in 1851 to £5,604 million in 1920.[40] Now, increasing advertisement also produced growing competition among newspapers in order to attract advertisement revenues, which increased from £20 million in 1907 to £59 million in 1938.[41] A war for promotional spending began between newspapers in the first half of the twentieth century, producing two major effects. The first was that the partisan press was supplanted in the market by industry, as it became too onerous for political parties and supporters to sustain the costs of newspapers. The second was the emergence of the era of press barons: huge media empires owned by powerful businessman who controlled the circulation of information.

If the nineteenth century consolidated the idea of the free press as the absence of state interference in its structure, organisation and functioning, the twentieth century consolidated a process of liberalisation that radicalised market logics. The industrialisation of the press produced structural forms of domination that manifest themselves today in different ways. The press became a multi-billion business controlled by powerful men who acquired not only immense fortunes, but also the power to influence the political, economic, cultural and moral spheres of the places where they based their operations. The 'press barons' of the beginning of the past century gave way to huge global conglomerates, which concentrated not only national but also international media markets of various types. One example is News Corporation. Owned by Rupert Murdoch, it is one of the world's biggest media conglomerates. Before its split in 2012, it counted among its assets Fox Entertainment Group, Fox News, News International, News Limited and HarperCollins Publishers. Its portfolio included hundreds of newspapers, television stations, one of the biggest film studios in the world, magazines and cable television channels, to mention just some. Its revenues in 2012 amounted to US $33.7 billion.[42]

For some time, it was thought that the emergence of the Internet could solve some of the problems of domination created by the liberalisation of the press. Digital technologies opened forms of communication that were unthinkable before. They promised a new era of political activism and a reinvigorated public

---

[40] ibid 32.
[41] ibid 44.
[42] News Corporation, Annual Report 2012, available at http://investors.newscorp.com.

sphere that would capture the diversity of views, opinions and ideas existing in society.[43] The fact is that the problems inaugurated by the industrial press have compounded in the digital era, as will be analysed in further detail in the next section. Although the Internet multiplied the platforms of communication and strengthened political activism and participation in public debate, it also inherited some of the vices of the traditional press. Just like the printing press, the Internet is showing a growing capacity to concentrate corporate control. According to Michael Wolff, 'the top 10 websites accounted for 31 percent of US pageviews in 2001, 40 percent in 2006 and about 75 percent in 2010'.[44] Google and Facebook concentrate online advertisement. While in 2015, 75 per cent of all new online spending on advertisement in the United States went to one of these companies, the numbers rose to 85 per cent in 2016.[45] The trends show that if anyone can make money out of online journalism, 'it will almost certainly be'—according to Robert McChesney—'as a very large, centralized operation, probably a monopoly or close to it. The Internet has proven to be more effective at centralizing corporate control than it has been at enhancing decentralization, at least in news media.'[46]

Market logics have created forms of domination in the media that, from the point of view of freedom as non-domination, have severely constricted not only media freedoms but also the freedom of citizens to inform themselves about social reality. These forms of domination, however, are not necessarily a problem from the point of view of freedom as non-interference. Ownership concentration, for example, is usually condemned from a non-interference perspective, as Baker argues, not on grounds of principle but for the consequences it may produce. It is condemned because it affects consumers' freedoms: their right to receive a wide range of content and diverse viewpoints. The problem with this position is that domination is qualified as an evil in consequentialist terms. Hence, if it is proved that concentration may produce viewpoint and content diversity, as has been suggested by some literature, then it ceases to be a problem.[47] From the point of view of freedom as non-domination, things are different. The central problem of media concentration is not related to its outputs. Concentration is an evil that must be

---

[43] See generally, C Shirky, *Here Comes Everybody* (New York, Penguin Press, 2009); Y Zheng, *Technological Empowerment* (Stanford, CA, Stanford University Press, 2010); TL Friedman, *The World is Flat* (New York, Farrar Straus & Giroux, 2007).

[44] M Wolff, 'The Web is Dead. Long Live the Internet', quoted in RW McChesney, *Digital Disconnect: How Capitalism is Turning the Internet against Democracy* (New York, The New Press, 2013) 190.

[45] M Meeker of Kleiner Perkins, Internet Trends 2017, code conference, available at http://www.kpcb.com/internet-trends.

[46] McChesney, above n 44, 190.

[47] For a long time now, there has been evidence suggesting that market concentration does not necessarily reduce diversity but sometimes stimulates it. See E Baker, *Media Concentration and Democracy* (Cambridge, Cambridge University Press, 2007) 16; PO Steiner, 'Program Patterns and Preferences, and the Workability of Competition in Radio Broadcasting' (1952) 66 *The Quarterly Journal of Economics* 194.

avoided even if dominant agents are able to provide a wide range of content to the public. This is because non-domination does not value the fact of having choice in itself (regardless of its conditions) but the fact of having un-dominated choice. Indeed, freedom as non-domination seeks to guarantee *unconditional* security against power. So, even if concentration can create viewpoint diversity, it still provides dominant agents the 'capacity' to interfere with people's choices arbitrarily. That capacity is enough to affect people's freedoms when we are dealing with such delicate matters as the construction of public opinion.[48]

Other forms of market domination affecting media freedoms have grown more relevant in the last few years. They will be explored in more detail in the next section in order to show how they have also affected the truth-seeking purpose of the press. As will be seen, extreme competition in the market has forced the industry to reduce costs and increase revenues, with detrimental consequences for serious investigative journalism.[49] To survive, newspapers must produce content that attracts the masses and cut spending on items that are no longer affordable. Doing so and renouncing their duty to adequately inform public opinion, not only is their capacity to decide for themselves the type of journalism they want to do radically stifled but so is the ability of citizens to access accurate depictions of social reality. The forms of domination created by the process of industrialisation of the press do not affect freedom from the point of view of freedom as non-interference. On the contrary, the production of news is not subject to direct interference from the state or third parties. Just like governments, advertisers do not directly decide what news is published by newspapers and websites, nor do they interfere with citizens' choices about what they read and see. However, from the perspective of the republican concept of freedom, the forms of domination created by the process of industrialisation and its consolidation have not only affected freedoms but have also affected the truth-seeking purpose of the press, as I shall now proceed to explain.

---

[48] Baker argues that when a democratic process under ideal conditions leads to content or viewpoint diversity, this diversity is valued because of the process itself, but if a democratic process does not lead to it, it simply does not require it. On the contrary, 'an absence of content or viewpoint diversity that reflects independent but congruent judgements of many people ... differs fundamentally from the same absence imposed by a few powerful actors': Baker, above n 47, 15.

[49] In their desperate attempt to make business profitable, news websites have borrowed from alien markets strategies designed to increase efficiency in the productive process. Outsourcing, for example, proved to be an efficient way of producing commodities like clothes or computers, has been tested in the United States for the production of news. Journatic (recently re-branded as LocalLabs) was an American local news provider whose business model was based on the assumption that it is no longer possible to provide local news with actual paid reporters. Hence, Journatic provided local stories produced by low-paid journalists and freelancers from the United States and the Philippines. The latter were paid 40 cents per piece, and they had to produce a minimum of 250 pieces a week. See McChesney, above n 44, 192.

IV. Domination and the Truth-seeking
Purpose of the Press

According to Pettit, non-domination is affected, amongst other ways, by the contraction of public space, and this happens when the information people receive about their social reality is biased.[50] But one could think that the causal relationship between the constriction of the public sphere and biased information works in the opposite direction. We get biased accounts of social reality when the public sphere contracts. Arendt argues that the public sphere is the space of appearances, that is, the space in which everything that appears can be seen and heard by everyone. The public sphere, from this point of view, is constitutive of reality because we can only have the sense that something is real when the things I see and hear are also things that other people see and hear. Therefore, when the public sphere deteriorates, when the space of appearances is constricted, so does our sense of reality. When the striking light that produces the gaze of the public is weakened, biased information or outright lies may find this crack and filter into the public space.[51] The purpose of this section is to show how the radicalisation of market logics has constricted the public space and so our sense of reality.

In March 2016, Emily Bell claimed that 'our news ecosystem has changed more dramatically in the past five years, than perhaps any time in the past 500'.[52] Some authors have seen in this transformation one of the explanations of the emergence of *post-truth politics*. Described by David Roberts as 'a political culture in which politics (public opinion and media narratives) have become almost entirely disconnected from policy (the substance of legislation)', *post-truth politics* has been associated with a media environment increasingly disconnected from truth and facts.[53] The so-called phenomenon has been a topic of intense debate since the 2016 Brexit referendum in Britain and the election of Donald Trump as President of the United States. During the Brexit campaign, it was falsely claimed that UK contributions to the EU were going to be spent on the NHS if the leave vote won. During Trump's election, false reports about the health of Hillary Clinton, of accusations that she had sold weapons to ISIS, and of the Pope's endorsement of Donald Trump were freely flowing on the Web. Whether this information was decisive for the result of these elections or not is something that we shall probably never know.[54] What interests us here is that the business strategies developed on

---

[50] Pettit, above n 5, 167–68.

[51] H Arendt, *The Human Condition* (Chicago, IL, University of Chicago, 1989) 50–52.

[52] E Bell, 'Facebook is Eating the World', *Columbia Journalism Review* (7 March 2016), available at https://www.cjr.org/analysis/facebook_and_media.php.

[53] D Roberts, 'Post-truth politics', 1 April 2010, available at http://grist.org/article/2010-03-30-post-truth-politics/.

[54] For an economic analysis of fake news in the 2016 US presidential election, see generally H Allcot and M Gentzkow, 'Social Media and Fake News in the 2016 Election' (2017) 31 *Journal of Economic Perspectives* 211.

the Internet and social media have created conditions that radicalised the tensions that always existed between freedom and truth.

Facebook's business model is built upon the interactions of individual users with their friends. Users receive in their news feed information provided by friends who tend to share similar ideas and views about the world. Users also receive information from other sources, such as news providers when, identified by powerful algorithms, they match their own recorded preferences and interests. At the same time, individual users do not interact with people who are not part of their network, and do not receive information that conflicts with their recorded preferences. This is how Facebook creates a *filter bubble* that is fundamental to its business model, which aims at keeping users permanently engaged with the information they are continually receiving.[55] This bubble is how not only social media, but also much of the Internet work. It tends to reinforce users' prejudices, as it prevents them from engaging with differently-minded people. Social media are reducing the scope for debate and interaction. They are isolating people within their own comfort zones, creating virtual communities separated by invisible walls that are eroding the vitality of the public sphere. The filter bubble also 'distorts our perception of what is important, true, and real', as Pariser claims.[56]

When the public sphere erodes, our sense of reality is affected. According to Arendt, the public sphere tolerates only that which is considered appropriate to be seen or heard by everyone. There are many things that cannot be exposed to the implacable and striking light produced by the constant presence of others in the public scene.[57] One of those things is the dissemination of outright lies, which are easily detected by a vibrant and critical public eye. This might explain the recent outburst of fake news on the Web and the phenomenon of post-truth. Indeed, the loss of what we have in common, expressed in the public sphere, occurs when people suddenly start behaving themselves as members of a family, each one multiplying and projecting only the point of view of her neighbour. In this context, everyone is walled within his or her own singular experience, which does not cease to be singular even if it multiplies innumerable times. Fake news can easily spread when it is directed only to those who see in it a confirmation of their own ideas and views about the world. Post-truth is nothing but a manifestation of the tensions between truth and freedom, which become more evident with the attrition of the public sphere.

The truth-seeking deficit of social media is also related to market concentration and the need of media platforms to obtain advertisement revenues. Facebook, which as of the fourth quarter of 2016 had 1.86 billion active users, has become the dominant way to find news on the Internet.[58] Now, competition for advertisement

---

[55] This term was coined and explored first in E Pariser, *The Filter Bubble* (London, Penguin, 2011).
[56] ibid 20.
[57] Arendt, above n 51, 50–52.
[58] K Viner, 'How Technology Disrupted the Truth', 12 July 2016, available at https://www.theguardian.com/media/2016/jul/12/how-technology-disrupted-the-truth.

revenue is as fierce on the Web as in the traditional press, and it also works on the basis of audiences. The more people go to a news site to follow a story that has appeared on their news feed, the larger audience the site gets and the bigger its advertisement revenues. News providers hence need to create stories that look attractive in order to increase their revenues. This has been a huge incentive to disseminate highly engaging material containing wild stories, scandals, intrusions into the private life of public figures, among others, for those stories have greater chances of receiving attention (clicks) than those lacking those features. The problem is that usually stories trying to capture the attention of people by way of scandal are not so worried about the truth of their claims. As Neetzan Zimmerman, a specialist in high-traffic viral stories, said, 'Nowadays it's not important if a story is real, the only thing that really matters is whether people click on it.'[59]

The shrinkage of the public sphere is not just a consequence of the social media business model. In his acute insight into news production in *Flat Earth News*, Nick Davies presents a bleak picture of the state of contemporary press: a press that is unable to fulfil its fundamental role, telling the truth about the world we live in. According to Davies, this is attributable to the 'forces of commercialism which now provide the greatest obstacles to truth-telling journalism'.[60] It is not that advertisers are pulling the strings of news behind the stage. What Davies describes as 'the global collapse of information gathering and truth telling' is the consequence of the radicalisation of the practices of collecting, processing and disseminating news due to the ever-growing pressures of the market.[61] But if the press has been under the control of commercialism for more than a century now, what has happened that its effects have been radicalised, as Davies describes? The answer can be found in what—for a significant number of authors—was at a recent point in time the promised path to media pluralism and diversity: the Internet.[62] Paradoxically, the Internet, and the emergence of digital technologies more generally, has turned out to be the worst enemy of a truth-seeking press. As McChesney suggests, 'the Internet has taken the economic basis away from commercial journalism, especially newspapers, and left the rotting carcass for all to see'.[63]

---

[59] Quoted ibid. Facebook's CEO, Mark Zuckerberg, claims that Facebook is not liable for fake news publications because '[n]ews and media are not the primary things people do on Facebook, so I find it odd when people insist we call ourselves a news or media company in order to acknowledge its importance'. 'Facebook's fake-news problem: What's its responsibility?', *Chicago Tribune* (15 November 2016), available at http://www.chicagotribune.com/bluesky/technology/ct-facebook-fake-news-20161115-story.html. A functionalist approach to the legal concept of media, such as the one defended by Oster, would lead to the opposite conclusion. See J Oster, 'Theory and Doctrine of Media Freedom as a Legal Concept' (2013) 5 *Journal of Media Law* 57.

[60] N Davies, *Flat Earth News* (London, Vintage 2009) 16.

[61] ibid 154.

[62] See, eg, J Jarvis, 'Foreword' to E King, *Free for All* (Evanston, IL, Northwestern University Press, 2010); C Shirky, 'Newspapers and Thinking the Unthinkable' in R McChesney and V Packard (eds), *Will the Last Reporter Please Turn Out the Lights* (New York, The New Press, 2011).

[63] McChesney, above n 44, 172.

Two important forces brought to bear by the Internet can explain the radicalisation of the processes of commercialisation of newspapers, which has exposed the precariousness of contemporary news production. The first one is speed. The Internet has accelerated the speed of communications on all media platforms. It is not that the information travels faster. Instant communication was introduced by the telegraph more than two centuries ago. What the Internet has accelerated is the process of news production. If before the Internet, news needed to be produced for newspapers once (or sometimes twice) a day, news websites now need to be constantly updating their information. This has introduced enormous pressure on newsrooms. Back in 2005, only six months after the BBC issued guidelines to its journalists in which it was established that accuracy was to be more important than speed, the service's chief editor, Rob Liddle, wrote a memo directed to the BBC's online news service, stating that '[w]e should be getting breaking news up within five minutes'. As Liddle himself clarified, this means that every five minutes the service should 'send an email to the news desk to warn them about the story; write a four paragraph version of the story and post it on Ceefax as well as on the website; and at the same time do "checking"'.[64] The number of journalists would have to multiply in proportion to the scope of the requirements introduced in news production by digitalisation if responsible journalism practices and investigative journalism were not to erode. Unfortunately, the number of journalists has not multiplied. On the contrary, the force of speed introduced by the Internet has been accompanied by a dramatic reduction in the number of correspondents, press bureaus and journalists working in newsrooms.[65]

The second force introduced by the Internet explains why the number of workers dedicated to the delicate process of news production has been reduced since its introduction. The Internet intensified competition for advertisement, competition that has radically affected the political economy of the press. This has been so strong in some places that it is jeopardising the existence of journalism itself. In the United States, as McChesney shows, daily newspapers received nearly $20 billion from classified advertisements in 2000. In 2011, they received only $5 billion. Over the same period, display advertisement revenue fell from around $30 billion to $15 billion. In the period stretching from 2003 to 2011, combined newspapers advertisement revenues were cut in half.[66] In contrast, online advertisement expenditure was $32 billion in 2011 and totalled $73 billion in 2016, half of which was received by Facebook and Google.[67] The freefall of newspapers'

---

[64] R Liddle, 'Memo to News Interactive editorial', 9 December 2005, quoted in Davies, above n 60, 69–70.

[65] See S Waldman, *The Information Needs of Communities* (Darby, PA, Diane Publishing, 2011) 44–45; RG Kaiser, *The Bad News about the News* (Washington, The Brookings Institution, 2014) available at www.brookings.edu/series/the-brookings-essay/.

[66] McChesney, above n 44, 172.

[67] M Meekers of Kleiner Perkins, Internet Trends 2017, code conference, available at kpcb.com/InternetTrends.

revenues is related to the migration of readers from newspapers to free websites.[68] This migration has produced dramatic transformations in the production and dissemination of news. These transformations explain why, according to Davies, truth telling has disintegrated into mass production of ignorance in such a brief period of time.

The structural forces of the political economy of the press that were shaken up by the emergence of the Internet have affected the process of production of news at several levels. In an effort to systematise this crisis, Davies has examined (at least) three elements involved in the production of news, the state of which can give us a hint of what is going on. The first is the level of workers, more specifically journalists. Journalists have become an automated link in the chain production of news. Unable to check the validity of the stories on which they are working, or to go out to gather information about them, journalists spend most of their time at their keyboards, merely reproducing information generated by third parties at a speed that has never been seen before.[69] A young graduate working at a regional daily tabloid produced for Davies a diary of his workload. In just a week, this journalist wrote 48 stories; he only spoke to 26 people to produce those stories; out of those 26, he only saw four of them face to face and spent just three out of 45.5 hours out of office.[70] The workload of journalists—and the impossibility of doing proper journalism that follows—is a direct consequence of the radicalisation of the processes of production unleashed by the forces of the Internet. Journalism has ceased to be a profitable investment, and in order to keep the system working, it is necessary to maximise the levels of production of journalists while at the same time reducing costs.[71]

Journalists are currently pumping out in great numbers stories that have not been checked, or merely recycling unchecked stories produced by third parties. According to Davies, 'the most respected media outlets [in Britain] are routinely recycling unchecked second-hand material'. He claims that 60 per cent of their stories 'consisted wholly or mainly of wire copy and/or PR [public relations] to which more or less other material has been added'. Only 12 per cent of the stories, he adds, are the product of work generated by reporters themselves.[72] It is easy to see that the dependence of (even the most respected) newspapers on third-party sources is the consequence of the radicalisation of the process of news production unleashed by the Internet. The cuts made by newspapers as a result of intense competition have drastically reduced the number of correspondents and journalists working in newsrooms. In the United States, '[t]he number of foreign bureaus

---

[68] For a study about the effects of the internet on daily print newspapers based on data from more than ninety countries, see D Cho, MD Smith and A Zenter, 'Internet Adoption and the Survival of Print Newspapers: A Country-Level Examination' (2016) 37 *Information Economics and Policy* 13.

[69] Davies, above n 60, 73.

[70] ibid 56–59.

[71] See McChesney, above n 44, 177.

[72] Davies, above n 60, 52.

and correspondents, Washington bureaus and correspondents, statehouse bureaus and correspondents, down to the local city hall, have all been severely slashed, and in some cases the coverage barely exists any longer'.[73] US News and World Report has, paradoxically, closed all its foreign bureaus.[74]

With the industry halving in size between 2005 and 2012, major shrinkage of foreign bureaus and local correspondents, and ever-increasing pressure for greater speed of production, the conditions for original reporting and investigative journalism could hardly be worse. But the problems do not stop here. The second element examined by Davies that explains what he calls *the mass production of ignorance* is the supply of news. Journalists rely mainly on two sources from which they produce or recycle stories. The first source is press agencies, the most important of which operating in the United Kingdom and Ireland is the Press Association (PA). According to a research commanded by Davies, 70 per cent of home stories in Britain from the most prestigious London papers are wholly or partially rewrites from wire copy, coming mainly from the PA.[75] The PA has such credibility that its stories are hardly checked by journalists. However, according to Davies, the PA is not 'reliable as a tool to dig out the most important and interesting events in [Britain]; and it is not reliable as a source of truth about those events which it does chose to cover'.[76] It is not reliable because the PA is not fitted to fill the gap that has been opened by the shrinkage of newspapers, reporters and bureaus. First, it does not have sufficient reporters and staff to compensate for this gap. Davies notes, for example, that the PA covers the whole area of Greater Manchester, Lancashire and Cumbria with only five reporters, including trainees. Secondly, the PA itself has fallen into the type of practices that have affected newspapers and which have eroded the truth-seeking purpose of the press. Intense pressure due to speed requirements in the production of information (file before the competition does), scarce resources and lack of time make fact checking as difficult as it is for commercialised media outlets. But perhaps what is most troublesome of all is that the function the PA was set to fulfil—reporting as accurately as possible what people say—has not changed, despite the influence it has acquired on the British media landscape. The role that the PA plays in the process of news production is to feed the system with information that is supposed to be processed, edited and complemented by newspapers or news sites in order to produce a final story that is delivered to the public. The problem, as Davies notes, is that an important number of stories delivered by newspapers are wholly rewritten from the PA's wires. This has detrimental effects on the truth-seeking function of the press.[77] Indeed, our comprehension of social reality cannot be anything but inadequate if it is construed (partly or wholly) on the basis of nude facts. The work of the journalist is

---

[73] See McChesney, above n 44, 180.
[74] Davies, above n 60, 100–04.
[75] ibid 74.
[76] ibid 76.
[77] ibid 81–83.

essential to feed those facts with context, confront them with opposed opinions, question their assumptions and so on. The progressive abandonment of that function distances newspapers from their truth-seeking function.

The changing conditions of the media landscape have enabled the emergence of another supplier of information that has acquired enormous importance: public relations (PR). Time constraints, insufficient resources available for the production of news and mounting competition, are all factors that have contributed to the rise of PR as a fundamental supplier of information to newspapers. The increasing dependence of newspapers on material delivered by PR for the production of their stories is proportionate to the growing ratio of PR people working for every journalist.[78] In the United States, according to McChesney, 'in 1960 there was only one PR agent for every working journalist, a ratio of 0.75 to 1. By 1990 the ratio was just over 2. In 2012, the ratio stood at 4 PR people for every working journalist'.[79] The growth of PR is a phenomenon that has taken place not only in corporations, but also in government agencies. And under current conditions of news production, it is a deadly weapon that threatens not only the watchdog role of the press but also its truth-seeking function. Indeed, PR material is produced to serve the interest of the supplier. As a consequence, not only is the information that is crafted and delivered by PR to press agencies or directly to newspapers always carefully looking after those interests, but information against those same interests is simply not released. Hence, the growing level of influence of PR in the media landscape is dangerous not only for its unreliability, but also for what it omits.

V. Re-thinking the Relationship between Truth and Freedom

If the concept of freedom as non-interference has contributed to creating multiple forms of domination that manifest themselves in the media system and that have affected not only freedom but also the truth-seeking purpose of the press, it is because this concept of freedom is perfectly compatible with them. Now, if domination is compatible with a concept of freedom as non-interference, it is not compatible with the republican concept of freedom as non-domination. To understand why this is the case, it is necessary to recall the difference between both concepts. First of all, both are negative concepts, both define freedom as the absence of something: of domination in the case of republican freedom and of interference in the case of freedom as non-interference. However, domination and

---

[78] For the expansion of public relations in Britain, see A Davis, *Public Relations Democracy* (Manchester, Manchester University Press, 2002).
[79] See McChesney, above n 44, 183.

interference are different categories. While interference is an external impediment to motion, domination is something else. According to Pettit, domination is exemplified by the master–slave relationship. In this relationship, the mastering part can interfere on an arbitrary basis in the decisions and choices of the slave. However, interference is not a necessary element in this relationship of domination. The benevolent master who allows his slave to do whatever he is willing to do represents a paradigmatic form of domination without interference.[80] As the republican concept of freedom as non-domination pays attention to the structure in which human relationships are framed, it will always qualify the master–slave relationship as un-free, regardless of whether the slave is interfered with or not by his master. Freedom as non-interference, on the other hand, only observes the contingent and material action of interference and is indifferent to structures of domination. Thus, it will qualify this relationship as un-free if, and only if, the master actually interferes in the slave's choices and decisions.

There is a second relevant difference between the concepts of freedom. As there can be domination without interference, like in the master–slave relationship, there can also be interference without domination.[81] According to Pettit, this may occur when 'another person or agency is allowed to interfere with me but only on condition that the interference promises to further my interests, and promises to do so according to opinions of a kind that I share'.[82] Law is the classic example of interference without domination. From the point of view of freedom as non-interference, as has been seen, law will always be a restriction on individual freedom. However, from a republican point of view, when the law is the product of the self-governing capacity of the people and is directed towards goals that are generally accepted as valid, although it will interfere with individual's choices and decisions, it will not affect freedom.

With these distinctions in mind, we are ready to spell out the reasons why a republican concept of freedom is better equipped to defend expressive freedoms on truth-seeking grounds than its counterpart, freedom as non-interference. First, republican freedom condemns all forms of domination. This includes not only domination coming from government, but also domination coming from the social and economic spheres. Secondly, in contrast to freedom as non-interference that sees the law as a necessary abridgement of individual freedoms, freedom as non-domination envisages the law as an instrument of freedom.[83] Consequently, the law could be used to regulate the press in order to remove forms of domination that affect its truth-seeking purpose. This, of course, would require interference

---

[80] Pettit, above n 5, 22.

[81] ibid 20.

[82] ibid 23.

[83] In a notable passage, Martin Loughlin draws the relationship between liberty and public law when he says that 'Just as the rules of grammar are not restrictions on speech but are possibility-conferring rules that enable us to speak with greater precision, so too should the rules and practices of public law be seen not as restrictions on power or liberty but as rules that are constitutive of the meaning of these terms.' M Loughlin, *Foundations of Public Law* (Oxford, Oxford University Press, 2010) 178.

with the structure of the press and also with its communicative practices. However, that interference would not be an abridgement of freedom as long as it is designed to overcome structures of domination when those structures restrain the truth-seeking practices of the press, as they actually do.

The forms of domination affecting the freedom of the press are the same affecting its truth-seeking practices. Although multiple in number, they are all related to the phenomenon of commercialisation. Not only does the survival of media outlets depend on their capacity to subject and constrain their modes of news production to ever-increasing market pressures, but those pressures have also eroded the capacity of the press to produce news that is the product of adequate investigative practices. If market domination of the press has affected not only freedom but also the truth-seeking purpose of the press, then the conditions necessary to guarantee a free press are also conditions necessary to enhance its truth-seeking practices and hence our understanding of social reality. In other words, freedom and truth can come closer if the press is thought of and subjected to regulation that is designed within the framework of freedom as non-domination.

The characteristic form of interference without domination is the law. The law as the product of collective self-government supposes a form of interference that is not arbitrary because, at least in principle, the properly constituted law is *controlled by the interests and opinions of those affected*. The law is, in Pettit's words, a non-mastering interferer. As a consequence, any form of interference aimed at removing structural relations of domination in the public sphere should be done by law. Interference in the form of law aimed at removing structural relations of domination in the public sphere, if effective, should enhance not only the freedom of citizens but also the freedom of media outlets. It should do so because market domination affects not only media freedom but also the development of truth-seeking practices, which are necessary to enhance citizens' understanding of social reality and to enable participation in the discussion and deliberation of public issues. In *Partial Constitution*, Cass Sunstein argues that legal regulation of media outlets not only is compatible with a free press, but it also strengthens its goals. His argument resembles the one developed here. However, its reach seems insufficient to deal with the problems currently affecting the press. According to Sunstein, there are forms of government interference with media outlets that enhance freedom, just as absence of interference may produce abridgements of freedom. The central point in Sunstein's argument is that from a First Amendment perspective, although threats to speech can only come from government action, the notion of 'government action' should be properly assessed. For in fact, when a broadcaster refuses to air the opinion of a relevant group in society, it is doing so only as a consequence of the current allocation of property rights, in this case a licence, which has been provided by government action. The same applies to newspapers, whose property rights, according to Sunstein, 'amount to a legally conferred power to exclude others'.[84] So, the state not only *acts* when it affects the existing distribution

---

[84] C Sunstein, *The Partial Constitution* (Cambridge, MA, Harvard University Press, 1993) 212.

of rights, it is also responsible for that very distribution and its effects. Therefore, the question is not whether government may or may not interfere with media markets, because it always necessarily does. The question is what type of interference is justified. Sunstein's answer is that interference is justified when its purpose is 'to promote democratic self-government by ensuring that people are presented with a broad range of views about public issues'.[85] If the market is able to guarantee that, there is no need for government action. Interference is only needed when markets fail. Sunstein argues that because the free press market is not good at providing quality information and diverse points of view, governments should interfere. This type of interference would not abridge free speech but promote it. Based on this argument, Sunstein justifies broadcasting regulation aimed at allocating time to issues of public importance, and defends campaign finance regulation and a right of access to the media, amongst other forms of media regulation.[86]

Sunstein is clearly sensitive to the limitations of media markets to properly guarantee a strong and pluralistic public sphere. Moreover, he seems to accept the 'freedom as non-domination' assumption that interference is compatible with freedom. However, it is not clear that his proposal is sufficient to remove the relations of domination currently plaguing media markets. Sunstein believes that media regulation (when aimed at enhancing public goods), although compatible with the central aims of free speech, affects the private autonomy of media outlets.[87] According to him, 'a core insight of the *Red Lion* case is that the interest in private autonomy from government is not always the same as the interest in free speech through democratic self government'.[88] Hence, promoting the latter may be incompatible with guaranteeing the former. This idea compels Sunstein to be very careful with the regulatory measures he chooses for enhancing public goods, as he needs to keep an adequate balance between the ends pursued by those measures and the intensity of the rights they affect (autonomy). A balancing exercise—that resonates with the principle of proportionality—forces him to choose only those measures that least affect the rights involved.[89] This may explain why Sunstein's regulatory proposals are only market 'correctives': they try to fix market failures—assuming that the market can be fixed—rather than overcoming the relations of domination produced by the market.

The problem with Sunstein's argument is that it loses a relevant part of the picture. Although it persuasively suggests that private autonomy is the consequence of the current distribution of ownership rights, hence the product of state action, it does not notice that extreme market logics, as seen in the previous

---

[85] ibid.

[86] See ibid 213–31.

[87] ibid 202, 212.

[88] ibid 202. In *Red Lion Broadcasting v FCC* 395 US (1969) at 390, the Court upheld the fairness doctrine, ie 'the right of the public to receive suitable access to social, political, esthetic, moral and other ideas and experiences'.

[89] See R Alexy, *A Theory of Constitutional Rights*, tr J Rivers (New York, Oxford University Press, 2002) 66–69.

section, have dispossessed media outlets of that very autonomy he claims to protect.[90] As seen in the previous section, conditions of work in newsrooms and news agencies have severely deteriorated as the motto of *reducing costs and increasing revenues* has eagerly spread throughout the press market due to extreme competition. The conditions under which journalists perform their work not only affect their capacity to produce stories that are the result of a serious and sustained effort to capture and reflect the intricacies of social reality. As previously seen, these conditions reduce media outlets' control over the production and publication of news. Much of what is published is unchecked stories coming from press agencies and from PR agents, who purposefully deliver material aimed at safeguarding the interests of the companies and government agencies for which they work.

The forces of commercialism have reduced the autonomy of media outlets. The conditions imposed by the market lessen, in the best case, their capacity to decide for themselves the quality of news they produce and print and, in the worst case, their editorial independence. Under these conditions, market correctives seem insufficient. Indeed, the problem is not merely the inability of the press to provide a wide range of views and ideas about the world in which we live; the problem is that it hardly possesses the resources needed to talk properly about that world. The type of regulatory intervention thus needed cannot be corrective, because this is not a problem of market failure. The problem is that the market 'cannot give us the journalism a self-governing society requires. What we need is a significant body of full-time paid journalists, covering their communities, the nation, the world, in competition and collaboration with other paid journalists.'[91] If markets have proved to be unable to fulfil this role, the question is how is it supposed to be done. History has taught us that state control of the press is not a good idea either. Media regulation should prevent the *possibility of arbitrary interference* (or domination) from both government and markets.

A free press, under a concept of freedom as non-domination, would require that the relevant views existing in a society possess proper means of communication under conditions that guarantee adequate control over the production and circulation of news. Media regulation would be compatible with freedom so long as it promotes these goals. Notice that this concept demands regulation at two levels. At a structural or external level, it would require proper distribution of media outlets subject to some democratic principle. At an internal level, it would require that editorial decisions respond first and mainly to the views of those who control singular media outlets. As editorial decisions should be freed from market constraints, guaranteeing a free press would require significant resources. Those resources should be distributed in such a way as to stimulate high-quality journalism. So, guaranteeing that all views of society possess adequate means of

---

[90] Although it is true that media market's conditions have changed radically since Sunstein wrote *The Partial Constitution*, it is also true that at that time, the critique of the political economy of the press was quite aware of the general loss of autonomy in media systems.

[91] McChesney, above n 44, 201.

communication, within those views, the ones that can produce high-quality journalism should be preferred over those that cannot. There have been some creative ideas about whence those resources might come.[92] The state, however, should guarantee their availability and provide for them if there is no alternative. The latter should always be done under mechanisms that prevent direct government involvement in their allocation.

If a republican notion of freedom provides the conceptual bases that are necessary for reducing the tensions between truth and freedom, it does not guarantee that a free press (in the republican sense) will ever fulfil its truth-seeking purpose. There are multiple obstacles that may prevent this from happening. Many of them were analysed throughout the book and are the consequence of the difficulties of harmonising conflicting values. Others emerge from the discussion presented here. The law is not an instrument that in every possible world will be the expression of a self-governing people and conducive to human emancipation. A number of conditions need to be fulfilled for that to occur, the analysis of which exceeds the scope of this book. However, as the illusion of the free press is an epistemological necessity, hence unavoidable, we have to confront the challenge of thinking about a world in which truths are things we do wish to defend. A republican notion of freedom may be only one of multiple possibilities for resisting the idea that the illusion is nothing but an empty epistemological hope.

---

[92] According to McChesney, journalism, like education, is a public good. Hence, just like with education, when journalism is subject to market logics, it fails. If journalism is considered a public good, the state has the duty to guarantee its adequate provision. See McChesney, above n 44, 193–94; for cooperative ownership see R Greenslade, 'If We Want to Save Newspapers How About Trying Cooperative Ownership', *Guardian* (8 May 2012) available at https://www.theguardian.com/media/greenslade/2012/may/08/downturn-local-newspapers.

Conclusion

The illusion of the free press is not merely a misapprehension of what the press really is. Neither is it the sole belief that social reality corresponds to its media portrayal. The illusion is the product of an epistemological necessity. We need to make sense of the world in which we live, to grasp political events as they unfold day by day, and to understand the different modes of life coexisting in our communities and the way they affect our own identity. We need to be able to organise the world as it appears in the media with the world as it is in itself, in a consistent unitary system in order to retain the sense of reality. The illusion of the free press is what allows us to do that and what keeps this system working. If we renounce the idea that the press is free and independent, if we reject the *illusion of the free press*, our sense of reality collapses and becomes a meaningless mess. This is why the illusion is neither renounceable nor disposable. This is why the illusion is an epistemological necessity.

The illusion of the free press explains the relevance that truth has in free-speech literature. In fact, as we saw throughout the chapters, the relationship between truth and freedom was identified in some of the most relevant theories of free speech that have been developed since the seventeenth century. But this relationship, as has been argued throughout the book, is problematic, because the modes of communication that characterise a free debate of ideas are in tension with those that define the discovery and dissemination of truths. In the literature, these tensions are reflected in different ways. As seen in Chapter 2, John Stuart Mill pays the price of ambiguity in order to justify the liberty of discussion as a means to discovering the truth. While some passages in *On Liberty* suggest that his theory is grounded on a correspondence model of truth, others suggest that he follows a subjective or perspective truth, one in which every opinion is as valid as any other as long as it is properly sustained.[1] As argued, Mill needs this ambiguity because it is what holds together the two conflicting values.

The tensions between freedom and truth are also identifiable in Holmes's marketplace of ideas. In his case, the tensions were dealt with by devolving truth to the competition of ideas in the marketplace. One of the most salient metaphors in American constitutionalism, the marketplace of ideas, has permeated not only

---

[1] See I Berlin, 'John Stuart Mill and the Ends of Life' in H Hardy (ed), *Liberty* (Oxford, Oxford University Press, 2002) 233.

the theory and implementation of the First Amendment, but also decisions of regulatory bodies like the FCC. The metaphor has legitimised the idea that the best test of truth is acceptance in the competition of the market, reinforcing the illusion (in the negative sense of the term) that an unregulated press is not only an equivalent to a free press but also a proper means of achieving intellectual progress in society. Seeing the marketplace of ideas as a form of intellectual degradation of the American people, democratic theorists sharply criticised it. In the democratic tradition, freedom of speech is defended as a means of developing and strengthening the democratic system. However, truth remains relevant in the theories analysed. It is no longer a truth that exists in the outer world, waiting to be discovered, but one that is supposed to be inscribed in the political system itself and that is identified as the central *motto* of a democratic society. Expressive freedoms are (or should be) instruments that contribute to unpacking this political truth, a truth that Meiklejohn called the 'plan of the constitution'. These freedoms are supposed to unveil the terms of cooperation that are inscribed in the plan of a self-governing society. However, within the framework of a coherence model of truth, democratic theories end up providing the conditions in which discussion is supposed to take place and what the public is entitled to know, so as to reproduce the democratic model in which they are inscribed.

Within autonomy theories the tension between truth and freedom appears most vividly in Raz's theory of personal identification. Raz believes that free speech serves the purpose of validating ways of life. When the media portray a form of life, this gives it a stamp of public acceptability that reaffirms personal identity. Individuals whose forms of life receive public validation have a greater chance of being true to themselves by identifying and remaining loyal to their plans of life. By contrast, individuals whose ways of life are excluded from public visibility have reduced chances of being true to themselves because, according to Raz, lack of public validation affects their sense of who they are. But Raz's defence of free speech is not limited to public validation. In fact, in his opinion, freedom of speech serves another purpose. This is to offer a variety of acceptable forms of life from which people can choose how to live their own; options that allow individuals to improve and even transform their lives. Drifting from the idea of a substantial self who has a clear sense of who he is and maintains it throughout his life to a 'flexible self' who modifies his plans of life according to the options offered in the public sphere, Raz is able to deal with the tensions between freedom and the true self. Just as Mill, Raz needs this ambiguous approach in order to defend freedom of speech as a way of validating personal identity—or the true self—without threatening the very freedom he defends.

As an epistemological necessity, the illusion is ingrained in the institution of the free press and manifests itself in the relevance that truth plays in free-speech literature. Truth takes different forms in the theory: correspondence with an outer world in the classic theory; coherence with a central judgement in democratic theory; authenticity in autonomy theories. Regardless of the form truth takes, its relationship with freedom is always problematic. But the problems between truth and freedom emerge not only in theory. The truth-seeking purpose of the actual press is often betrayed in those societies that are proud to affirm that a free press is a fundamental, constitutive liberty of their political systems. The free press has been understood as the absence of state interference in the functioning and structure of the press. Historically, it has been claimed that the press achieved its freedom once the laws and regulations affecting it were repealed or amended. This understanding of the free press is inspired by a concept of freedom as non-interference. Created by Hobbes in the seventeenth century to justify absolute forms of government, freedom as non-interference was revived by Bentham after almost two centuries of obscurity. It became the modernist instrument by which the freedom of the press was conceived, defined and articulated. Although this notion of the free press inspired the fights to liberate the press from undue forms of government interference, it was also instrumental in the creation of new forms of domination.

As argued in Chapter 5, the concept of freedom as non-interference has contributed to legitimising forms of domination that have severely constricted the public sphere. By equating the freedom of the press with the absence of state regulation of the media, market logics have shaped the structure, organisation and functioning of the media in the last two centuries. In the market, media ownership is highly concentrated, the interests of advertisers define the business strategies of media outlets, and the profit-seeking impulses delineate the terms of selection, production and dissemination of news. Market logics have built into the system structural conditions of domination that prevent media outlets from freely deciding the type of journalism they wish to pursue. And these conditions have radicalised since the emergence of the Internet and the consolidation of social media.

Currently, the public sphere is showing alarming sings of deterioration. Whilst the Web intensified time pressure in the production of news, it was also increasing competition for advertisement revenues. Mounting competition has forced media outlets to reduce costs. Consequently, news organisations have slashed staff. With fewer journalists subject to ever-increasing pressures for the production of news, investigative journalism has become moribund. Journalists have become, according to Davies, an automated piece in the process of news production. They do not have the time to do reporting, and are basically reproducing information coming from unknown or unchecked sources. The weakening of journalism has strengthened public relations efforts. Powerful corporations and government agencies can see their views easily bypass the media's filters. With reduced capacity and resources to process information coming from PR sources, media outlets are prone to reproducing information that has been crafted especially to protect the interests of big economic conglomerates and government agencies. The business strategies of social media have also contributed to damaging the health of the public sphere. Walled within secluded spaces of communication that protect like-minded people from ideas, opinions or information not attuned with their interests and tastes, social media have contributed to creating filter bubbles that have fragmented the public sphere.

The deterioration of the public sphere has eroded our sense of reality. Indeed, the public sphere, as Arendt claims, is the space where everything that appears is seen and heard by everyone. The public sphere is constitutive of reality because in a shared world what is real is that which is subjected to the common gaze. Therefore, when the public sphere deteriorates and the prominent light that allows the scrutiny of everyone dims, biased information, hyperbole, scandal and the dissemination of outright lies can flourish. This is why it was argued that although the phenomenon of post-truth is nothing new, the increasing erosion of the public sphere in the last few years has made it more prominent.

From the perspective of freedom as non-interference, structural domination of the media is not necessarily a problem, for no one is directly defining the content that media outlets should publish or censoring them. Moreover, from this point of view, any form of state interference aimed at reducing domination in media markets would be qualified as a restriction of media freedoms. Things change, however, when viewed from the perspective of republican freedom, because the latter depends on the structures in which human relationships are framed. Therefore, structural forms of domination, especially those that affect the vitality of the public sphere, necessarily constrict freedom. And it is not only the freedom of the media to perform their vital functions in a democratic society that is affected, but also the freedom of citizens to participate in an informed way in the discussion of those issues that define the life in common.

When the law is the expression of a self-governing society, it may interfere in the structure and functioning of media markets in order to reduce domination. As seen in Chapter 5, this would be compatible with freedom as non-domination when it guarantees that the relevant views in a society possess a proper means of communication and adequate control over the selection, production and dissemination of news content. Now, mechanisms aimed at reducing domination not only increase freedom, they also promote the truth-seeking purposes of the press. A media system enhances our understanding of social reality when it is designed to strengthen the capacities of media outlets to perform their functions in a democratic society by distributing media ownership, exposing citizens to the multiple views existing in a society, directing communication towards issues that are relevant to the life in common and reporting on them in ways that improve our understanding about them.

The republican concept of freedom is one way of handling the epistemological necessity inscribed in the illusion of the free press, a way that actively promotes our desire to live in a world in which truths are things we wish to stand for and defend. By translating the illusion into a public concern about the forms of domination affecting the media and their capacity to describe the world in which we live, the republican concept of freedom reduces the distance that separates truth and freedom. A free press, from this point of view, is not the equivalent of an unregulated press. A free press is that which is not subject to forms of domination that prevent it from performing one of its basic functions in democratic societies: to broaden our understanding of social reality. If a republican concept of freedom has its own difficulties in guaranteeing a truth-seeking press, it at least provides the ingredients to transmute the illusion into a productive idea—an idea that reaffirms and actualises the long-standing struggle for a free press.

BIBLIOGRAPHY

Adorno, TW and Horkheimer, M, *Dialectic of Enlightenment* (London, Verso Books, 1997).
Alexy, R, *A Theory of Constitutional Rights*, tr J Rivers (New York, Oxford University Press, 2002).
Allcot, H and Gentzkow, M, 'Social Media and Fake News in the 2016 Election' (2017) 31 *Journal of Economic Perspectives* 211.
Allison, HE, *Kant's Transcendental Idealism: An Interpretation and Defence*, rev'd edn (New Haven, CT, Yale University Press, 2004).
——, 'Transcendental Realism and Transcendental Idealism' in P Kitcher (ed), *Kant's Critique of Pure Reason: Critical Essays* (Lanham, MD, Rowman & Littlefield, 1998).
Alschuler, AW, *Law Without Values: The Life, Work, and Legacy of Justice Holmes* (Chicago, IL, University of Chicago Press, 2000).
Althusser, L, *On Ideology*, tr B Brewster (London, Verso, 2008).
Amdur, R, 'Scanlon on Freedom of Expression' (1980) 9 *Philosophy & Public Affairs* 287.
Arendt, H, *Eichmann in Jerusalem: A Report on the Banality of Evil* (London, Penguin, 2006).
——, 'Truth and Politics' in *Between Past and Future*, rev'd edn, (London, Penguin Books, 2006).
——, 'What is Freedom?' in *Between Past and Future*, rev'd edn (London, Penguin Books, 2006).
——, *The Human Condition* (Chicago, IL, University of Chicago, 1989).
——, 'Truth and Politics' in *Between Past and Future: Eight Exercises in Political Thought* (New York, Penguin Books, 1977).
Atria, F, 'La verdad y lo político (I). La verdad y su dimensión constitutiva' (2009) 23 *Persona y Sociedad/Universidad Alberto Hurtado* 21.
Bacon, F, *The Essaies of Sr Francis Bacon* (Edinburgh, AndroHary, 1614).
Bagdikian, B, *The New Media Monopoly*, 7th edn (Boston, MA, Beacon Press, 2004).
Baker, CE, *Media Concentration and Democracy* (Cambridge, Cambridge University Press, 2007).
——, *Human Liberty and Freedom of Speech* (Oxford, Oxford University Press, 1989).
Balibar, É, *Spinoza and Politics*, tr P Snowdon (London, Verso, 1998).
Barendt, E, *Freedom of Speech*, 2nd edn (Oxford, Oxford University Press, 2007).
Baudrillard, J, *Simulacra and Simulation*, tr S Glaser (Ann Arbor, MI, The University of Michigan Press, 1994).
Benjamin, W, 'Two Types of Popularity' in MW Jennings, B Doherty, and TY Levin (eds), *Work of Art in the Age of Its Technological Reproducibility, and Other Writings on Media* (E Jephcott tr, Cambridge, MA, Harvard University Press, 2008).
Benjamin, W, 'Work of Art in the Age of Its Technological Reproducibility' in MW Jennings, B Doherty, and TY Levin (eds), *Work of Art in the Age of Its Technological Reproducibility, and Other Writings on Media* (E Jephcott tr, Cambridge, MA, Harvard University Press, 2008).

Bentham, J, 'On the Liberty of the Press' in J Bowring (ed), *The Works of Jeremy Bentham* (Edinburgh, William Tait, 1843).

Berlin, I, 'John Stuart Mill and the Ends of Life' in *Liberty*, ed H Hardy (Oxford, Oxford University Press, 2002).

——, *Four Essays on Liberty* (Oxford, Oxford University Press, 1969).

Berry, D, 'Radical Mass Media Criticism, History and Theory' in J Klaehn (ed), *The Political Economy of Media and Power* (New York, Peter Lang, 2010).

Berry, D and Theobald, J, *Radical Mass Media Criticism: A Cultural Genealogy* (Montreal, Black Rose, 2006).

Blackstone, W, *Commentaries of the Laws of England, 1765–1769*, vol 4, ed WC Jones (San Francisco, Bancroft-Whitenet, 1916).

Blasi, V, 'Holmes and the Marketplace of Ideas' 2004 *The Supreme Court Review* 1.

——, 'The Checking Value in First Amendment Theory' (1977) 2 *American Bar Foundation Research Journal* 521.

Bollinger, LC, *The Tolerant Society: Freedom of Speech and Extremist Speech in America* (New York, Oxford University Press, 1986).

Bourdieu, P, *On Television* (Cambridge, Polity Press, 2011).

Bork, R, 'Neutral Principles and Some First Amendment Problems' (1971) 47 *Indiana Law Journal* 1.

Bowring, J (ed), *The Works of Jeremy Bentham*, vol II (Edinburgh, William Tait, 1843).

Boyer, D, *The Life Informatic: Newsmaking in the Digital Era* (London, Cornell University Press, 2013).

Brison, SJ, 'The Autonomy Defense of Free Speech' (1998) 108 *Ethics* 312.

Burke, E, 'Reflections on the Revolution in France' in *The Works of the Right Honorable Edmund Burke*, vol 2 (London, Henry G Bohn, 1855).

Carlile, R, *The Republican* (London, 1 March 1822).

——, *The Republican* (London, 26 April 1822).

——, *The Republican* (London, 19 July 1822).

——, *The Republican* (London, 6 September 1822).

Cassian, J, 'First Conference of Abbot Moses' in H Wace and P Schaff (eds), *A Select Library of Nicene and Post-Nicene Fathers of the Christian Church*, vol 11 (Oxford, Parker, 1893).

Castells, M, *The Rise of the Network Society* (Oxford, Blackwell Publishing, 2010).

——, *Communication Power* (Oxford, Oxford University Press, 2009).

Charney, J, 'The Tensions Between Free Speech and the Protection to One's Reputation: Importance and Limits of the Exceptio Veritatis' (2016) 29 *Revista de Derecho (Valdivia)* 175.

Cho, D, Smith, MD and Zenter, A, 'Internet Adoption and the Survival of Print Newspapers: A Country-Level Examination' (2016) 37 *Information Economics and Policy* 13.

Chomsky, N and Herman, ES, *Manufacturing Consent: The Political Economy of the Mass Media* (London, Vintage, 1994).

Christman, J, 'Autonomy in Moral and Political Philosophy' in EN Zalta (ed), *The Stanford Encyclopedia of Philosophy* (2011), at plato.stanford.edu/archives/spr2011/entries/autonomy-moral/.

Christman, J and Anderson, J (eds), 'Introduction' in *Autonomy and the Challenges to Liberalism* (Cambridge, Cambridge University Press, 2005).

Coase, RH, 'The Market for Goods and the Market for Ideas' (1974) 64 *The American Economic Review* 384.

Compaine, BM, *Who Owns the Media?: Competition and Concentration in the Mass Media*, 3rd edn (Mahwah, NJ, L Erlbaum Associates, 2000).

Copeland, DA, *The Idea of a Free Press: The Enlightenment and Its Unruly Legacy* (Evanston, IL, Northwestern University Press, 2006).

Curran, J and Seaton, J, *Power Without Responsibility*, 7th edn (Oxford, Routledge, 2010).

Davies, N, *Flat Earth News* (London, Vintage, 2009).

Davis, A, *Public Relations Democracy* (Manchester, Manchester University Press, 2002).

Debord, G, *Society of the Spectacle*, tr K Knabb (London, Rebel Press, 2006).

Dews, P, 'Adorno, Post-Structuralism and the Critique of Identity' in S Žižek (ed), *Mapping Ideology* (London, Verso, 1994).

Doyle, G, *Understanding Media Economics* (London, Sage Publications Ltd, 2002).

Duncan, C, *Duncan and Neill on Defamation* (London, Butterworths, 1983).

Dworkin, G, 'The Concept of Autonomy' in J Christman (ed), *The Inner Citadel: Essays on Individual Autonomy* (New York, Oxford University Press, 1989).

——, *The Theory and Practice of Autonomy* (Cambridge, Cambridge University Press, 1988).

——, 'Autonomy and Behavior Control' (1976) 6 *Hastings Center Report* 23.

Dworkin, R, 'The Coming Battles over Free Speech', *The New York Review of Books* (11 June 1992), available at http://www.nybooks.com/articles/1992/06/11/the-coming-battles-over-free-speech/.

——, *A Matter of Principle* (Oxford, Clarendon, 1986).

Eagleton, T, *Ideology: An Introduction*, 2nd edn (London, Verso, 2007).

——, *The Illusions of Postmodernism* (Oxford, Blackwell, 1996).

Elkins, J, 'Concerning Practices of Truth' in J Elkins and A Norris (eds), *Truth and Democracy* (Philadelphia, PA, University of Pennsylvania Press, 2012).

Fenwick, H and Phillipson, G, *Media Freedom Under the Human Rights Act* (Oxford, Oxford University Press, 2006).

Firth, CH and Rait, RS (eds), *Acts and Ordinances of the Interregnum, 1642–1660*, vol 1 (London, Stationery Office, 1911).

Fiss, O, *The Irony of Free Speech* (Cambridge, MA, Harvard University Press, 1996).

——, 'Why the State?' (1987) 100 *Harvard Law Review* 781.

Forst, R, 'Political Liberty: Integrating Five Conceptions of Autonomy' in J Christman and J Anderson (eds), *Autonomy and the Challenges to Liberalism* (Cambridge, Cambridge University Press, 2005).

Foucault, M, *The Politics of Truth* (Los Angeles, CA, Semiotext(e), 2007).

——, 'Truth and Juridical Forms' in JD Faubion (ed), *Power: Essential Works of Foucault 1954–1984*, vol 3 (R Hurley tr, London, Penguin, 2002).

——, 'Truth and Power' in JD Faubion (ed), *Power: Essential Works of Foucault 1954–1984*, vol 3 (R Hurley tr, London, Penguin, 2002).

Frankfurt, HG, 'Freedom of the Will and the Concept of a Person' in *The Importance of What We Care About: Philosophical Essays* (Cambridge, Cambridge University Press, 1988).

Freedman, D, *The Politics of Media Policy* (Cambridge, Polity Press, 2008).

Friedman, TL, *The World is Flat* (New York, Farrar Straus & Giroux, 2007).

Freud, S, *The Future of an Illusion*, trs JA Underwood et al (London, Penguin Books, 2008).

Gray, J, *Mill on Liberty: a Defence*, 2nd edn (London, Routledge, 1996).

Greenawalt, K, 'Free Speech Justifications' (1989) 89 *Columbia Law Review* 119.

Habermas, J, *The Structural Transformation of the Public Sphere: An Inquiry into a Category of Bourgeois Society*, tr T Burger (Cambridge, MA, MIT Press, 1989).

Haller, W (ed), *Tracts on Liberty in the Puritan Revolution*, vol I (New York, Columbia University Press, 1934).

Harnett, B, and Thornton, JV, 'The Truth Hurts: A Critique of a Defense to Defamation' (1949) 35 *Virginia Law Review* 425.

Haworth, A, *Free Speech* (London, Routledge, 1998).

Himmelfarb, G, *On Liberty and Liberalism: The Case of John Stuart Mill* (New York, Knopf, 1974).

Hitchens, L, *Broadcasting Pluralism and Diversity: A Comparative Study of Policy and Regulation* (Oxford, Hart Publishing, 2006).

Hobbes, T, *Leviathan* (London, Penguin Books, 1985).

Holmes, OW, *Speeches* (Boston, MA, Little, Brown & Co, 1934).

——, 'Natural Law' (1918) 32 *Harvard Law Review* 40.

Ingber, S, 'The Marketplace of Ideas: A Legitimizing Myth' (1984) 1984 *Duke Law Journal* 1.

Jameson, F, 'Postmodernism and the Market' in S Žižek (ed), *Mapping Ideology* (London, Verso, 1994).

Jenkins, R *Convergence Culture* (New York, NYU Press, 2006).

Johnston, D, *The Idea of a Liberal Theory: A Critique and Reconstruction* (Princeton, NJ, Princeton University Press, 1994).

Kaiser, RG, *The Bad News about the News* (Washington, The Brookings Institution, 2014) available at www.brookings.edu/series/the-brookings-essay/.

Kalven, H, 'The New York Times Case: A Note on "The Central Meaning of the First Amendment"' (1964) *The Supreme Court Review* 191.

Kant, I, *Critique of Pure Reason*, trs P Guyer and AW Wood (Cambridge, Cambridge University Press, 1998).

——, *Groundwork of the Metaphysics of Morals*, tr M Gregor (Cambridge, Cambridge University Press, 1998).

——, 'Perpetual Peace: A Philosophical Sketch' in H Reiss (ed), *Kant Political Writings*, 2nd edn (HB Nisbet tr, Cambridge, Cambridge University Press, 1991).

Kendall, W, 'The "Open Society" and its Fallacies' (1960) 54 *The American Political Science Review* 972.

King, E, *Free for All* (Evanston, IL, Northwestern University Press, 2010).

Korsgaard, CM, *Creating the Kingdom of Ends* (Cambridge, Cambridge University Press, 1996).

Lessig, L, *Free Culture: How Big Media Uses Technology and the Law to Lock Down Culture and Control Creativity* (New York, Penguin Press, 2004).

Levinson, S and Posner, RA, 'Strolling down the Path of the Law (and Toward Critical Legal Studies?): The Jurisprudence of Richard Posner' (1991) 91 *Columbia Law Review* 1221.

Locke, J, *An Essay Concerning Human Understanding*, ed AC Fraser (New York, Dover, 1996).

Loughlin, M, *Foundations of Public Law* (Oxford, Oxford University Press, 2010).

Loveland, I, *Political Libels: A Comparative Study* (Oxford, Hart Publishing, 2000).

——, *Constitutional Law: A Critical Introduction* (London, Butterworths, 1996).

Lovgen, S, '"War of the Worlds": Behind the 1938 Radio Show Panic', *National Geographic* (17 June 2005), available at http://news.nationalgeographic.com/news/2005/06/0617_050617_warworlds.html.

Lyotard, JF, *The Postmodern Condition: A Report on Knowledge*, trs G Bennington and B Massumi (Manchester, Manchester University Press, 1984).

Marcuse, H, 'Repressive Tolerance' in A Feenberg and W Leiss (eds), *The Essential Marcuse: Selected Writings of Philosopher and Social Critic Herbert Marcuse* (Boston, MA, Beacon Press, 2007).

Marx, K, *Capital: Critique of Political Economy*, vol 1, new edn (B Fowkes tr, London, Penguin Classics, 1990).

McChesney, RW, *Digital Disconnect: How Capitalism is Turning the Internet against Democracy* (New York, The New Press, 2013).

——, *The Political Economy of Media: Enduring Issues, Emerging Dilemmas* (New York, Monthly Review Press, 2008).

McChesney, RW and Packard, V (eds), *Will the Last Reporter Please Turn Out the Lights* (New York, The New Press, 2011).

McLuhan, M, *Understanding Media*, 2nd edn (New York, Routledge, 2001).

Meiklejohn, A, 'Free Speech and its Relation to Self-Government' in *Political Freedom: The Constitutional Powers of the People* (New York, Oxford University Press, 1965).

——, 'The Freedom of the Electorate' in *Political Freedom: The Constitutional Powers of the People* (New York, Oxford University Press, 1965).

——, 'The First Amendment Is an Absolute' 1961 *The Supreme Court Review* 245.

Mill, J, 'Government' in T Ball (ed), *Political Writings. Cambridge Texts in the History of Political Thought* (Cambridge, Cambridge University Press, 1992).

——, 'Liberty of the Press' in T Ball (ed), *Political Writings. Cambridge Texts in the History of Political Thought* (Cambridge, Cambridge University Press, 1992).

Mill, JS, *On Liberty* (New York, Cosimo Classics, 2005).

——, 'The Spirit of the Age, V [Part 1]' in AP Robson and JM Robson (eds), *Newspaper Writings: Collected Works of John Stuart Mill*, vol XXII (Toronto, University of Toronto Press; London, Routledge & Kegan Paul, 1986).

——, 'De Tocqueville on Democracy in America [II]' in JM Robson (ed), *Essays on Politics and Society: Collected Works of John Stuart Mill*, vol XVIII (Toronto, University of Toronto Press; London, Routledge & Kegan Paul, 1977).

——, in FE Mineka and DN Lindley (eds), *The Later Letters of John Stuart Mill: Collected Works of John Stuart Mill*, vol XV (Toronto, University of Toronto Press; London, Routledge & Kegan Paul, 1972).

——, 'Essays on Ethics, Religion and Society' in *Collected Works*, vol 10 (London, Routledge, 1969).

Milner-Gibson, T, HC Debates 15 April 1850, vol 110, col 378.

Milton, J, *Areopagitica* (Champaign, IL, Standard Publications, Inc, 2008).

——, 'The Tenure of Kings and Magistates' in *The Prose Works of John Milton*, vol 1 (London, Methuen, 1905).

Mitchell, P, *The Making of the Modern Law of Defamation* (Oxford, Hart Publishing, 2005).

Napoli, PM, 'The Marketplace of Ideas Metaphor in Communication Regulation' (1999) 49 *Journal of Communication* 151.

Negroponte, N, *Being Digital* (New York, Knopf, 1995).

Noam, EM, *Media Ownership and Concentration in America* (New York, Oxford University Press, 2009).

Norrie, AW, *Punishment, Responsibility, and Justice: A Relational Critique* (Oxford, Oxford University Press, 2000).

Norris, P, *Democratic Deficit: Critical Citizens Revisited* (Cambridge, Cambridge University Press, 2011).

O'Neill, O, 'News of This World', *Financial Times* (18 November 2011), available at https://www.ft.com/content/25c0d316-0ec6-11e1-9dbb-00144feabdc0.

O'Rourke, KC, *John Stuart Mill and Freedom of Expression: The Genesis of a Theory* (London, Routledge, 2001).

Oster, J, 'Theory and Doctrine of Media Freedom as a Legal Concept' (2013) 5 *Journal of Media Law* 57.

Pariser, E, *The Filter Bubble* (London, Penguin, 2011).

Pettit, P, *Republicanism: A Theory of Freedom and Government* (Oxford, Oxford University Press 1997).

Phillipson, G, 'Leveson, the Public Interest and Press Freedom' (2013) 5 *Journal of Media Law* 220.

Posner, RA, *The Problems of Jurisprudence* (Cambridge, MA, Harvard University Press, 1990).

Post, R, 'Participatory Democracy and Free Speech' (2011) 97 *Virginia Law Review* 477.

——, 'Democracy and Equality' (2005) 1 *Law, Culture and the Humanities* 142.

Postman, N, *Amusing Ourselves to Death* (London, Methuen Publishing Ltd, 1987).

Powe, LA, *The Fourth Estate and the Constitution: Freedom of the Press in America* (Berkeley, CA, University of California Press, 1992).

Radin, MJ, *Contested Commodities* (Cambridge, MA, Harvard University Press, 1996).

Raz, J, 'Free Expression and Personal Identification' (1991) 11 *OJLS* 303.

——, *The Morality of Freedom* (Oxford, Clarendon, 1986).

Redish, MH, *Freedom of Expression: A Critical Analysis* (Charlottesville, VA, Michie Co, 1984).

Rees, JC, *John Stuart Mill's On Liberty* (Oxford, Clarendon Press, 1995).

Richards, DAJ, *Free Speech and the Politics of Identity* (Oxford, Oxford University Press, 1999).

Rorty, R, 'Feminism, Ideology, and Deconstruction: A Pragmatist View' in S Žižek (ed), *Mapping Ideology* (London, Verso, 1994).

Salecl, R, *The Spoils of Freedom: Psychoanalysis and Feminism After the Fall of Socialism* (London, Routledge, 1994).

Scanlon, T, 'Freedom of Expression and Categories of Expression' (1979) 40 *University of Pittsburgh Law Review* 519.

——, 'A Theory of Freedom of Expression' (1972) 1 *Philosophy & Public Affairs* 204.

Scott, A, 'The Same River Twice? Jameel v Wall Street Journal Europe' (2007) 12 *Communications Law* 52.

Sehnbruch, K and Donoso, S, 'Chilean Winter of Discontent: Are Protests Here to Stay?' (2011) *Open Democracy*, available at https://www.opendemocracy.net/kirsten-sehnbruch-sofia-donoso/chilean-winter-of-discontent-are-protests-here-to-stay.

Shapiro, I, *Politics Against Domination* (Cambridge, MA, Belknap/Harvard, 2016).

Shiffrin, SV, 'A Thinker-Based Approach to Freedom of Speech' (2011) 27 *Constitutional Commentary* 283.

Shirky, C, 'Newspapers and Thinking the Unthinkable' in R McChesney and V Packard (eds), *Will the Last Reporter Please Turn Out the Lights* (New York, The New Press, 2011).

——, *Here Comes Everybody* (New York, Penguin Press, 2009).

Siebert, F, *Freedom of the Press in England 1476–1776* (Urbana, IL, University of Illinois Press, 1965).

Silverstone, R, *Media and Morality: On the Rise of the Mediapolis* (Cambridge, Polity Press, 2006).

Skinner, Q, *Hobbes and Republican Liberty* (Cambridge, Cambridge University Press, 2008).
——, *Liberty before Liberalism* (Cambridge, Cambridge University Press, 1998).
Sloterdijk, P, *Critique of Cynical Reason*, tr M Eldred (Minneapolis, MN, University of Minnesota Press, 1987).
Spinoza, B de, *Ethics*, tr E Curley (London, Penguin, 1996).
Steiner, PO, 'Program Patterns and Preferences, and the Workability of Competition in Radio Broadcasting' (1952) 66 *The Quarterly Journal of Economics* 194.
Sullivan, KM, 'Two Concepts of Freedom of Speech' (2010) 124 *Harvard Law Review* 143.
Sunstein, CR, *Republic.com 2.0* (Princeton, NJ, Princeton University Press, 2007).
——, *The Partial Constitution* (Cambridge, MA, Harvard University Press, 1993).
——, *Democracy and the Problem of Free Speech* (New York, The Free Press, 1995).
Taylor, VE and Winquist, CE (eds), *Encyclopedia of Postmodernism* (London, Routledge, 2001).
Thomas, W, *The Philosophic Radicals: Nine Studies in Theory and Practice, 1817–1841* (Oxford, Clarendon Press, 1979).
Volokh, E, 'In Defense of the Marketplace of Ideas/Search for Truth as a Theory of Free Speech Protection' (2011) 97 *Virginia Law Review* 595.
Waldman, S, *The Information Needs of Communities* (Darby, PA, Diane Publishing, 2011).
Waldron, J, 'Moral Autonomy and Personal Autonomy' in J Christman and J Anderson (eds), *Autonomy and the Challenges to Liberalism* (Cambridge, Cambridge University Press, 2005).
Weber, M, *Economy and Society*, eds G Roth and C Wittich (Berkeley, CA, University of California Press, 1968).
Welles, O, 'Orson Welles—War of the Worlds—Radio Broadcast 1938—Complete Broadcast', available at www.youtube.com/watch?v=Xs0K4ApWl4g&feature=yout ube_gdata_player.
Wickwar, WH, *The Struggle for the Freedom of the Press, 1819–1832* (London, Allen & Unwin Ltd, 1928).
Wonnell, CT, 'Truth and the Marketplace of Ideas' (1986) 19 *UC Davis Law Review* 669.
Wuerth, J, 'The Paralogisms of Pure Reason' in P Guyer (ed), *The Cambridge Companion to Kant's Critique of Pure Reason* (Cambridge, Cambridge University Press, 2010).
Zheng, Y, *Technological Empowerment* (Stanford, CA, Stanford University Press, 2010).
Žižek, S, *Mapping Ideology* (London, Verso Books, 2012).
——, *The Sublime Object of Ideology*, 2nd edn (London, Verso Books, 2008).
——, *Tarrying with the Negative: Kant, Hegel and the Critique of Ideology* (Durham, NC, Duke University Press, 1993).

INDEX

Note: Alphabetical arrangement is word-by-word, where a group of letters followed by a space is filed before the same group of letters followed by a letter, eg 'free thought will appear before 'freedom'. In determining alphabetical arrangement, initial articles and prepositions are ignored.

www.ingramcontent.com/pod-product-compliance
Lightning Source LLC
Chambersburg PA
CBHW050442280326
41932CB00013BA/2212